ANCIENT AMERICA'S LOST COLONIES

DISCOVERING ANCIENT AMERICA

ANCIENT AMERICA'S LOST COLONIES

FRANK JOSEPH

Rosen YA
New York

This edition published in 2018 by
The Rosen Publishing Group, Inc.
29 East 21st Street
New York, NY 10010

Library of Congress Cataloging-in-Publication Data

Names: Joseph, Frank, author.
Title: Ancient America's lost colonies / Frank Joseph.
Description: New York : Rosen Publishing, 2018. | Series: Discovering Ancient America | Includes bibliographical references and index.
Identifiers: LCCN 2017002102 | ISBN 9781499466751 (library-bound)
Subjects: LCSH: America—Antiquities. | United States—Antiquities. | Antiquities, Prehistoric—America. | Prehistoric peoples—America. | Indians—Antiquities. | America—Discovery and exploration. | Curiosities and wonders—America.
Classification: LCC E21.5 .J67 2018 | DDC 970.01—dc23
LC record available at https://lccn.loc.gov/2017002102

Manufactured in the United States of America

First published as *The Lost Colonies of Ancient America: A Comprehensive Guide to the Pre-Columbian Visitors Who Really Discovered America* by Career Press © 2014 by Frank Joseph

Contents

Please note:

The terminology included herein is common parlance in the scientific discourse of the fields of anthropology and forensics. In every instance, the author has endeavored to use valid and accepted terminology. Nevertheless, the reader should be advised that this text contains references to controversial theories on racial classifications and human migration that should be approached with a healthy degree of skepticism.

To Laura,
the love of my life

Acknowledgments

Special thanks to Wayne May for publishing more than 20 years of *Ancient American* magazine, and to Larry Gallant for painstakingly indexing every issue; Gunnar Thompson, PhD, whose classic *American Discovery* inspired this latest effort; and senior acquisitions editor, Michael Pye, for assigning me the satisfying task of writing it.

Introduction:
Recovering from Cultural Amnesia

"Much of how we reconstruct the past is based on how we perceive it."

—President of the World Explorers Club,
David Hatcher Childress[1]

This book is intended to acquaint readers with the monumental dramas of human achievement and tragedy that played out across our land many hundreds, and even thousands of years ago. These grand events are generally unknown, because humanity's last 25 generations have been schooled to believe that Christopher Columbus was the first and only discoverer of the New World. For them, American history began in 1492, and nothing of equivalent significance supposedly took place here before then.

Such ignorance is understandable, when we learn that the ancient Old World colonizers who repeatedly landed on our shores arrived with their own, very specific agendas. They sought to monopolize American resources of high-grade copper, precious gems, powerful narcotics, agricultural products, or any other native riches, just as modern corporations guard against one another's industrial espionage. Navigational directions were state secrets, and rumors of boiling seas filled with monsters or sailing off the edge of the Earth were deliberately spread to discourage competition. Transatlantic voyages were covert operations undertaken only by the most capable maritime kingdoms, each jealous of the others' success.

But the colonizers' trade secrets were lost with the catastrophic close of the Bronze Age, around 1200 BCE, when its thorough and widespread collapse ushered in a dark age that virtually wiped clean all memory of contact with the Americas. Two millennia of transoceanic accomplishments were reduced to legends, until first the Phoenicians, followed by Latin and then Keltic, sailors found some old sea-lanes back to the Opposite Continent. With the late 5th Century fall of the Roman World, another, deeper dark age ensued to yet again cast its shadow over all previous knowledge of the New World. Scandinavian Vikings made an exception, of course, but, like their Bronze Age forerunners, their voyages were mostly described in sagas, the stuff of which myth was made.

It was against this backdrop of cultural amnesia that Christopher Columbus challenged the Atlantic Ocean. Although he was by no means the first to discover America—but rather the last—the greatness of his personal achievement has not been diminished by any Ancient World predecessors, because their oversea link had been broken and forgotten long before his time. On the contrary, he single-handedly accomplished what all of them had failed to do—namely, open up America to the rest of humanity. Seen in this context, Columbus stood triumphantly at the apex of a maritime tradition that went back many thousands of years. Regardless of whoever came before or of its consequences for native peoples, his success still deserves proper homage.

Richard Greenough's 1856 "Bust of Young Christopher Columbus" at Indiana's Fort Wayne Museum of Art portrays the future admiral as a self-assured 14-year-old. By then, he was already a veteran mariner of nearly five years at sea. Photo courtesy of Wikipedia.

But the reader interested in such pre-Columbian voyages must wonder: Why do no history textbooks in the United States so much as mention any of them? An answer lies in the conditioning of modern, accredited archaeologists, who cannot deviate from an academic party line without jeopardizing their professional careers. Their attitude is crystallized in a response Dr. Michael Waters made to data contradicting a 1929 theory he and his colleagues embrace as scientific dogma. It holds that the first humans settled North America no earlier than 13,500 years ago. When the director of the Center for the Study of the First Americans at Texas A&M University was presented with credible materials for a quarter-million-year-old or older man-made habitation site outside Mexico City, he declared, "I don't care what the evidence is, I can't believe the old dates, because they refute everything that's known about archaeology and anthropology. I could never bring myself to believe those old dates."[2]

Tragically, this shockingly unscientific mindset is not confined to a few fringe theorists or dotty professors, but characterizes most U.S. archaeologists, who recognize only those facts that support mainstream opinion. Worse still, these are the people writing our textbooks and telling us what to think based more on their academic authority than fact. A reverse, opposite approach is taken herein, which begins with no preconceived notions, but allows instead for conclusions to arise from available evidence, regardless where that process may lead—even to possibilities for the arrival on our shores of ancient Old World visitors.

Their impact on the development of the Americas is as unacknowledged as it is nevertheless immutable and enduring. Volumes could be written on any one of these numerous culture-bearers, who forever transformed our land and its great variety of peoples during antiquity. Instead, not all the evidence for their influential legacies, but among the latest and best is offered in the following pages. May they open our eyes to the ancient human adventure enacted on the very ground we walk today, and may they also enable us to appreciate the inherent fragility of all civilizations, past and present, including our own!

Chapter 1:
Sumerians

They created the first human society known to have met all the fundamental requirements for modern civilization. They built the earliest city-states overseen by ruling dynasties; carved out empires and engaged in foreign relations; instituted a legal code and administrative systems, complete with courts, jails, and government records; instituted military science with divisions of infantry, transport (carts drawn by pairs of desert *onagers,* Asiatic wild asses), and spear-throwers; invented systems of weights and measures; created accounting and record-keeping, and published histories in an original written language; organized agriculture and irrigation; warehoused produce for general distribution; engaged in long-distance commerce; ran a merchant fleet; established an economy based on the various trades of its subjects; employed skilled artisans for public works projects; organized large-scale labor and hierarchical management for the construction of monumental temples and palaces, some with arches, domes, and buttresses, thousands of years before these architectural components were re-discovered by Roman building engineers; provided welfare for the underprivileged; protected women under the law and allowed them to achieve much higher status than in other, contemporaneous societies; taught navigation, mathematics, geometry, algebra, surveying, and astronomy with abacus and slide rule; specialized in decorative arts; and codified religion.

Who were these inventive people? And how did they come to take the first step from pre-civilized to civilized humankind?

The Sumerians called themselves the *Uĝ saĝ gíg-ga*, or "black-headed people," though surviving examples of their painted statuary depict them with blue eyes, and poems celebrated their "fair-headed lads and maidens."[1] Nor did they ever refer to the territories they occupied in what is today modern Iraq as "Sumer." The name is Semitic, after the later Akkadian *Šumeru*, itself derived from the earlier Hittite *Šanhar* and Egyptian *Sngr.* To these "Sumerians," their domain was originally known as *Ki-en-ĝir*, or "land of the civilized kings," a name reflecting their self-conscious identity as culture-creators.

They were a non-Semitic folk from Samarra, in northern Mesopotamia, their lineage going back to a Sanskrit-speaking, Aryan homeland in the Southern Urals Steppe region. These roots in south-central Russia account for the ubiquitous appearance of the swastika, that emblematic symbol of all Indo-European tribes, among the inhabitants of Samarra. Paleo-linguists Hyatt and Ruth Verrill have demonstrated the relationship "between Sumerian and Sanskrit."[2]

The proto-Sumerians of Samarra flourished as able farmers, weavers, leatherworkers, masons, and potters. Such skills led to increasing population pressures that forced some, after 4500 BCE, to leave Samarra for less crowded conditions at the southern end of the Fertile Crescent. There, the immigrants drained the marshes, established their industries, and traded with their neighbors—indigenous peasants in mud-brick huts, together with nomadic Semites, pastoralists living in black tents and following herds of sheep and goats. The newcomers' innovative management of storable food fostered a demographic expansion constrained within settled areas, with consequent development of extensive labor forces required to serve the diversifying needs of burgeoning community life. Rising levels of material success had gradually matured into prosperous urban centers sprouting along the Persian Gulf. Here history merged with myth to explain the birth of civilization on the Euphrates-Tigris alluvial plain, south of Baghdad.

Although archaeologists and paleo-anthropologists are unable to definitively trace the Sumerians' ethnic or linguistic roots, the Sumerians themselves told how their first city was built in the south, from whence spread high culture northward throughout the Fertile Crescent. Their claim was borne out by field investigators, who identified Eridu as the oldest city not only in Mesopotamia, but in the world. It was established around 5400 BCE, near the mouth of the Euphrates River and the seacoast, but lies now some distance from the Persian Gulf, due to the accumulation of silt at the shoreline over the last 74 centuries. Eridu, according to the Sumerians, was founded by Adapa, a representative from the far-off land of Dilmun, revered as the seat of Creation.

It was from this "place where the Sun rises" that "the first man" landed with the seeds of a technological society that soon after blossomed between the Tigris and Euphrates rivers. Although scholars have not yet determined the location of Dilmun, its culture-bearers appear to have indeed gained a foothold in coastal Iraq nearly one thousand years before immigrants from Samarra arrived at Eridu, where a synthesis of Adapa's sea-faring people from Dilmun with the *Uĝ saĝ gíg-ga* of Samarra resulted in Sumerian civilization. This conclusion is underscored by the excavation at Eridu of abundant fish middens containing the mid-sixth-millennium BCE skeletal remains of deep-water ocean catch made by a sailing folk fitting Adad's characterization and believed to have been ancestors of the Sumerians.

Two thousand years later, *Ki-en-ĝir* was divided into about a dozen independent city-states ruled over by either an *ensi,* a kind of priestly governor, or a monarch, known as the *lugal.* These were transitional to their First Dynasty, circa 2900 BCE, and Sumer flourished for more than 400 years, until violence began to wash over the "land of the civilized kings" with the onset of the 26th Century BCE. Cities grew suddenly overpopulated and threw up formidable defensive walls, while undefended villages disappeared. An aggressive Semitic kingdom, Akkad, was making its bid for supreme power.

Around 2500 BCE, Eannatum of Lagash endeavored to unify all of Sumer against this dire threat by taking most of his fellow city-states by force. His dynamic action saved *Ki-en-ĝir* for the next 230 years. But with the appearance of Sargon the Great, the ancient "land of the civilized kings" was completely overpowered in 2270 BCE. The Akkadians themselves went into steep decline just 52 years later, only to be replaced by the non-Semitic Gutians. Successful revolts against the Gutians were led by the *lugals,* Ur-Nammu and Shulgi, who expelled the occupiers around 2047 BCE. Their triumph unleashed a national revival of civilization that flourished for more than 100 years.

But renewed, mid-20th-century-BCE bickering between quarrelsome city-states doomed this "Sumerian Renaissance." In 1940 BCE, another Semitic people, the Amorites, overwhelmed *Ki-en-ĝir,* which would never rise again, although the elegance of its speech would linger on in revered use for centuries to come among the Babylonians, much as Latin is still the language of the arts and sciences in our modern world. Thus vanished a formerly great people, who lost their birthright for all time, because they preferred relatively petty disputes among themselves to unity in the face of a growing menace threatening their common existence. The Sumerians squandered the heritage of their forefathers and posterity of their children on behalf of issues less important than their own survival.

The Sumerians left their foremost surviving memorial to themselves in a place known 4,000 years ago as Urim. Today shortened by archaeologists to "Ur," it was originally a very populous and prosperous coastal urban center on the Persian Gulf, until millennia of silting stranded it far inland, 10 miles from the Iraq city of Nasiriyah, south of the right bank on the Euphrates River. It was here that labor teams and building engineers constructed *E-temen-niguru,* the "House Whose Foundation Creates Awe," now known as the "Great Ziggurat of Ur." The term is Akkadian, from the verb *zaqāru,* "to build on a raised area." It describes a step-pyramid of large, layered platforms ascending in successively receding stories or levels.

Built mostly of mud bricks set in bitumen (mortar manufactured from a naturally occurring tar), the 210-foot-long structure stood more than 100 feet high in three terraces. Each of its baked bricks measured 11.5 by 11.5 by 2.75 inches and weighed about 33 pounds. Approximately three million six hundred thousand of them were carried by an estimated 10,000 workers—not slaves—laboring year-round to complete their monument in a single generation. Unguessed thousands of cut stones additionally went into its construction. As a Khan Academy writer observes, "The resources needed to build the Ziggurat at Ur are staggering."[3]

Image 1-1: Iraq's Ziggurat of Ur. Photo courtesy of Wikpedia.

Across the front of its 150-foot expanse angled a series of ramps priests and privileged worshippers—though not the general public—used to climb from its base to the first tier, from which they continued their ascent via grand stairways, eventually reaching a shrine for the moon god, Nanna, at the flat summit. Thirty-two ancient ziggurats have been identified, but in only one other place outside Iraq and Iran: South America.

The pre-Inca peoples of coastal Peru built stone and mud-brick step pyramids of similar design and proportions. Like their Middle Eastern counterparts, the Andean versions were part of temple complexes surrounded by other buildings to serve as city administrative centers. These included courtyards, storage rooms, bathrooms, and living quarters, likewise among Sumerians and Peruvians, even to the shared use of massive ramps. Writes Jim R. Bailey in his acclaimed *Sailing to Paradise*:

> But it is not only the general form of these pyramids that is common to the Middle East and to America. In both regions there was a temple on top for the benefit of the god that—again in both regions—was also used by the priests for astronomy. In both regions the sides of the temples were often accurately aligned with the four points of the compass. In both regions a broad flight of steps, a Jacob's ladder, led from the ground to the temple at the summit.[4]

The most cogent such comparison is found in the Supe Valley, Barranca province, about 130 miles north of Lima, some 13 miles from the Pacific coast. Although discovered in 1948, the ruins at Caral—part of a high culture referred to by U.S. archaeologists as "Norte Chico"—were not truly appreciated for their high significance until the early 21st Century, when Ruth Shady Solís, director of Peru's Museum of Archaeology and Anthropology at the National University of San Marcos, re-examined their plazas, mud-brick buildings, and stone monuments.

Towering above them all is the 59-foot-tall *Pirámide Mayor.* Made of quarried stone and river cobbles, it stands 490 feet long and 520 feet wide, and covers more than four acres (or nearly four football fields). As described by *Archaeology* magazine's Roger Atwood, "Armies of workers would gather a long, durable grass known as *shicra* in the highlands above the city, tie the grass strands into loosely meshed bags, fill the bags with boulders, and then pack the trenches behind each successive retaining wall of the step pyramids with the stone-filled bags."[5]

Image 1-2: Peru's Pirámide Mayor *at Caral was under construction at the same time King Sargon built the ziggurat of Ur, in what is now Iraq. Photo courtesy of Wikipedia.*

The discovery of these sacks in situ at the site accurately disclosed the structure's age, because they were woven of reeds, a readily carbon-datable material that allows for a high degree of accuracy. Repeated C-14 testing consistently revealed that the *Pirámide Mayor* was built in 2627 BCE. This year is remarkable not only for identifying Caral as the oldest urban center in the Americas, but because it perfectly coincides with crucial changes brought about with Mesopotamia's transition to the Dynastic IIIa period. At that time, its city-states were beginning to engage in warfare among themselves, spoiling the previous two centuries of relative harmony and cooperation typified by Early Dynastic II. To escape these worsening conditions, it would appear some Sumerians emigrated from "the land of the civilized kings," even as far as the other side of the world. That they possessed the means whereby to carry themselves anywhere they chose is beyond question. "Cuneiform inscriptions tell of vessels large enough to carry twenty-eight tons of cargo," writes Dr. Gunnar Thompson in *American Discovery.*[6]

Archaeologists know that the Sumerians were highly skilled mariners, operating four different classes of vessels. These included eminently seaworthy boats constructed from animal skins; virtually identical craft were used many centuries later by Christian missionaries for regular crossings of the treacherous Irish Sea, 150 miles of open water, often in the company of cows or horses. The Sumerians also built deep-keel (for ocean-going), wooden-oared warships and freighters capacious enough for carrying fully armed troops or livestock.

Some Sumerian hulls were clinker-built, stitched together with onager hair and waterproofed with bitumen. Also known as *lapstrake,* clinker building fixes wooden planks one to another, enabling them to overlap along their edges. The entire length of one such composite plank is called a strake. This technique was invented for navigating transoceanic swells and high waves, as dramatically demonstrated by the Viking long-ships. In fact, clinker-built vessels were formerly associated with Norse seafaring to such an extent that they were believed to have originated in Northern Europe sometime during the early second century AD, as suggested by Denmark's Nydam Bog find, until their discovery in ancient Mesopotamia.

The Sumerians also successfully operated large reed boats, as re-created by Dr. Thor Heyerdahl for his "Tigris Expedition." In 1978, his 55-foot-long re-creation cruised down Shatt-el-Arab from Iraq into the Persian Gulf, continuing on to Pakistan's Indus Valley, before sailing back over the Indian Ocean to Africa. Heyerdahl covered 4,225 miles in five months, demonstrating his reed vessel's capabilities by successfully voyaging to pre-planned harbors, regardless of contrary winds and ocean currents. The same could have been identically achieved in the Atlantic Ocean.

According to Dr. Thompson, "Sumerian tablets of the 3rd Millennium B.C. tell of voyages 'beyond the western sea,'" an apparent reference to the Mediterranean.[7] In fact, the discovery of resin from Mozambique in the tomb of Puabi, an *eresh* (queen) at Ur, showed that her people were capable of navigating equivalent distances as far east as the South China Sea or as far west as the Canary Islands. Bailey compares 22 Sumerian gold weights with their virtually exact counterparts among the Ashanti, a strong indication that merchants from Ur not only visited Ghana, but made a lasting impression there. As long ago as 1935, Willibald Wanger's Comparative Lexical Study of Sumerian and Ntu documented the relationship "between Sumerian and black African Bantu languages...."[8]

Hugh Fox, PhD, a professor at Michigan State University and the author of six published anthropology books, wrote of the Sumerians' "connection to West Africa, then the leap across the Atlantic (carried by friendly currents) to the New World."[9] Writing in *The Western World Review,* Robert Sagehorn cited Hugh Fox as "...one of the foremost authorities (perhaps the foremost authority) on pre-Columbian American cultures."[10] During his extensive research into parallels between the ancient Middle East and pre-Columbian South America, Fox made an important, relative find in Dr. Thor Heyerdahl's *Early Man and the Ocean*: "Con-Ticci-Viracocha is a composite of three names for the same white and bearded deity. In pre-Inca times, he was known on the coast of Peru as Con and in the highlands as *Tici* or *Ticci*, but when Inca rule and language (Quechua) spread to encompass the entire territory, the Incas recognized that the names *Con* and *Ticci* referred to the same deity as the one they themselves called *Viracocha*. They therefore grouped the three names together, to the satisfaction of all the people of their empire."[11]

The original *Con* and the later, amalgamated *Con-Ticci-Viracocha* was revered as the founding father of Andean society—described in native traditions as a tall, red-bearded, fair-skinned culture-bearer, who bequeathed to their ancestors all the benefits of civilization, which had been developed in his overseas' kingdom. This was important news to Fox, who read in L.A. Waddell's *The Makers of Civilization in Race and History* that "the second pre-dynastic Sumerian king is known as Kon."[12]

Appropriately, the Andean Con was known on the Peruvian coast, the location of Caral, the significance of which was not learned until after Heyerdahl's death. Fox expanded his investigation to another pre-Inca site in western Bolivia, near Lake Titicaca, the highest navigable body of water on Earth. Tiawanaku, from the Aymara *taypiqala,* "stone in the center," once belonged to a huge ceremonial and administrative center of grand staircases, sunken courtyards, monumental stone gates, sprawling plazas, and monolithic statues. Scholars are divided over the age of its ruins, dating them to as long ago as 15,000 BCE or as recently as the 7th to 11th Centuries CE.

They are in agreement, however, that Tiawanaku was once a powerful city of great influence long before the Incas rose to prominence. Intrigued by the appearance of Sumer's pre-dynastic King Kon as coastal Peru's Con, Dr. Fox found that "the area around Titicaca is the very center of the Bolivian tin country. All the ancient folklore epithets associated with Titicaca, in fact, center around its connection with tin: *Titi-Tata,* 'Father of Tin'; *Titi Wiyana,* 'Altar of *Tin* to Adore the Sun, Our King;' *Titi-Kaka/ Thithi-Ccotta,* 'Tin-Plated Cup that Contains All the Waters Reunited by the Four Winds of the Intis, Antillis, or Andes.'"[13]

Fox discovered further revelations in the classic Sumerian story of Gilgamesh, a saga of the historical King of Uruk, who traveled westward sometime between 2750 and 2500 BCE over the sea to a distant land referred to in the epic as *Anaku.* Its philological and geographical resemblance to *Tiawanaku* seemed self-evident:

> And Oruru, in Bolivia, not far from Tiawanaku, another Bolivian mining center (where, incidentally, the School of Mines is located), is derived from another Sumerian word, *urruru,* "to smelt." So, we have the tin at Tiawanaku/Anaku, and the smelting at Oruru/

> urruru, although Arthur Posnansky, the great scholar, who devoted so much of his life to a study of Tiawanaku, was impressed by the size of the heaps of slag he saw at Tiawanaku, when he first arrived there...the Sumerian epic tale of Gilgamesh is about a voyage to Tiawanaku.[14]

Tin was vitally important to the Sumerians in their production of bronze, together with copper and zinc. Bronze was the nuclear fission of its day, a commodity more valuable than gold for making tools, weapons, lamps, and a wide variety of essential goods. "If it seems strange that an important center of a civilization should have been at such a height," Bailey writes, "more than twelve thousand feet above sea-level, the first answer is simply the excellence of the supplies of metal nearby. They are some of the biggest deposits of silver, copper and alluvial tin anywhere in the world."[15]

The Lake Titicaca area, as Fox pointed out, is abundant in tin resources, more than enough economic incentive for metallurgists from the ancient Old World to brave the hazards of transoceanic voyages, if only because such resources were far less rich in Mesopotamia. In fact, the Sumerian Anaku from which Bolivia's Tiawanaku derives means, literally and descriptively, "Tin Lands." Bailey writes how "Sargon himself mounted overseas' expeditions to secure supplies of tin. Contemporary inscriptions record that he crossed the sea in the west, and in a general review of his empire, he is credited with control of two 'lands beyond the Upper Sea,'" a reference to western territories outside the Mediterranean.[16]

Despite its high altitude in the Andes Mountains, the area was easily accessible to Sumerian sailors rounding Africa's Cape of Good Hope and crossing the South Atlantic to South American shores. Bailey explains that "the headwaters of the Amazon and its tributaries reach within a hundred miles of Lake Titicaca. So, too, do those of the River Paraná, which runs southeastward to empty into the Atlantic at Buenos Aires, from whence the traders could have made use of the South Atlantic circle of winds and currents...."[17]

David Hatcher Childress concludes

> that Tiawanaku, Pima Punku [a nearby ruined ceremonial center] and possibly some sunken cities in Lake Titicaca were part of an early transoceanic quest for metals that culminated in the creation of a huge metallurgical plant and ceremonial city that processed metals from around the lake. According to my theory, many mines were located in the large region in all directions from Lake Titicaca.[18]

"In the innumerable inscriptions dealing with Sumerian history," the Verrills wrote, "frequent references are made to the 'Lake of Manu' sometimes associated with a 'cloud lake,' and usually designated as being in the 'Mountains of the Sunset,' a semi-fabulous or traditional land which, apparently, the Sumerian explorers were seeking on voyages to the 'Sunset Land.'"[19] Bailey observed, "Lake Titicaca is the only lake that fits the description..."[20]

Ur's Queen Puabi died around 2600 BCE, the same period assigned to Peru's *Pirámide Mayor.* Although it certainly resembles her city's Great Ziggurat, *E-temen-niguru* was built 600 years later, which is, in any case, no cause for discrepancy, because such step-pyramids were introduced at the very start of Sumer's First Dynasty. Iran's Sialk ziggurat, in Kashan, the oldest known of its kind, was built circa 2900 BCE, pre-dating Caral by three centuries. In fact, Sumerian chronology is a perfect template for "Norte Chico" time lines, particularly in consideration of Mesopotamian impact on pre-Columbian South America. As already pointed out, Caral burst upon the scene in Peru just as the Middle East's Early Dynastic II period shifted into Early Dynastic IIIa.

"Ur was the largest city in the world from circa 2030 to 1980 B.C. Its population was approximately sixty-five thousand...2011 research indicates that the area was struck by drought conditions from 2200 to 2000 B.C. The population dropped by ninety-three per cent."[21] An environmental catastrophe so severely reduced agricultural output that most of Ur's residents were forced to leave. Strangely, their emigration had no demographic effect on any of Mesopotamia's other city-states. Where did these people go? Their disappearance coincides with a sudden population surge on the other side of the Atlantic Ocean, when Norte Chico may have been the most densely populated area of the world. Sumerians appear to have sailed *en masse* from Ur to Caral, in the same way human migration has been prompted for time immemorial by the irresistible pressures of events, man-made or natural.

The Sumerian Renaissance in 2047 BCE and its violent termination by Amorite conquerors likewise coincided with the end of Peru's Norte Chico Civilization. Previous to their simultaneous demise, the Sumerians found more than refuge or tin in west coastal South America. They were great lovers of cotton, which the Middle East's arid climate prevented them from growing, and so were forced to import it at no small cost all the way from India. But in the Supe Valley, they found conditions ideal for a species of *Gossypium barbadense*, enabling them to produce the soft, tough fabric on a massive scale. It is this love for cotton found in common among the Norte Chico and Sumerian populations that helps identify them as the same people. Cotton manufacture may not have been known in South America before its sudden introduction at Caral, certainly not to the broad extent seen there.

Bailey explains:

> All domestic American cottons are what are known as *tetraploids*...that is, they contain two sets of recognizably distinct genes. One set resembles the genes of American wild cottons, the other the genes of all Asiatic cottons, domestic and wild. There is no possible way this could have come about except by the inter-breeding of the two stocks. We know that

> cotton was being used in Peru in the 4th Millennium B.C. using fibers from the crossbred Asian-American plant. The conclusion seems to follow without doubt: at some time before that the seeds of Asian cotton had been brought into America, and they did not come by natural means. Even if a few seeds had managed to drift all the way across the Pacific they could never have remained fertile after months of immersion in salt water.... The cotton grown in America was a hybrid between a Southeast Asian cotton and a native American cotton, and thus also points to transoceanic contacts.[22]

His important observations not only reveal the foreign origins of American cotton; they also imply that the Sumerians may not have reached the Americas only by sailing across the Mediterranean Sea and out into the Atlantic Ocean, but continued on from their known ports of call in India into Southeast Asia, then beyond across the Pacific. Alternatively, the Sumerians brought their own cotton, imported from Southeast Asia, in their transoceanic voyages to coastal Peru.

In any case, cotton was used there during the third millennium BCE to make strong nets for deep-sea fishing, yet another cultural trait characteristic of the maritime Sumerians, whose temple at Ur "contained immense amounts of luxury items made out of precious metals, and semi-precious stones, all of which would have had to been imported from long distances—Iran, Afghanistan, India, Asia Minor, the Persian Gulf.... All the wealth which came to Mesopotamia by sea had to pass through Ur."[23]

So, too, the ancient *Caralinos* pursued far-flung commerce, much of it by water routes, at least as far as the Amazon, where they brought back such bizarre luxury items as monkeys and hallucinogenic snuff. Indeed, narcotics may have been yet another attractive commodity in the New World. Fox cites Gilgamesh, "who voyages across the ocean to Anaku, the tin lands, searching for a spiny thorn-apple that makes old men young again, an 'apple' of eternal youth. And behind this 'myth' about the apples is another reality about the taking of psychedelic drugs as part of an initiation ceremony at the time of the winter solstice, also hidden under layers of metaphor."[24]

The inhabitants of Caral supplemented their diet of squash, beans, lucuma, apple guava, pacay, camote, avocado, and achira with deep-ocean catch. During her excavation of the ruins, Ruth Shady Solís learned how "animal remains are almost exclusively marine,"[25] an observation that confirmed archaeologist Michael E. Moseley's belief in the "maritime foundation of Andean civilization."[26]

As some indication of their sea-faring proficiency, Caral's ancient inhabitants made furniture from the hearing vertebrae of blue whales. Accordingly, the *Caralinos* seem indistinguishable from Sumerian sailors making their way to similarly remote markets across the Indian Ocean and beyond. These comparisons were remarkably underscored by two, separate finds of ancient cuneiform in South America during the mid-20th and early 21st Centuries. The script derived its name from *cuneus*, Latin for "wedge," because its characters—impressed into clay tablets by a stylus—were wedge shaped. They belonged to the earliest known written language, which was invented by the Sumerians about 3000 BCE, just prior to the founding of their First Dynasty.

The first discovery of its kind occurred in 1959, when a construction worker found a chestnut-brown, fired ceramic vessel at Magna Fuente, or the "great fountain" area of the Manjon family property, about 50 miles from the Bolivian capital at La Paz. Over the next 42 years, the 2.4-inch-deep, 5-inch-wide bowl received little attention, even though it had been accidentally dug up not far from the pre-Inca ruins of Tiahuanaco, long ago the ceremonial and administrative capital of a great kingdom.

The object languished in virtual obscurity until January 4, 2002, as archaeologists excavated a site known as Pokotia, again near Tiahuanaco, less than 4 miles west of the ruins.

Inside a pyramidal hill, director Bernardo Biados and his colleagues found

> a three hundred fifty-pound, five-foot-tall, two-foot-wide statue made of red granite, broken at the feet and neck. The male figure with almost entirely eroded facial features stands upright with his arms at his sides, ribs indicated by four lines on either side of the chest, wearing a loincloth-like garment about his hips, and simple armbands at both wrists. The puffy headgear atop his head is identical to similar representations found at Tiahuanaco's semi-subterranean court. Inscrutable symbols and cuneiform script spill over his back, the front of his legs below the hands, and on both thighs.[27]

Publicity surrounding the discovery of the Pokotia Monolith prompted renewed interest in the Magna Fuente vessel, because it had been

> engraved overall with zoological motifs and anthropomorphic characters intersecting two, different scripts...one is entirely unlike any comparable written language, but the other is identifiably cuneiform.... Dr. Alberto Marini, a recognized authority in ancient Mesopotamian languages, determined that the Magna Fuente inscription was Sumerian, and identified the artifact as a libation bowl.... When the Pokotia Monolith was removed to La Paz's Museum of Precious Metals (formerly known as the Gold Museum) on Calle Jaén, it was joined by the Magna Fuente object in 2007.[28]

According to a writer for *Kemo's Journal,* "the two languages on the bowl are apparently Sumerian and the local

Aymara language; the two appear to be related, with the local dialect apparently derived from Sumerian."[29]

While inscriptions on the bowl and statue await full translation, the mere existence of such finds in the Andes, to say nothing of their discovery near one of South America's foremost archaeological sites, alone represents potent proof for the arrival of visitors from third millennium BCE Mesopotamia. But when combined with the monumental evidence at Caral, a Sumerian impact during early pre-Columbian times seems undeniable. That impression is reinforced by yet more correspondences with the ancient Middle East. The very name, "Pokotia," appears to be an Aymara derivation of *patesi*, Sumerian for a "priest king."

"Quechua, the other principal language still spoken in the Andes," states Fox, "is filled with...Sumerian cognates."[30] For example, the Verrills compare the Sumerian word for "lord"—*apu*—with the Quechua *Apu Inca*, or "Lord Inca."[31] The Sumerian earth-mother-goddess was *Mami*; *Mama* was her name in pre-Columbian Peru.

"Both Sumerians and Peruvians," Dr. Thompson observes, "believed in the existence of a holy mountain with twin peaks, where the Sun rested during the night. Sumerians called their twin peaks Mashu; among the Inca, it was known as Machu Picchu."[32] Mario Montaño, associate professor in the department of anthropology at Colorado College (Colorado Springs), "has found startling linguistic evidence that indicates a Sumerian substratum in the Aymara and Quechua languages."[33] Examples of cuneiform occur outside Bolivia, into Argentina, according to Dr. Thompson, attesting to the Sumerians' broad impact, which extended far beyond South America.

After Hin-mah-too-yah-lat-kekt of the Wal-lam-wat-kain, a band of Nez Perce Indians, surrendered to units of the U.S. Cavalry near Chinook in the north of what is now Montana on October 5, 1877, his "medicine bag" containing a 1-inch-square baked clay tablet was stolen. Better remembered as Chief Joseph, he explained that the tablet, engraved on both sides with then inscrutable texts, "had been passed down in his family for many generations, and that they had inherited it from their white ancestors. Chief Joseph said that white men had come among his ancestors long ago, and had taught his people many things."[34] Today, his ancestral heirloom is still warehoused at New York's West Point Museum.

In 2000, Robert D. Biggs, an Assyriology professor at the Oriental Institute of the University of Chicago, with a PhD from Johns Hopkins University, and editor of the *Journal of Near Eastern Studies,* was able to translate the texts of Chief Joseph's tablet, because they had been inscribed in cuneiform. They recorded the sale of a lamb for sacrifice on behalf of a person named *Enmahgalanna* to celebrate her promotion as a high priestess of Nanna, the same moon-god enshrined at Ur's Great Ziggurat. Professor Biggs dated the Sumerian inscription to approximately 2042 BCE.[35]

Native American pouches such as the one Chief Joseph carried "contained items that would remind the warrior of home, of where he came from," according to historical writer Mary Gindling. "The mundane nature of the contents of the tablet argues against forgery. Cuneiform had only been deciphered in 1846, and the process was far from complete even in 1877, so a would-be forger would had to have been an extremely well educated individual, familiar not only with the ancient language itself, but with the shape of the tablets created by the ancient scribes."[36]

Not long after the Cherokee artifact came to light, "a Sumerian tablet with cuneiform writing was found beside ancient stone projectile points near Lexington, Georgia," writes Dr. Thompson. "The tablet is from Ur-Nammuk, Iraq, and dates to 2040 B.C."[37]

Cultural diffusionist researcher Gloria Farley tells of a similar discovery in the same state made by a Mrs. Joe Hearn:

> In 1963, while digging a new flower bed on her property in northwestern Georgia, not far from the Chatahoochee River, her shovel had struck a small, pillow-shaped tablet made of lead.... The cuneiform script, according to Dr.

> Curtis Hoffman, describes how a scribe named *Enlila* was aware that it was the thirty-seventh or thirty-eighth year of the reign of King Shulgi of Ur, which by our reckoning, would have been about 2040 B.C. It recorded the sale of sheep and goats, which apparently had been transported overseas to America, for sacrifice to Utu, the sun-god, and the goddess, Lama Lugal [a Sumerian deity of intercession and protection].[38]

Although Shulgi actually ruled from 2029 to 1982 BCE, Georgia's Hearn object and Chief Joseph's tablet both date to within 11 years of each other; their discoveries were separated by many hundreds of miles and two centuries, underscoring a common authenticity. LaGrange College, Georgia's oldest private college, founded in 1831, today owns the Hearn Tablet.

Near Quaker City, Ohio, an amateur Indian arrowhead collector discovered a cuneiform tablet in 1978. Its ancient provenance was established by David Owen, professor of Near Eastern studies at Cornell University, in Ithaca, New York. He translated the Sumerian text, which had been composed "by a man named *Ur-e'e* in the month of Dumuzi [late June], in the year [circa 2030 BCE] the *ensi* [ruler] of Karzida was elevated."[39] Karzida was the second city of worship for Nanna, the same moon-god likewise referenced by the inscription on Chief Joseph's tablet, suggesting a relationship between his family heirloom and the Quaker City find, which came to light years after his death. That relationship is remarkably cogent to our discussion, because they, together with the Lexington and Hearn tablets, were all inscribed within 12 years of each other, between 2042 and 2030 BCE. They define the most appropriate segment of time for voyages to America, because it matches the dynamic outset of the Ur III Period, or "Sumerian Renaissance."

It began in 2047 BCE, just after the Sumerians liberated themselves from Akkadian domination and experienced their most energetic outward expansion, as exampled by the specimen of South African resin found in Queen Puabi's tomb at Ur. "Many such Ur III tablets have been found in the U.S.," states Professor Owen, "including some tablets dug up a few years ago from the ruins of an old apartment house in Auburn, New York."[40]

So many tablets spread over half a continent—from Montana to Georgia, Ohio, and New York—do not suggest some lone survivor of shipwreck, blown far off course during some otherwise-normal trading mission in the Middle East, but indicate rather the deliberate arrival of numerous Sumerian visitors, all from the same capital of Ur's Third Dynasty. If the appearance of genuine cuneiform in North America and South America emphasizes the broadly populous impact they made during early pre-Columbian times, that impression is supported by additional finds made between both continents, in Central America.

In his report for the Epigraphic Society's Occasional Publications, Clyde Keeler writes:

> I learned from twenty-two expeditions to the Cuna Indians, on the offshore San Blas Islands of Eastern Panama, that this tribe has a Turning Tree of Life religion similar to that of ancient Sumer, 3400 B.C. Like Ishtar, the Cuna Earthmother bears in her womb a Tree of Life on which grow plants, animals and Man. It also bears the Golden Apples of Immortality. One must obtain permission from the Cuna Earthmother to pick the apples. The Tree is guarded by a dog, corresponding to Cerberus, that must be appeased before the Golden Apples (*Olo Wini*) can be picked.
>
> As in Sumer, Ishtar had to carry a leafy branch from the Tree of Life (the Golden Bough) in order to be able to return to the surface of the earth, so the Cuna High Priest (*kantule*) must break off for protection a golden branch so freshly developed that it has no chlorophyll ("so freshly developed," say the Cunas,

> "that no bird has yet sat upon it"). The Cunas originally lived in Columbia that borders on Peru. Evidence also comes from seventy-four words of native Peruvian that have identical or similar sounds and meanings with words in Sumerian. A list of forty-two cultural identities or similarities in culture have been described for Peruvian and Sumerian.[41]

The "Ishtar" Keeler mentions was actually the later Babylonian version of Sumer's "Queen of Heaven," Inanna, goddess of sexual love, fertility, and warfare. Her worship preceded Babylon's rise during the late 23rd Century BCE, going back to the Uruk period, beginning around the turn of the fourth millennium BCE. Inanna's symbol, signifying the planet Venus, was an eight-pointed star, which also appears on an Inca *uncu,* or high priest's 38-inch by 30-inch tunic displayed at New York's American Museum of Natural History Library, Division of Anthropology, originally from Bolivia's Lake Titicaca region, the same general area where the Magna Fuente Bowl and Pokotia statue covered with cuneiform texts were found.

A revealing comparison is made between the origins of civilization at Mesopotamia and in the Supe Valley: The former has been traced back to long periods of gradual pre-development. A growing coalescence of sea-farers from Dilmun, agriculturalists from Samarra, indigenous peasants, and nomadic Semitic herders progressively matured from the mid-6th and 5th Millennia BCE to the rise of city-states during the mid-4th Millennium BCE and the establishment of Sumer's First Dynasty around the turn of the 3rd Millennium BCE.

Mesopotamia's extended cultural evolution was in sharp contrast to the abrupt florescence of Caral. It appeared without precedence and full-blown in the middle of the 27th century BCE, minus any traces of previous development, giving every indication that Norte Chico Civilization was imported into the Supe Valley by outsiders, who cultivated it elsewhere over time. This impression is deepened by Caral's complimentary chronology with Sumer, *Pirámide Mayor*'s unmistakable resemblance to a Mesopotamian ziggurat, and all the other cultural commonalities—as numerous as they are cogent—both civilizations shared.

These comparisons amount to credible, even overwhelmingly convincing evidence for the early-fourth-millennium BCE arrival of culture-bearers from the Middle East on the northern Pacific coast of South America, where they proliferated over 15 centuries and influenced another three millennia of Andean Civilization. Its Norte Chico beginnings began to flourish around 3000 BCE, an era parallel to Sumer's late Uruk period and its pre-dynastic King *Kon,* who is credibly identified with *Con,* the racially alien culture-bearer known in the same area of coastal Peru.

Over the next thousand years, the colonizers he personified grew in numbers, as the needs of their Mesopotamian homeland expanded to include tin, cotton, and hallucinogenic plants. So, too, the final collapse of Sumer in the mid-20th century BCE coincides with Caral's abandonment. As such, the simultaneous rise and fall of the first known civilizations in the Old and New Worlds was a shared experience.

Chapter 2:
Egyptians

Conventional archaeologists unanimously insist that the same Egyptians who raised the Great Pyramid were incapable of building a ship that could cross the sea. Although this general consensus is still emphatically upheld by mainstream scholars, it was effectively demolished almost 60 years ago. In 1954, a magnificent vessel more than 140 feet long and nearly 20 feet wide was discovered near the base of a pyramid assigned by Egyptologists to Pharaoh Khufu (also known as "Cheops"), who ruled the Old Kingdom's Fourth Dynasty for at least 26 years. On public display since 1982, following painstaking reconstruction at the Giza Solar Boat Museum, it had been sealed with all its 1,224 perfectly preserved pieces still laid out in their original order, minus any human remains, inside a deep pit carved from the local bedrock around 2580 BCE.

As some indication of its pristine condition as the world's oldest intact ship, conservators found that it is still seaworthy,

Image 2-1: Great Pyramid ship. Photo courtesy of Berthold Werner, via Wikipedia.

despite the passage of more than 45 centuries. In fact, they noticed sure signs of water wear on the hull, indicating that it had done its fair share of sailing at one time. The ancient builders had lashed planks and frames of cedar together with tough "needle grass" and used unpegged tenons made from a species of a deciduous shrub known as the "Crown of Thorns" to fix the boards. This maritime technology, surprisingly advanced for mid-third millennium BCE shipwrights, went beyond the needs of leisurely cruising down the mostly placid River Nile. Instead, it met criteria for negotiating far more challenging open-water voyages by allowing the hull to twist and wriggle its way through high swells and wave action. In other words, King Khufu's royal yacht is actually an ocean-going vessel. Nor is it the only one of its kind known.

Joining it around the peripheral base of his Great Pyramid are four more boat pits, each still containing its own ship, and deliberately left undisturbed to maintain their hermetically sealed environments for continued preservation. The nearby and only slightly smaller Khafre pyramid, officially associated with Khufu's successor, is accompanied by three boat pits, with two more on the south side of his mortuary temple; the ships in these subterranean chambers have long since disappeared.

A virtual flotilla of 14 identically constructed, if less perfectly intact, but much older examples was found during 1991 in the desert near Abydos, predating Khufu's specimen by some 500 years. The 75-foot-long, 9-foot wide craft goes back to the start of the First Dynasty, around 3100 BCE, and proves that the Egyptians already possessed a high level of applied marine technology at the very outset of their civilization. Other Egyptian cargo-carriers were capacious enough for stowing several chariots, including stalls for their horses. That these large ships could have and did engage in extensive missions overseas is beyond question. But King Khufu's royal ship reveals far more about dynastic origins.

As mentioned previously, its timber planks were sewn together with a tough "needle grass" identified by Egyptologists as *Stipa tenacissima*. Paleo-botanists, however, point out that this perennial plant is not native to Egypt. Instead, it grows in Atlantic coastal Spain, Morocco, Cape Verde, the Azores, Madeira, and Canary Islands.[1] These origins for the grass imply that either Khufu's yacht must have been constructed outside the Straits of Gibraltar at an Atlantic location, or that *Stipa tenacissima* was imported from that region into the Lower Nile Valley more than 4,500 years ago. Trace evidence suggesting the former conclusion is provided by David Hatcher Childress: "This vessel also has scraping damage on its forward underside that ship experts have claimed could only have been caused by a coral reef."[2] The nearest coral reef to Egypt grows in the Canary Islands.

Although orthodox scholars insist that no dynastic Egyptians had any direct contacts beyond the Eastern Mediterranean world, alternative researchers have wondered if the ships found around the base of the Great Pyramid were deliberately entombed there because they were the same vessels that transported its builders from some overseas homeland. Manetho, a third-century-BCE compiler of the Egyptians' earliest traditions, told how they believed their civilization was initiated by the *Smsu-Hr*, or "Followers of Horus," and the *Mesentiu*, "Harpooners," two related peoples who landed at the Nile Delta in great fleets of ships before the dawn of recorded history. They arrived from a so-called "Primal Mound" (mountain), cited additionally in the Egyptian Book of the Dead as *Sekheret-aaru,* an island of deep wisdom, because this "Field of Reeds" was sinking into the seas of the "Distant West." Reeds were used as writing utensils; hence, a field of reeds signified a place of great literacy.

Manetho's foundation account seems borne out by the anomalous appearance of a non-Egyptian grass originating in the "Distant West" for construction of Khufu's yacht. The only civilization conceivably responsible for its construction more than four millennia ago lay, in Plato's words, "beyond the Pillars of Heracles"—where *Stipa tenacissima* was a native plant and coral reefs were capable of marring the underside hull of Pharaoh's ship.

Hardly less notorious than mere allusion to Atlantis among cultural isolationists were Dr. Thor Heyerdahl's experimental voyages demonstrating the transatlantic capabilities of ancient Old World seamanship. Not as well known, however, was the failure of his first attempt in 1969. Although it was the faithful re-creation of a reed sailing vessel designed according to temple art illustrations and models from pharaonic Egypt, *Ra-I* was constructed on the northeastern border of Nigeria. Heyerdahl had wrongly assumed that the natives there preserved valid traditions of ancient boat-building, when, in fact, they did not even make skiffs capable of venturing across Lake Chad, their residence for time out of mind. They even lacked local, raw materials for the job, and he had to fly in papyrus reeds all the way from Ethiopia's Lake Tana. After a few weeks at sea, *Ra-I* was taking on water and began to sag, then broke apart.

Undeterred, Heyerdahl went to Bolivia's Lake Titicaca, where the natives did in fact enjoy a long tradition of making reed boats surprisingly similar to the design plans he brought from Egypt. The Aymara Indians told him that they continued to reproduce the same kind of vessels sailed by their fair-haired culture-bearer, Con-Ticci-Viracocha, who arrived long ago from over the sea. Engaging their inherited expertise, he commissioned them to build another re-creation, this one built of totora reeds that still grow around Lake Titicaca. In 1970, the resulting *Ra-II* left the shores of Morocco, from whence it was inexorably carried by the Canary Island Current across the Atlantic

Ocean to land at Barbados in good time and without incident. Long after *Ra-II* was still seaworthy, mainstream archaeologists argued that its voyage failed to prove that pharaonic Egyptians traveled to America.

The skeptics either missed Heyerdahl's point or endeavored to distort it, because his announced intention had been only to demonstrate that mariners from the Nile Delta possessed the means by which such crossings could have been successfully undertaken. This he and his reed-boat established beyond a shadow of a doubt. At least as early as the beginning of Khufu's Fourth Dynasty, surviving records indicate that ships very much like *Ra-II* were bringing back cargoes of gold to the Nile Delta from the distant "Land of Punt." Generations of Egyptologists have been unable to pinpoint its location, but today wonder if *Pwenet* or *Pwene*, as the country was also known, lay in northern Somalia, Djibouti, Eritrea, and the Red Sea coast of Sudan. Others believe the Arabian Peninsula is a more likely candidate. All their suppositions are partially based on occasional dynastic definitions of Punt as *Ta netjer*, the "land of the god," perhaps alluding to Egypt's solar deity, Ra, who rises in the East.

But these academic speculations are rendered suspect by original source material accounts describing voyages to Punt lasting 36 months. Even given the admittedly slow progress Egyptian freighters undoubtedly made—especially when sailing in convoys, their speed determined by the slowest vessel—they would not have required as many as three years to complete an 800-mile round trip to Djibouti, much less the shorter distances to and from the Arabian Peninsula. Egyptian freighters averaged 100 to 140 miles per day[3]; sailing distances from the Nile Delta to the Horn of Africa are roughly 1,500 miles. As such, round-trip voyages even as far as Somalia would have required only a few months at most, hardly three years to complete. Revealingly, when the 26th Dynasty Pharaoh Nekau II dispatched his own expedition to Punt circa 600 BCE, his seamen sailed around the African Continent inside three years—21 centuries before the famous Portuguese mariner, Vasco de Gama, unknowingly duplicated the same feat.

The length of their voyage suggests that all previous expeditions to the "land of the god" were not confined to the Red Sea, but also circum-continental. This implication is supported by some of the listed goods with which the ancient Egyptians returned. Chapter 1 told how Puabi was entombed at Ur with rare, aromatic resins imported from Mozambique, 3,000 miles south from northern Somalia; these resins were likewise brought back to Egypt in the same period cited as the first recorded voyage to Punt, and contemporary with the Sumerian Queen. The large quantities of gold said to have been taken from Punt more likely originated further away still, because Eritrea or the Arabian Peninsula is not especially endowed with mineral wealth, unlike South Africa and especially Ghana.

"Punt," writes Egyptologist Dimitri Meeks, "we are told by the Egyptians, is situated—in relation to the Nile Valley—both to the north, in contact with the countries of the Near East of the Mediterranean area, and also to the east or south-east, while its furthest borders are far away to the south."[4] The same texts describe Punt as simultaneously located southeast and northeast of Egypt, extending into Lebanon and Asia. These vast territories never comprised a single country, but were made up of vastly different peoples, as numerous as they were diverse and, to a large extent, unrelated.

It seems clear then, that Punt was not a "land," but a term for commercial expeditions to Lebanon, down the Red Sea to Mozambique and around the Cape of Good Hope, up the entire length of West Africa, then through the Straits of Gibraltar eastward across the Mediterranean Sea, back to the Nile Delta, accumulating stores of exotic luxury items and rare supplies at every stop along the way. Only such a far-ranging trade mission would have needed three years to complete. Thus understood, the lands of Punt included transatlantic detours to America for otherwise-unavailable commodities highly prized by Egypt's priestly and professional classes. For the last documented expedition of its kind under the auspices of Rameses III, about 1185 BCE, the 20th Dynasty Pharaoh spoke of his convoys traveling into the "inverted waters."

Dr. Thompson affirms:

> This confirms knowledge of the Earth's spherical shape, because vessels sailing to America were actually beneath Egypt, or "inverted," relative to Egypt's position on the globe. From the vantage point of Egypt, the western Atlantic lies on the opposite side of the globe. In other words, it appears "inverted" from the perspective of Egypt. The expression "inverted waters" is an accurate description of the western Atlantic, and it confirms Egyptian knowledge of the Earth's spherical shape.[5]

Rameses III's relationship with an American Punt was affirmed by a Pakistani scholar, whose thorough research won even the respect of cultural isolationists. R.A. Jairazbhoy states:

> In Peru, the Egyptian presence is evident at both the coastal region and in the high Andes. Recently (1994), I analyzed the plan of a pre-Inca site, *Huaca de los Reyes* [Pyramid of the Kings, or Sun], in the Moche Valley. There, I found a series of precise correlations in architectural layout with the grounds of Pharaoh Rameses III's Victory Temple at Medinet Habu, in the Upper Nile Valley. The plan of the Huaca, with its three plazas arranged in increasing elevation, decreasing size and decreasing access, has no antecedents in the previous Initial Period and is therefore unique. Yet another feature of Peru's *Huaca de los Reyes* is now observable on a recent diagrammatic reconstruction. It is the twin flanking towers at the entrance to the second court, a feature which exactly parallels the pylons at Medinet Habu.[6]

Foremost among the exotic imports brought back to the Nile Valley from beyond the "inverted waters" was cocaine. Although the plant has never grown in North Africa and is, in fact, unique to northern Peru, Ecuador, and Colombia, traces began to emerge in ancient dynastic human remains during the late 20th Century. Dr. Carl L. Johannessen, professor emeritus in the department of geography at the University of Oregon, in Eugene, conducted one of the most thorough investigations of the anomalous substances. He concluded:

> The chemicals related to coca and nicotine found in several Egyptian mummies, dating over a period of fourteen hundred years, is reciprocal proof of the trade in medicinal plants that existed between the Old World, specifically the Mediterranean Basin, and the Americas, specifically the Peruvian peoples, before Columbus. German forensic researchers discovered the chemicals from digested residue of tobacco and coca, and even pieces of tobacco leaf, in the back of the mummified abdominal cavity of Rameses II.
>
> The relevant chemicals associated with the ingestion and use of the coca plant have been found in numerous Egyptian mummies of the New Kingdom that date from approximately 1070 B.C. to 395 A.D. This could not have been contamination, as the metabolites [digested particles] were found inside the body tissues of the radio-carbon-dated mummies, showing that the living person (including children) partook of the plants prior for a significant period of time until their deaths. The presence of the coca products in the Egyptian mummies makes it highly likely, given the cotenien (metabolized nicotine) in the mummies as well, that both products were traded at the

> same time from the Americas to Egypt. The three plants all show marked use in the highest levels of Peruvian and Egyptian societies, a steady supply, and understanding of the effects of the plants on the persons using them.[7]

Whereas surgeons in ancient Egypt treated their patients with cocaine as a form of anesthesia, priests sought it to achieve altered states of consciousness for the practice of ritual and ceremonial magic. That narcotic connection between pre-Inca South America and Pharaonic Egypt was monumentalized in perhaps the single greatest masterpiece of Andean art: The 7-foot-high Raimondi Stela is made of highly polished granite lightly incised with an almost-unnoticeable imagery of extraordinary complexity and craftsmanship. During an Italian geographer's 1840 visit to Peru, he was appalled to see that the incredible sculpture was being used as a mere table top in a private home. His efforts to secure its removal to the courtyard of Lima's *Museo Nacional de Arqueología Antropología e Historia del Perú* resulted in the masterpiece being named after its rescuer, Antonio Raimondi. The Stela was also the first artifact associated with the Chavín Civilization, a culture of ecstatic ritual practices fueled by local psychoactive plants.

Reflecting these hallucinogenic rites, the Raimondi Stela depicts a short, squat figure standing with a stave in either hand, as energetic forms rise high from his head. Its resemblance to temple art representations of the ancient Egyptian god of pleasure is inescapable. Like his Peruvian counterpart, Bes was envisioned as a dwarf holding lily garlands that rise up and above him, as an energy form ascends from his head. Dwarves, especially black ones imported from Nubia, were associated in the ancient Egyptian mind with hilarity and highly valued as entertainers. Whether the Raimondi Stela figure derived from Bes, or the Egyptian deity was influenced by drug contacts in Peru, their visual relationship is underscored by Chavín Civilization itself, which began to flourish around 1200 BCE, just when Pharaoh Rameses III launched the last, documented Punt

Image 2-2: by Gunnar Thompson, PhD (www.alanticconference.org) *from his book* Nu Sun.

expedition. Clearly, narcotics were sufficiently needed to justify long-distance travel for their transatlantic importation. But cocaine, despite its importance, was not the only good brought back to Egypt from the Punt expeditions.

In a report on ancient Old World maize farming for Washington State's New World Discovery Institute in Port Townsend, Dr. Thompson announced his discovery of 21 identifiably American corncobs depicted throughout Nile Valley art. His two-year investigation included temples, tombs, and papyrus scrolls, some dating back more than 4,000 years. "The Egyptian corncobs are actually derived from a New World crop plant," he explains. "They aren't supposed to be in Egypt. This is conclusive evidence that the Egyptians were farming New World corn thousands of years before Columbus was born. All the modern, European historians have claimed that Columbus brought the first Indian corn, or maize, to the Old World. That's a total mistake that needs to be corrected."[8]

Dr. Thompson cited earlier, joint research by ancient art experts from the New York Metropolitan Museum of Art and the National Museum of Scotland at the 18th Dynasty temple of Queen Hatshepsut at Deir el-Bahri, near Thebes, where foreign corncobs are portrayed along with pineapples and other New World plants in their displays of religious offerings. A highlight of the Foremost of Noble Ladies' reign from 1492 to 1458 BCE was her lavish trading mission to Punt, which she had illustrated and documented on the walls of her temple. In 2006, Thompson

> noticed an unusual photograph of a mural that was taken inside the Queen's Temple almost a hundred years ago.
>
> The mural included a Nubian servant who was carrying a platter of fruits, vegetables, and breads. On the very top was balanced a single corncob. Bingo! I knew they had corn. The golden color of the corncobs, the parallel rows of large kernels, the tapered shape, and the green husk leaves all confirm that this grain is the New World maize plant. Indian maize was more resilient than the common Old World staples, such as wheat, barley, and millet. Eventually, maize farming spread throughout the Mediterranean Region, where the foreign grain was affectionately known as "barbarian corn," or "Turkey wheat."... [I]t was a key ingredient in the growth and survival of Old World civilizations.[9]

Similar corncobs have been identified at the Temple of Pharaoh Seti I (reigned 1294 BCE–1279 BCE), near Abydos, and at the Tomb of Rekhmire (an 18th Dynasty nobleman, 1504–1425 BCE), not far from Thebes, where he was governor. Still more examples appear on papyrus scrolls dating to Rameses II, mentioned by Dr. Johannessen for the pieces of tobacco leaf found in the mummified Pharaoh's abdominal cavity. Rameses himself boasted of gardens with plants from Punt.

He and his fellow countrymen not only took from ancient America, but gave to it. The world-famous walls raised by Andean city-builders were pattern developments from predecessors originally designed by Egyptian construction engineers. Their massive blocks used to build the Osireon temple complex, in the Upper Nile Valley, and those at Machu Picchu or Cuzco, which eventually became the capital of the Inca Empire, are equally and irregularly studded with small protuberances, whose function neither conventional nor alternative investigators are able to explain. The comparison is valid, as this feature occurs at no other ancient sites in the world, and because the Osireon is a ceremonial structure built by Seti I, the same Pharaoh who commissioned a Punt expedition to Peru. Also noted previously, mummies from his 18th Dynasty reveal traces of Bolivian cocaine.

Other, indelible cultural traces left behind in pre-Columbian South America by dynastic Egyptians were important loanwords, such as their name of Paradise: *iaro. Yaro* also means "paradise" in Quechua.

Hector Burgos-Stone writes in *Ancient American* that an early title for the Egyptian god of the afterlife, Anubis, was "Guardian of the Lineage," Willkanu, or Willka-Anu. *Anubis* was Greek for the original Anpu, or Anu.

> Later on, the symbolic figure of a jackal, an attentive watcher or guardian, was replaced by that of a dog. Hence, the Jackal Star, or Dog Star; that is, Sirius.... *Willkanu* is derived from the nouns *willka*—"lineage," "ancestry," "inheritance"—and *anu*—for jackal or dog. Therefore, *illka-Anu* is a jackal or [more generally, canine] guardian of lineage. However, *Willkanu* is not an exclusively Egyptian name, but occurs in Equatorial America [as *Willkanu-ta*].... The suffix particle, *ta*, has the value of the definite article, "the," according to the agglutinant structure of native American languages.

> *Willkanu-ta* should consequently be understood as "the Dog" (or "Watch Dog") of Lineage, or, literally, the "Lineage Dog."[10]

Willkanu-ta was additionally the original name of the Urubamba Valley, the Sacred Valley of the Incas, in the Peruvian Andes, because it encompassed the heartland of the Inca Empire with its leading sacred sites, including the capital at Cuzco, Machu Picchu, Pisac, Ollantaytambo, and many other important locations. Vast numbers of Inca and pre-Inca mummies were buried in the Urubamba Valley, attesting to Willkanu-ta's philological and mortuary connections with the Egyptian god of the dead. Perhaps it is more than coincidence that the shipyard in Egypt from which most of the vessels for the Punt expeditions were launched was called *Peru-nefer*, literally "Peru the Beautiful." But the name of Punt's monarch—Parihu—has more than an echo of "Peru," as does the Egyptian word for "king" (*perhoe*). So many similar names associated with complimentary meanings seem to constellate around important connections linking pre-Columbian South America with ancient Egypt.

Maize was more available in North America, from where Dynastic Egyptians obtained the corncobs depicted in temple art. And here, too, traces of their presence are still etched into the very landscape, particularly in the Middle West, where most corn was and still is grown. James P. Scherz, PhD, professor emeritus of civil and environmental engineering at the University of Wisconsin, in Madison, discovered a revealing relationship between the largest structures in the prehistoric New World and the ancient Old World. He observes that Ohio's Newark Earthworks, 25 miles east of Columbus, encompass approximately 3,000 acres to create the largest enclosure complex of its kind on Earth. It consists mainly of 8-foot-high walls defining a perfectly executed circle 1,054 feet across, surrounded by a 5-foot-deep moat and connected by linear embankments to an octagon of equivalent extent. Together, they form the largest earthen enclosures in the world.

As an archaeo-astronomer, Professor Scherz confirmed surveys conducted in 1982 by archaeologists from Earlham

College, in Richmond, Indiana, demonstrating that the site was originally designed as a lunar observatory. It had been designed to track motions of the Moon, including the northernmost point of the 18.6-year cycle of the lunar orbit. The moon then rises within one-half of a degree of the octagon's exact center, making the Newark Earthworks twice as precise as the astronomical complex at Britain's Stonehenge. Scherz was also aware of various lunar relations associated with Egypt's Great Pyramid, the western and eastern sides of which align with True North to within three arc-minutes, one-tenth the width of the full Moon. The Great Pyramid also expresses the ratio in size between the Earth and the Moon by "Squaring the Circle," or constructing a square with the same area as a given circle by using only a finite number of steps with a compass and straightedge. Remarkably, both of these features recur at the Midwestern site.

Scherz's careful survey of the earthworks at Newark, Ohio, revealed a solution to the ancient Old World geometrical riddle of "Squaring the Circle" by use of rope geometry, as associated with Egypt's foremost structure. Ross Hamilton, curator of the state's Great Serpent Mound, added that

> the Great Pyramid of Cheops appears in scale with the Newark circle-octagon to demonstrate an almost eerie commonality of (1) area, (2) measurement and (3) angularity between the two sites. With its earthen walls at full thickness, the Pyramid is wholly contained by the Great Circle. Similarly, yet in a more linear fashion, twin Great Pyramids hypothetically placed side-by-side would nicely span the twin circles, leaving little footage between them. Then (3), the angle of True North off the central axis, is very close, if not the same as the slope of the Great Pyramid; i.e., between 51.5 and 52 degrees.[11]

Clearly, the Newark Earthworks were constructed using the same, monumental measurements incorporated on the other side of the world in the Nile Delta's Great Pyramid. The only discrepancy is Modern Man's. The Ohio location has been assigned by mainstream archaeologists to the Native American Hopewell Culture that flourished in the Middle West from around 300 BCE to 400 CE, whereas Egyptologists believe Giza's Great Pyramid was built about 2560 BCE. The more than two millennia separating these sites makes any kind of perceived relationship between them, at best, entirely circumstantial. Yet, that relationship is indisputable, unlike methods used to date prehistoric locations. In the absence of organic materials at the Newark Earthworks relative to their construction or prehistoric habitation, conventional scholars infer that the geometric figures must have been created by members of the Hopewell Culture, only because its leaders were known mound builders in Ohio. In fact, no real evidence has been found to determine the site's true age anymore than the construction date officially assigned to the Great Pyramid is an assumption based on its alleged connections, as flimsy as they are sparse, to King Khufu, who may have reigned from 2589 BCE to 2566 BCE.

These date parameters for building the Great Pyramid were called into question during the fall of 1990, when a large, perfectly preserved vase was found in the desert west of the Nile, north of Thebes. It was one of many surviving examples of Gerzean ware manufactured before and right up to Egypt's First Dynasty. Such pottery often portrays scenes of life, painted in bold, black lines on bright orange surfaces, on the Nile. Typical are depictions of palm trees and animals along the banks, together with many-oared rafts or boats floating down the river. Presently on display at the Luxor Museum, 1990's 3-foot tall, 10-inch wide (at the mouth) discovery is not unlike dozens of similar examples, save that it portrays three delta-shaped figures—two side by side of relatively equal size, the other one much smaller—standing above the Nile. If they are not the pyramids of the Giza Plateau, it is difficult to imagine what else they were intended to represent. The Gerzean pot on which they were illustrated was dated from 3200 BCE to 3000 BCE, a transitional period known as Naqada III-c, when Egypt was changing from a pastoral society into a high culture.

If, in fact, the pottery drawing does depict the Giza pyramids, then they must have been observed by a Gerzean artist at the very dawn of Egyptian civilization, at least 500 years before textbook opinion posits their construction. Thorough radio-carbon testing of datable material retrieved from the Great Pyramid late last century by an American archaeologist came as something of a shock to his colleagues. "It is a safe assumption," says Dr. Mark Lehner, "that the material [collected from the exterior covered by decorative casing stones until their removal in the 13th century] is from the original construction."[12]

The high calculation he and his team found was 1,244 years older than the official date for building the Great Pyramid, placing its construction around 3009 BCE. This scientifically ascertained date not only removes the Pyramid's origins outside the Fourth Dynasty, but beyond dynastic civilization altogether. It nonetheless corresponds with a low date for the Gerzean illustration, mentioned prior, of the same era. Dr. Lehner's findings were dismissed as unacceptable by most Egyptologists, who still cling to their less-well-ascertained belief in Khufu as pyramid-builder.

"Despite claims that these dates were incorrect," Florida scholar Kenneth Caroli asserts, "the mortar from the Great Pyramid averaged to about 2988 B.C, once calibrated ... Conservatively, the Great Pyramid's calibrated date falls between 2850 and 3050 B.C., and so is three hundred to five hundred years older than the date agreed upon by standard chronologies. 2950 B.C. might be treated as the absolute calibrated median."[13]

This deeper antiquity for the Great Pyramid is important to appreciate, if we mean to understand the reappearance of its measurements at the Newark Earthworks, which either date to around the turn of the fourth millennium BCE, or were brought from the Nile Valley to the Ohio Valley by someone who understood the Pyramid's arcane significance in time to incorporate its features in the Great Circle and Octagon at the start of the Hopewell Culture during the late fourth century BCE. We may never know, but the truth may fall somewhere in between these two extremes, which are open to a variety of options. Even so, if correspondences between Newark and Giza consisted of the only evidence for viable connections between pre-Columbian Ohio and ancient Egypt, honest skeptics might be disposed to consider them as intriguing possibilities, at best. But a profusion of additional evidence—physical, oral, and linguistic, as different as it is persuasive—clearly discloses a serious pharaonic presence in North America.

During early summer 1934, about 350 miles southwest of the Newark Earthworks, construction engineers were in the process of clearing land for a large, public irrigation project in eastern Tennessee when they inadvertently unearthed a Hopewell cemetery. Further labors were temporarily halted, while a "mad rush was on by archaeologists to find and excavate as many Indian burial mounds as they could," reported Jake Hopping for *Ancient American:* "These mounds would soon be submerged by water" from the nearby Clinch River, slated for damming by summer's end. "After excavating one mound, the archaeologists kept digging. Several feet below, they uncovered a more unusual and much older building. The men had found a group of large blocks and columns laid out to form the perimeter of a rectangle," approximately 95 feet long by 55 feet wide.[14]

They enclosed the ruins of a monumental, stone building that obviously had nothing whatsoever to do with Hopewell Indians. The strange discovery was reported by several newspapers, most prominently the *New York Times,* which featured a photograph with extensive caption of the site in the July 1, 1934 edition. It eventually came to the attention of James Rendel Harris, a professor of ancient languages, whose series of essays was published by the University of London Press. He was also manuscript curator at the University of Manchester's John Rylands Library, a position requiring familiarity with the institution's "special collections, believed to be among the largest in the United Kingdom, such as medieval illuminated manuscripts and examples of early European printing, including a Gutenberg Bible.... The Rylands Library

Papyrus P52 is believed to be the earliest extant New Testament text," which Harris himself was instrumental in finding, together with three, other lost manuscripts he found entirely on his own.[15]

Educated at Clare College, Cambridge, where he was a fellow in mathematics, he went on to become a professor of New Testament Greek at Johns Hopkins University in Baltimore, Maryland. Not content with a sedentary academic existence, he traveled extensively throughout the Near East, learning dozens of unfamiliar dialects, personally investigating numerous archaeological sites, and making new discoveries. At his own expense, and following years of research, Harris purchased 47 rolls and codices written in Hebrew, Latin, Arabic, Syriac, Armenian, and Ethiopic, all of which he read, then donated them to Pennsylvania's Haverford College, where they are still held by the college library's Quaker Collection. After teaching theology at Leiden University, the oldest university in the Netherlands, which includes John Quincy Adams, René Descartes, and Rembrandt among its alumni, he was appointed director of studies at the Society of Friends' Woodbrooke College, near Birmingham. This brief sketch of the man's lofty and brilliant life provide credence to his published statements concerning the eastern Tennessee discovery, which he studied a full year before writing anything about it in his seventh "After-Glow Essay" of 1935.

The Hopewell, Harris writes, were late-comers, who raised their mounds of earth over a much older temple built by pharaonic Egyptian émigrés to their most important deities—Isis, the Queen of Heaven, and her husband, Osiris, the god of resurrection. The *New York Times*' photograph (plus information possibly sent to him from U.S. field investigators) clearly defined many of the architectural features with which he was intimately familiar from his years of study in the Nile Valley. He refers to the excavated location's "monolith, if such it be, which the photograph clearly shows us, is a Pillar of Osiris," who was, indeed, worshipped as a column depicted in temple art very much like the site's standing stone.[16]

Harris found that the Volunteer State's very name corresponds precisely and without interpolation from the Egyptian *tenn esse*, literally, "the land" (*tenne*) of Isis (Greek for the original *Esse*). In *Ancient American*, Russell Bennett Stafford observed that Iroquois Indian reverence for five, ancestral clans, each one signified by a specific animal, recalls another name for the Egyptian king of the gods—*Iroqoai*—one of five totem animals associated with Amon.

Stafford continues:

> Pauti was a primeval god who created himself and all that is; he ruled Upper and Lower Egypt. *Pauti-Taui* was a title of Amon-Ra [supreme god of the sun], as an agent for this very early god; his title means, "the Beginning of Time," Primeval Time, the Time of Creation. In the Western Hemisphere, *Pautiwa* is the Chief Council of Deities among the Zuni [a pueblo tribal people residing in western New Mexico]. Pautiwa symbolizes the Sun Father's power, kindness, dignity and beauty. In the village of Zuni, Pautiwa is associated with *katchinas* (spiritual figure). He is present during ceremonies celebrating the solstices.[17]

Harris continued to pursue such revealing parallels:

> [T]he names *Suwanee* and *Savannah (Sawannah)* are philologically equivalent. The ground for in either case is *Sawan*, which has been affected by the adjectival termination in *Suwanee*, and by a re-duplication in *Savannah*. These can easily be explained from an Egyptian standpoint. It is, however, the ground form that attracts our attention. The traveler up the Nile commonly makes his destination to be the town of Assuan, at the foot of the First Cataract. The Arabic article

has been prefixed to the name *Suan*, which the Greeks, on their part, transliterated as *Suene* (Syene). Whatever it may mean, it is clearly the same name we found in Florida and in Georgia; so that in the last two cases, we are on the track of Egyptian colonists. If we write it in the form Sauan, it will divide at once into *Sau* + *An*; that is, "the Children of Osiris."[18]

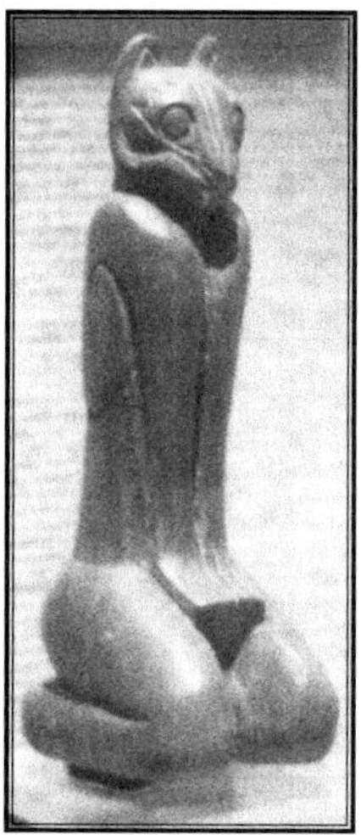

Image 2-3: Florida's ancient statuette of the popular Egyptian cat goddess, Bast. Photo courtesy of the author.

The ancient Egyptian colonization Harris traced into Florida through variations of *Suwanee* had already materialized off the state's southwestern coast, in the Gulf of Mexico. Adjacent to Marco Island was a large shell works forming its own artificial island, at the center of which lay a small pond, covering less than 1 acre. Key Marco yielded the largest number of wooden artifacts from any prehistoric archaeological site in the eastern United States. During 1896, Smithsonian Institution excavators dredging the "Court of the Pile Dwellers," as they called it, recovered more than one thousand wooden artifacts, the most extraordinary of which was the representation of an anthropomorphic cat.

The brown-red, 6-inch-tall figure features a feline head on a human torso, arms together and descending directly over the chest, with both hands palms down atop the thighs, which sit on bent-back calves, knees protruding. Everything about the Florida statue resembles the ancient Egyptian goddess of protection against contagious diseases and evil spirits. Bast was likewise portrayed in temple art as a woman with the head of a cat, a singular configuration found nowhere else in the ancient world outside the Nile Valley and Florida. If recovered from inside a tomb at the Nile Valley, instead of a pond at an artificial island in the Gulf of Mexico, archaeologists would have unhesitatingly recognized the statue as a depiction of the famous Egyptian cat-goddess.

Though the workmanship of the Court of the Pile Dwellers' version is decidedly more complex than other pre-Columbian artwork found in the continental United States, it was dredged up amid a profusion of cords, ropes, nets, net floats, fishhooks, and other items associated with the sea-farers to whom it belonged. Although its pristine condition in muck was fortunate, techniques for preserving very old wood had not been developed when excavation took place in the late 19th Century. Moreover, the object was manhandled and stored in a variety of environments that additionally rendered accurate dating with modern methods impossible. Radio-carbon attempts during the 1960s and 1970s produced unmanageable time spreads from 55 CE to 1670 CE. More useful was a closely associated site at Horr's Island, where related, undisturbed organic materials dated to circa 1450 BCE. This period corresponded to Queen Hatshepsut's 18th Dynasty and to within 50 years of her great expedition to the Lands of Punt.

Less than 60 miles due east from Miami lies Bimini, famous for its controversial "Road" or "Wall," located just off the northern point of this small Bahama island and 19 feet beneath the surface of the Atlantic Ocean. Its fresh-water springs and ideal position in the current that courses along North America's Eastern seaboard would have made an ideal stop-over for transoceanic voyagers plying the ocean between the ancient Old World and pre-Columbian America. These ancient navigational features are underscored by the roots of its name in the Egyptian *Baminini*, or "Homage to (*ini*) the Soul (*ba*) of Min," the divine patron of long-distance travelers, appropriately enough.

About the same time Tennessee's Egyptian temple was uncovered, Armand Viré, a geology professor from the University of Paris, was hired by Haitian government officials to find new sources of fresh water. While digging a 10-foot trench on a small island near Haiti's northeast coast, he was surprised to find the black stone statuette of a dog, 10 inches long and 6 inches high.[19] The workmanship and execution of all its anatomical details were different from Carib or Arawak Indian artifacts. The animal was portrayed in a calm, recumbent posture, head held high, tall ears standing alert, and long muzzle pointing straight ahead in the classical pose of Anubis, the ancient Egyptian god of the dead.

Expanding his paleo-linguistic investigation beyond North America, Harris observed that the name of the Central American country, Guatemala, is a local native derivative of the original Egyptian *Watem-Ra*, the "Way of Ra's Rest," a name that does, indeed, conform to Guatemala's western location in relation to travelers from the distant Nile Valley. He found, too, that the Bay of Campeche in the Gulf of Mexico is accurately described in the ancient Egyptian *khampetche* for a curving body of water.

These geographical cognates combined with a large body of supportive source materials to persuade Harris that pharaonic culture-bearers from the Nile Valley established themselves in many parts of Middle and North America, where they built a large stone temple in Tennessee.

"It would be fascinating to relocate this structure," Hopping states. "Unfortunately, it now resides under the dam-swollen waters of the Clinch River. The [*New York Times*'] photo shows what looks to be a plowed field behind the structure. The caption says that it was found near the banks of the Clinch River. That would be the riverbank before it was dammed up."[20]

Despite such a dramatic loss of evidence, the linguistic trail to ancient Egyptians in America blazed by Rendel Harris was taken up four decades later by another British-born professor. During the early 1970s, Barry Fell began to detect strangely familiar details in *komq-wej-wi'k-as-ikl*, or "sucker-fish writings," named for their general resemblance to tracks *Catostomidae* leave on muddy river bottoms, and used by an east-coast Canadian tribe. The Mi'kmaq, along with the Algonkians, were the only Native Americans to use an indigenous, written language. It was logographic, or composed of single symbols representing entire words or phrases (for example, the symbol % meaning "percent").

This, Fell knew, was the same kind of system developed by the early dynastic (perhaps proto-dynastic) Egyptians. When he compared their hieroglyphs to Mi'kmaq "sucker-fish writings," he was shocked to find that they not only had many characters in common, but that these shared logograms had identical or equivalent meanings. After publishing these comparisons, Professor Fell was emphatically condemned by mainstream scholars, who devoted less energy endeavoring to disprove his observation than attacking him personally.

Because he was not an official archaeologist—only a university-trained scientist and world-class marine biologist at the Harvard Museum—his conclusions, they decreed, were unworthy of consideration. The implication here is that only the opinions of experts in a particular field should be considered, a point of view that, if logically followed from the beginning of civilization, would have thwarted any scientific development for all time. In similar cases, critics invariably avoided mentioning that any one of their own colleagues who dared to utter statements such as those made by Barry Fell would find his or her professional career terminated in the blink of an eye.

Skeptics further argued that *komq-wej-wi'k-as-ikl* was neither indigenous nor ancient, but merely invented by modern European Christian missionaries as an aid in proselytizing non-Christians. Perceived similarities between "sucker-fish writing" and any ancient Old World logograms were dismissed as entirely accidental. Or they may have come about when Church leaders surreptitiously borrowed some Egyptian hieroglyphs, which they revered as sacred symbols, in their efforts at conversion. But Father le Clercq, a Roman Catholic missionary on the Gaspé Peninsula in New France, personally witnessed Mi'kmaq children "writing symbols" with porcupine quills pressed directly into birch bark, in 1675.

His observation occurred not only before he began preaching to the Native Americans, but 15 years prior to the birth of Jean-François Champollion, who first translated

Egyptian hieroglyphs. Le Clercq adapted "sucker-fish writing" to writing prayers, discarding those symbols he could not use and replacing them with new ones of his own invention, until today's Mi'kmaq script ended up in a modified version of the now mostly incomprehensible original. Any remaining Egyptian hieroglyphs survive only because le Clercq still found use for them. As a sure sign of its ongoing deterioration and inevitable disappearance, *komq-wej-wi'k-as-ikl* is now written using most letters of the standard Latin alphabet.

Other skeptics believe another Catholic priest actually fabricated "sucker-fish writing" for the same reasons, but physicist William R. Corliss points out that Pierre Maillard

> actually had died sixty-one years before Champollion first published his decipherment of Egyptian hieroglyphics. It is unreasonable, therefore, to believe that Maillard could have invented Mi'kmaq writing with its Egyptian affinities. Either these affinities are the product of chance, or pre-Columbian contacts occurred between the Mi'kmaq and Egyptian voyagers. In the latest volume of Epigraphic Society papers, Fell discusses many additional similarities between Mi'kmaq and Egyptian hieroglyphics—so many more, that the "Chance" theory seems most unlikely.[21]

Conventional archaeologists nonetheless brush aside these discrepancies, while continuing to fault Professor Fell for his willful distortion of "sucker-fish writing," the work of 17th Century missionaries, for Egyptian hieroglyphs.

According to David Warner Mathisen, a graduate of the United States Military Academy at West Point, where he now teaches in the English department:

> By this sort of criticism, it is implied that the symbols selected by the priests were merely Christian symbols (such as a triangle for the Trinity or a *Globus Cruciger* for the concept of

> "holy"), and that these selections only coincidentally resembled Egyptian hieroglyphs for the same concepts. However, this argument becomes more difficult to maintain when other Mi'kmaq symbols are examined. For example, prominent in the Mi'kmaq version of the Lord's Prayer...is the symbol for "name" (as in, "hallowed be thy name"'. The Mi'kmaq symbol recorded by Father Maillard in 1762 is extremely suggestive of the ancient Egyptian symbol for a name, which is the symbol known as a *cartouche*.[22]

This is an oval with a horizontal line at one end, indicating that the text enclosed is a royal name. The earliest known cartouche dates back to the beginning of the Fourth Dynasty under Pharaoh Sneferu, who reigned from 2613 BCE to 2589 BCE. The French term derived from observations made by Napoleon's men during the Battle of the Pyramids, in 1798, when his soldiers noticed that the often-encountered symbol resembled a muzzle-loading firearm's paper powder cartridge, or *cartouche*. Appropriately, the pre-Columbian implications presented by their language are underscored by the Mi'kmaqs themselves. Their tribal name is rooted in the word *megu-ma-waach*, for "spiritual power," associated with the *Megu-Mu-Wesu*—recalled in oral traditions as master magicians, fair-skinned foreigners who arrived from over the Atlantic Ocean very long ago, when they bequeathed their magical powers to the earliest Mi'kmaq wizards. In the Mi'kmaqs' spoken language, *waban, muskun*, and *oweaoo* are identical to the same ancient Egyptian words for "sunrise," "heaven," and "circle," respectively.

"Fell theorizes that Egyptian merchants taught natives a few words and symbols useful for trading," according to Dr. Thompson.[23] The Mi'kmaqs are indigenous to Canada's Maritime Provinces and the Gaspé Peninsula of Quebec, a region they know as *Mi'kma'kik*. It was here that the ancient sea-farers first touched land in North America upon entering the St. Lawrence River on their way through the Great Lakes to the great copper mines of Michigan's Upper Peninsula.

Mathiesen concludes:

> In the end it does not really matter whether one is convinced by the evidence of ancient contact present in Mi'kmaq script. One piece of evidence, on its own, can be explained away as an incredible coincidence. The important perspective to adopt when examining such evidence is the understanding that each such clue is "one data point." When viewed in conjunction with all the other data points found in the Americas, which point to deliberate ancient contact, the Mi'kmaq writing system is far more powerful evidence.... Taken in context with all the other evidence, then, the case of the Mi'kmaq hieroglyphics is another blow to the isolationist position, and a powerful blow at that.[24]

Chapter 3: Minoans

Although human habitation on the Eastern Mediterranean island of Crete goes back at least 130,000 years, not until the advent of the Bronze Age did its pastoral societies coalesce into one of the most attractive high cultures in history. Only since Sir Arthur Evans discovered its ruins in 1900, however, has this premiere Aegean civilization been recognized as "Minoan." He coined that appellation after Minos, the mid-third-millennium-BCE king, who built a great labyrinth the British archaeologist found while excavating Knossos, ancient Crete's foremost city. Precisely how the pre-Classical natives actually referred to themselves is not known, although their name may have been phonetically akin to the contemporaneous Egyptian *Keftiu* and Semitic Akkadian *Kaptara*. The *Eteocretans*, or "true Cretans," were the island's original, pre-Greek inhabitants in Homer's *Odyssey*, the last of a dying breed by the close of the 8th Century BCE.

Eighteen hundred years before, a profusion of monumental architecture began to arise in the island's first urban centers, which were connected by stone-paved roads made of cut blocks. Minoan cities were surprisingly modern, with efficient drainage sewer systems, and clay-pipe plumbing for running water in fountains and baths, public or private. Crete's many large villas were smaller, almost as lavish copies of palaces, which were less royal residences than centers of government, with administrative offices, shrines, workshops, and granaries. These multi-story complexes—with floors of plaster, wood, or flagstone—included gypsum, sandstone, and limestone in their construction of open courts, grand staircases, large archives, indoor garden areas, and airy spaces to admit as much daylight as possible.

Characteristically, the Minoan pillar was wider at the top than the bottom, mounted on a stone base, and topped with a pillow-like, round capital. These "inverted columns" were made of wood and painted a remarkable shade of bright, brownish red, sometimes known as "Tuscan." Walls and ceilings were brightly painted in a variety of pigments, with which the Minoans excelled in painting large, lively murals. Artists strove to out-do each other in the depiction of pleasure cruises, religious processions, banquets, social outings, sporting events—such as boxing and bull-leaping—or natural scenes of fish, squid, birds, and lilies. Elegantly shaped pottery was adorned with spirals, rosettes, triangles, curved lines, crosses, and fishbone motifs, whereas anthropomorphic statuary foreshadowed later developments in Classical times.

Men went about in the Mediterranean climate wearing loincloths and kilts, but women wore a strapless, fitted bodice. Less often, they donned short-sleeved robes or layered, flounced skirts that were open to the navel, though perhaps only during ceremonial occasions. Attire for both sexes was dyed in several different colors, and they appear to have been a very fashion-conscious folk. They developed polyculture, growing more than one crop at a time, which allowed for a bounty of continuous food production, supplemented by fishing, together with fig-, olive-, and grape-orchard farming. Luxury foods included the local production of honey and wine, plus the importation of date palm trees, quinces, and pomegranates from the Near East. Fed for generations on such a varied and healthy diet, regional populations swelled, until Homer could record a tradition to the effect that the island once boasted 90 cities.

This same tradition described Crete as entirely surrounded and powerfully protected by a vast, wooden wall—an analogy for its coast guard fleet, less a military navy than a floating police force that fought piracy and kept the sea-lanes open for commerce. Its heavily armed, well-trained, and disciplined marines aboard their speedy warships were also formidable enough to keep the threatening forces of Mycenaean Greece at bay.

Crete herself was conspicuous in a warlike age for her domestic tranquility, so much so that she possessed no army to intimidate her own people or wage foreign campaigns, unlike every other contemporaneous kingdom. What Evans called a *pax Minoica*, or Minoan Peace, dominated the Eastern Mediterranean for one thousand years. But the Minoans were under no circumstances pacifists. Their mass-produced swords were the finest in the Aegean world. Recent experimental testing of accurate replicas demonstrated that they were capable of cutting down to the bone, and scoring its surface, without damaging the blades themselves. Crete's arsenal also included 3-foot-long rapiers superior to anything of the kind wielded by other powers. Detailed frescoes depicted these and other weapons borne by determined men-at-arms outfitted with metal helmets, breastplates, greaves from ankles to knees, while carrying figure-eight-shaped shields made of stretched, layered cowhide impervious to most arrows and capable of fending off many sword strikes, yet light enough for agility in combat. If, uncommonly, the Minoans did not abuse their military strength with internal oppression or outward aggression, the *pax Minoica* was nonetheless firmly rooted in their superior weapons and, more importantly, the spirit to use them ruthlessly against any and all attackers.

That spirit was tested in 1628 BCE, when recorded history's most powerful volcanic explosion detonated on an island just 68 miles away. The eruption ejected 24 cubic miles of superheated material in a 22-mile-high ash plume, literally vaporizing the center of Thera, from which a resultant tsunami 200 feet high radiated across the Aegean Sea. This cataclysmic event is still regarded by a dwindling number of believers who equate it with the destruction of Atlantis. They are contradicted, however, by widespread, important remains found above the Theran ash layer, proving that Cretan society survived the eruption and flourished. No more than 0.20 inches of ash fell anywhere on Crete, insufficient to depose its high culture.

Indeed, the centuries immediately after the natural catastrophe represent the apex of Minoan civilization. Although most if not all of its cities suffered damage, with north coast settlements particularly hard hit (having taken the brunt of a 500-mile-per-hour tsunami), reconstruction began at once, resulting in a general upgrading of quality workmanship. "Even this disaster didn't discourage the Minoans: the palaces were again rebuilt and were made even greater than before."[1]

Far from having been obliterated, as Plato described Atlantis, which some researchers identify with Crete or one of its smaller islands, the Minoans went on to bigger and better things. Even Thera, where the event occurred, survived and is still inhabited under its post-Classic name (Santorini). Although comparisons with Atlantis are invalid, because Thera's eruption did not topple Minoan civilization, but, on the contrary, invigorated it, Bronze Age Crete's downfall 200 years later was brought about by more seriously effective geologic upheaval. Around 1450 BCE, major earthquake activity destroyed the living quarters at Knossos and badly damaged the other major cities of Mallia, Tylissos, Phaistos, and Hagia Triade, forcing their abandonment. The most vital naval bases along the north coast were wiped out.

Weakened after 30 years of painstakingly slow rebuilding efforts, plus the loss of virtually the entire coast guard fleet, the Minoans offered little resistance to a Mycenaean Greek invasion that quickly subdued the whole country circa 1420 BCE: "The Mycenaeans generally tended to adapt, rather than destroy, Minoan culture, religion and art, and they continued to operate the economic system and bureaucracy of the Minoans. After about a century of partial recovery, most Cretan cities and palaces went into decline in the 13th [c]entury B.C."[2]

Knossos lingered on as a drastically diminished administrative center until 1200 BCE, when it was finally abandoned forever. Minoan civilization vanished into the dark ages that followed during the next four centuries, faintly re-emerging in myth with the gradual rise of classical antiquity. But Bronze Age Crete remained lost until Evans identified it little more than 100 years ago.

Certainly, it would seem strange if, over the course of their thousand-year history, such outgoing sea-farers should have restricted their commercial instincts to the Aegean world and not gone beyond its geographical limitations as far as America. Their ships were small, but eminently seaworthy, with deep keels for stability in oceanic swells and brails at their sails for tacking against the wind.

More of their maritime technology was alluded to in Homer's *Odyssey*. He describes the *Lapis Heracles,* or "Stone of Hercules," a gold cup filled with some kind of liquid on which floated an arrow-shaped magnet used by sailors to pass safely through night and fog over great distances, far beyond sight of land, or without recourse to navigating by the stars.[3] The existence of this mariner's compass went back at least as long ago as the Late Bronze Age, during the mid-13th century BCE, in the aftermath of the Trojan War (1250 BCE to 1240 BCE) Homer narrated, when such a device would have been available to seafarers from Crete for oceanic voyages.

Indeed, they marked their penetration of the Atlantic by engraving the likeness of a labrys on one of the great megaliths at Britain's Stonehenge, whose builders were contemporaries of the Minoans. The Labrys lent its name to the famous Labyrinth, at the ritual center of which stood the sacred double-headed ax—a stylized symbol of the moon goddess, whose quest for enlightenment was the spiritual significance of the intricate complex. Inside, seven young boys and as many girls were devoured each year by the Minotaur, a bull-headed monster, on the anniversary of a Minoan prince's murder at the annual Olympics; Greek royals had allowed his killer, one of their own, to escape justice, for which the Athenian children were sacrificed as atonement. The Labyrinth in which they underwent their ordeal was depicted as either a circular or square maze. That this uniquely emblematic imagery should find itself expressed anywhere outside the Eastern Mediterranean can only mean that it was left behind by a people for whom it was their cultural icon.

As Harold Sellers Colton, an archaeologist reporting for *Science* magazine, writes, "[I]t is hard to believe that such complicated labyrinths similar in every detail could have had separate origins."[4] Yet, they appear throughout North America's "Four Corners Area," where Arizona, New Mexico, Colorado, and Wyoming touch, and the oldest, known specimen was incised on the adobe walls of a prehistoric city outside Phoenix. One thousand years ago, Casa Grande, the "Big House," was built by the Hohokam, as they are still remembered by modern-day Pima Indians, who are partially descended from these long-vanished "Ancient Ones." Highly civilized irrigationists and construction engineers of monumental ceremonial structures, the Hohokam decorated their pottery, fragments of which still survive, with images of the Labyrinth. It is commonly replicated today by several Southwestern tribal peoples as symbolic of the unending quest for wisdom, a connotation derived from an ancient, native pastime no longer played and otherwise entirely forgotten.

An anonymous Spanish traveler passing through Arizona during the early 1760s observed a Pima Indian drawing a maze "in the form of a whorl arising from a center called *Tcunni Ki*, the council house," as part of *Tculikwikut*, the "House of *Tcuhu*," or *Tcuhiki*.[5] Although the details of this old dart game have been lost, its central figure was Tcuhuki, a cultic hero who gave his name to the "House of *Tcuhu*," the object of which was to rescue some innocent children imprisoned inside the maze by a ferocious monster. The similarity of this old game to the Minoan Labyrinth grows closer in Tcuhuki's fundamental resemblance to Theseus, the Greek mythic hero who freed the young Athenian captives by killing the Minotaur. There is even the suggestion of a philological relationship between the Native American *Tcuhuki* and the ancient Old World

Theseus, whose liberating victory signified a triumphant quest over confusion and ignorance implicit in the maze.

Although more than 20 centuries separated Minoan Crete from Hohokam Arizona, the survival of a labyrinthine design at Casa Grande suggests that Bronze Age visitors from the Eastern Mediterranean made an impact, as indelible as it was profound, on native cultures in the American Southwest, so much so that the influence was carried forward over time unto today's Pima Indians.

Image 3-1: Arizona's Casa Grande petroglyph. Photo courtesy of the author.

Another iconic proof of Minoan influences at work in North America was discovered in October 2006 by Daniel Byers. He was looking for old coins and lost jewelry by sweeping a suburban Cleveland high school practice football field with his metal detector. When its alarm indicated something metallic beneath the surface, he dug down about 18 inches to find a small, metal, delta-shaped pendant approximately 2.4 inches long by 1.5 inches wide, with a single perforation at the top. Weighing 1.4 ounces, the bronze object "has no casting marks around the edge, and shows clear working marks," he observed, "so it seems to be carved into the metal, not cast."[6]

On one side appears the image of a shirtless figure striking what appears to be a dancing pose, his hair styled into long locks hanging beneath a headgear of some kind, a belted skirt at his slim waist, and pectoral around the shoulders. This imagery resembles nothing, if not the so-called "Prince of Lilies," a dancer portrayed in painted fresco on the palace walls at Knossos. To the lower right of the Ohio figure is something resembling an inverted question mark partially contained inside a semi-circle. Both are recognizable glyphs from a written language epigraphers refer to as "Linear A," an official script for cult purposes and palace administration in Bronze Age Crete.

Although Linear A still defies translation, the semi-circle defines things lunar, an identification reflected in the Minoan moon-goddess. An inverted questionmark likewise appears in Linear A, but its significance is unknown. The appearance of these glyphs on the Ohio pendent dates it from circa 1900 BCE to 1700 BCE, because Linear A was only current during the Middle Minoan Period. On the opposite side of the object appears a stylized, double-headed axe, Minoan Crete's emblematic symbol.

Byers endeavored to have his discovery identified by experts, "including Sotheby's Auction House.... I have tried, repeatedly, to have it examined by certified archaeologists, but the 'pros' absolutely refuse to even have their names associated with any kind of site that might turn up the 'wrong' kind of evidence."[7]

Nothing about the suburban Cleveland find suggests modern manufacture, and comparisons with possible 19th- or 20th-century reproductions have not been found. As such, it must be admitted into evidence for a Minoan presence in ancient America. Nor is the Ohio artifact the only one of its kind that has come to light. Thirty-one years earlier, Michael Rose was digging 12 feet down into a house foundation on the banks of Maine's Penobscot River, near Old Town, 10 miles north of Bangor, when he made a related discovery. His shovel unearthed a curious, metallic rectangle about 1 inch long by three-quarters of an inch wide, and as thin as a dime. The obverse features the image of a woman dressed in a flounced skirt and wearing a high, pointed headgear, with a large necklace hanging to her midriff. Her right hand is extended beyond or before an open, over-arching doorway in which she stands framed, while her left hand holds either a snake or a fan with serpentine handle.

That so much detail could be skillfully executed in nickel-iron and encompassed by such a tiny space seems remarkable. By contrast, the obverse is only a rough-cut indentation for the complex image embossed in relief on its opposite side. As such, the Penobscot River object resembles a type font more than anything else, a comparison that—far from affirming modern origins for Mr. Rose's find—supports its Bronze Age Cretan provenance: The Minoans invented movable type. Their variety of metal fonts was not used for the ink printing of books or newspapers, but impressed into soft, clay roundels that were hard-baked in kilns. Their only surviving specimen, the so-called Phaistos Disc, is emblazoned, on either side, with signs of the Zodiac, identifying it as a horoscope. The fonts represented astrological symbols, glyphs, or associated imagery all pertaining to Bronze Age Cretan cosmology and the individual's destined relationship with it.

Gregory De LaCastro writes in *Ancient American* "that the writing style of the Phaistos Disc is related to the ceremonial wrappings of a planetary ritual stone that was used as part of a Native American astrological patterning frame...."[8]

The Maine object is just such a piece of movable type, even matching its Phaistos Disc correspondents in size. One side of the Maine artifact has been also embossed, its high-relief features sufficiently prominent to distinctly impress themselves into soft clay. Such fonts allowed Minoan astrologers to virtually mass-produce personal horoscopes in what must have undoubtedly amounted to many thousands of such discs over the centuries, when their civilization flourished from circa 2600 BCE to shortly after 1200 BCE. The figure shown on Mr. Rose's discovery is self-evidently a version of the famous Minoan snake-handler portrayed identifiably in statuary and on pottery recovered from archaeological zones at Knossos, Tylissos, Mallia, and many other locations on the Aegean island.

In every instance, she is characteristically depicted wearing a flounced skirt, while wielding a serpent in each hand, as part of an ecstatic cult for achieving altered states of consciousness, probably not all that different from present-day snake-handing Pentecostal Christians in the rural backwaters of the United States. Minoan renditions suggest either a priestess of such a cult or its goddess—perhaps both, as the former may have striven to merge with and become the latter. In any case, the appearance of movable type from Bronze Age Crete near Old Town says almost as much for its ancient authenticity, as does its quite-accidental discovery one dozen feet beneath the banks of the Penobscot River. The artifact was found just 30 miles inland from the shores of the Atlantic Ocean, where related finds have been made.

Another *Ancient American* writer, W. Mead Stapler, tells how a scuba diver in coastal Maine, not far from where the Penobscot River type font emerged,

> was searching among the rocks of the outer harbor of Pemaquid, hoping to spear a succulent lobster for dinner, when he came across a tumbled stack of odd-shaped stones. There were about eight in all, and just below the surface at low tide. With great labor and the assistance of a friend with a tow-truck, he came back later to haul three specimens out of the water, up to the beach, and home to his wife's rock garden. Going back at a later time for one or two more of the oddly shaped stones, the remaining examples were lost under continually shifting harbor sands.... The three stones are similar but not identical. They are all cut from the same granite or banded gneiss common to the Pemaquid area, but with varying degrees of detail, quality and craftsmanship.
>
> Thus, they are not the work of one individual, even though the design indicates a common purpose. The commonality of design is a trian-

> gular pie shape with two, flat and parallel sides, and an arc at the base. A large, circular hole at about the center of gravity is cut through each... they are the blades of an ancient form of stone anchor. For this use, a rounded, wooden shank would have been fitted through the center hole, and locked in place by a cross-pin. Pemaquid has a sheltered harbor that would have been an attractive landing place for any seamen, either ancient or modern. It is the sight of an early colonial trading settlement and fort, circa 1623.[9]

Stapler's description perfectly matches stone anchors of the Late Bronze Age of the kind recovered from the bottom of the waters around Crete, although the New England specimens were not from Europe or the Near East, but made, as he mentions, of "the same granite or banded gneiss common to the Pemaquid area." In other words, the design was Old World, but the manufacture was North American. Perhaps the metal font retrieved from beneath the banks of the Penobscot River had been discarded by an ancient Old World visitor who arrived in a Minoan ship that dropped and lost its anchor off the coast of Maine some 35 centuries ago.

Nine years before Michael Rose's small artifact surfaced, a related object was found under equally convincing circumstances, when Manfred Metcalf hiked into Georgia's vast Fort Benning military reservation, just south of Columbus, probing among the ruins of the abandoned Underwood Mill, built on Pine Knot Creek, in 1820. According to *Ancient American* writer James Miles, he "searched the area for rocks for use in a barbecue he was constructing in his backyard. He built a portion of it, then dismantled the barbecue. Returning to the project in September 1966, he flipped a stone over and noticed [the image of] a sun burst symbol inscribed on it."[10]

The red sandstone measured about 9 square inches, weighed approximately 11 pounds, and was cut on one side only with 17 characters. Metcalf carried his find to Dr. Joseph B.

Mahan, a distinguished Columbia State University anthropologist, who subjected it to microscopic scrutiny. He was convinced that the inscribed marks "were not made in recent times," due to their severe weathering. One of them, a double-headed axe, suggested a Minoan pedigree. "Another argument against the inscription being a modern hoax," writes Miles, "were traces of red clay and mortar, which had cemented the stones together, found embedded in the symbols. 1889 was the latest date for the mill and other structures where the stone was found. Sir Arthur Evans did not locate the first clay tablets containing Linear A until ten years later."[11]

By 1968, the Metcalf Stone had sufficiently impressed Dr. Mahan for him to share it with Cyrus Gordon, a Brandeis University professor and renowned authority on ancient linguistics. Although unable to make a translation, Gordon agreed with Mahan's initial impression: "...[I]f we compare the symbols on the rock with the known scripts of the world, the symbols most closely resemble Minoan."[12] Gordon then consulted Stanislav Segert, a professor of North-West Semitic languages at the University College of Los Angeles and formerly at the University of Prague, Czechoslovakia. Dr. Segert affirmed that the glyphs were an early form of Linear A, some four thousand years old.

The Metcalf Stone joins equally authenticated artifacts from Maine and Ohio, together with Arizona's Hohokam labyrinths, to document visitors from Bronze Age Crete in North America. The future decipherment of their written language will not only shed new light on the Minoans' high culture, but simultaneously reveal something about the impact they made on the American continent so long ago.

Chapter 4: Phoenicians

The sudden collapse of the Bronze Age around 1200 BCE took with it virtually every civilized society throughout the Peloponnesus, the Aegean world, and Asia Minor. Minoan Crete, Mycenaean Greece, Homeric Troy, the Hittite Empire, and numerous kingdoms across Anatolia and the Near East were toppled, and Pharaonic Egypt slid into a decline subsequent dynasties would be unable to check. Thus freed from the domination of these suddenly defunct superpowers, other peoples waiting in the shadows filled the commercial vacuum by exploiting trade routes pioneered and guarded by their deposed predecessors. History remembers them as "Phoenicians," a Semitic folk residing in Canaan, a region roughly corresponding to the present-day Levant of modern Israel, Palestinian territories, Lebanon, and the western parts of Jordan and Syria.

"The Phoenicians were the Canaanites, and the ancestors of today's Lebanese," concluded geneticist Spencer Wells in

2004, after an extensive DNA study of Phoenician origins sponsored by *National Geographic Magazine*.[1] Their name is Greek—*Phoiníkē*—for "people of the purple (*phoínios*)," signifying a violet-purple dye used by Athenian aristocrats to color their garments, and imported from the Levantine city of Tyre. *Phoiníkē* derived from the earlier Mycenaean *po-ni-ki-jo*, itself a derivation of the still older Egyptian *fenkhu*, denoting Asiatic Semites. This venerable lineage of nomenclature demonstrates how the Phoenicians were already well known to the outside world for exportation of the costly purple dye (extracted from a marine gastropod, the *pupur murex* mollusk, only at their cities of Tyre, on the shores of Lebanon, and Mogador, in far-off Morocco) long before their rise to prominence in the early 12th Century BCE.

They never called themselves "Phoenicians," but identified instead with any one of their numerous cities. Hence, they were Tyrians, Sidonians, Carthaginians, and so forth. They nonetheless comprised, in the aggregate, an identifiable entity. According to the 2011 census, only 12 percent of today's population in Lebanon are Arab. DNA studies reveal "overwhelming" genetic similarities between Phoenicians and most modern Lebanese.[2]

They regard Arabization as merely a shift to the Arabic language as the vernacular of their people, according to a Reuters News Service report, and believe that no actual shift of ethnic identity, much less ancestral origins, took place. Phoenicianists agree that Arabs in Lebanon, Syria, Palestine, Egypt, Sudan, Tunisia, and Iraq are different people, each descended from indigenous, pre-Arab populations, with their own histories and cultural identities. Consequently, these groups never belonged to a single, pan-Arab ethnicity, an erroneous and inapplicable categorization.[3]

The ancient Phoenicians built a loose confederation of casually affiliated, ethnically and culturally related, if independent urban centers. These were collectively known as *Khna* (the ancient equivalent of "Corporate Empire") or, to outsiders, as "Phoenicia," that spread from the Levant to the Atlantic coasts of Iberia and North Africa. It was organized into politically self-contained, metropolitan states collaborating in leagues or alliances, dominated by what was ever the most economically influential city at the time. Each one was alike, however, in its hierarchy of a king, followed in order of rank by temple priests and council elders. Their first successful city, which dominated trade routes from the Eastern Mediterranean into the Red Sea routes, was also where the earliest known inscription in the Phoenician alphabet—on a sarcophagus—was found and dated to circa 1175 BCE. Benefiting from the prosperity of Byblos, Tyre began its rise to influence, which spread as far north as Beirut and part of Cyprus.

Phoenician affluence depended on sturdy cargo vessels manned by well-trained, experienced sailors. It was to them that all the city-states of Khna owed their wealth. They sold cedars of Lebanon and wine to the Egyptians, who were unable to grow grapevines or quality timber in the Nile Valley, and for Nubian gold. The Phoenicians merchandized tin from Britain and slaves from Somalia for millions of customers in between, and built whole fleets for the Persian navy. In response to such widespread commerce, more Phoenician cities began to flourish along the southern and northern coasts of the Mediterranean Sea, but Carthage (from the Phoenician *Kart-hadasht*), founded in 814 BCE, was the greatest of them all. Its immense prosperity showed that the Phoenicians were less warlike than mercantile, chiefly interested in amassing riches, not territories, and conquest by foreign trade, not military invasions.

Their commercial preferences did not spare them from the armed aggression of others, however, when the Persians conquered most of Phoenicia in 539 BCE. After Cyrus the Great divided Khna into four vassal kingdoms, many Phoenicians migrated to Carthage, making it even grander and more powerful, with its own navy, as efficient as it was huge. Over centuries of escalating might, alternating conflicts and alliances with colonists from Greece and Etruscans from western Italy eventually burgeoned into competition with Rome. Three Punic Wars ended in 146 BCE, when Carthage was razed to the ground, its ruins vengefully ploughed under, and 50,000 of its residents were sold into slavery. But the Phoenicians' story did not end with this catastrophe, which their reputation as the foremost mariners of the Classical World outlived.

Given their expansive commercial instinct and the hardy ships they sailed so expertly, scholars have long wondered if

Carthaginian entrepreneurial ambition might have stretched to the other side of the world. Greek geographer Strabo wrote in the first Century BCE, "[F]ar-famed are the voyages of the Phoenicians, who, a short time after the Trojan War, explored the regions beyond the Pillars of Heracles, founding cities there and in the central Libyan seaboard."[4]

As an indication of their early transoceanic ambitions (inherited directly from Bronze Age sea-farers), very shortly after they began to break out of the Levant around the turn of the 12th Century BCE, the Phoenicians had already founded the city of Cádiz on the Spanish coast, from which they were poised to cross the Atlantic, around 1100 BCE. To be sure, critics of the "Columbus Was First" school of thought continue to argue that he was preceded 2,000 years or more by Phoenician traders. Most of those critics, however, have not been professional researchers. But when someone with Dr. Mark A.S. McMenamin's scientific background went public with the same conclusion, the Phoenician impact on pre-Columbian America gained substantial credibility. As a professor of geology and paleontology at Mount Holyoke College, in South Hadley, Massachusetts, he was not immediately drawn to questions of overseas' arrivals in the Western Hemisphere from the ancient Old World.

In 1996, Dr. McMenamin was on expedition in Mexico, where he excavated the fossilized remains of a 600-million year-old terrestrial vertebrate, the oldest and most complete found until then. His discovery pushed the timetable for animal evolution back much earlier than previously believed. Together with his wife, Dianna, who holds a master's degree in geology, he authored *Hypersea: Life on Land,* which convincingly argues that life on Earth pursued an evolutionary course through aquatic, as well as terrestrial phases. Their theory was selected by *Discover* magazine as among the "seven ideas that changed the world."[5]

Impressive as the professor's accomplishments have been, they brought him nowhere near the Phoenicians. His interest in them was accidentally sparked by a children's encyclopedia he happened to be consulting in preparation for educating his daughter at home. It mentioned that Carthaginian coins from the fourth Century BCE had been uncovered in the Azores, on the island of Corvo, some 800 miles from the European mainland. The hoard was discovered by Portuguese sailors during the early 1750s. The coins have long since been lost, although Dr. McMenamin established the authenticity of their discovery through personal research that found them described in the 1778 diary of Swedish sailor Johannes Podolyn.

In absence of the coins themselves, McMenamin made an in-depth study of Carthaginian currency, even going so far as to become fluent in the Phoenician language. At the University of Massachusetts Library, he studied a book illustrating gold coinage from the first few centuries BCE. Finding nothing to match Podolyn's description, McMenamin was in the process of returning the book when he noticed very small markings at the bottom of the reverse, or "tails," side of several *staters*. *Stater* is actually a Greek term that referred to coins made of precious metal.

The markings he examined have long been known to numismatists, but not generally understood. Most expert coin collectors dismiss them as errors in production. The markings attracted McMenamin's attention, because they seemed vaguely familiar. Only after he had them enlarged on his computer screen did he recognize them for what they really were. McMenamin was astounded to realize that tiny dots on the Carthaginian staters were elements of a map—and not just any map, but a world map similar to one compiled by the second-century Greek geographer Ptolemy.

Through further close scrutiny of the hitherto neglected metallic blobs on all 14 of the known specimens of a particular type of Phoenician *stater*, McMenamin was able to identify the entire Mediterranean region, including the Straits of Gibraltar, Sardinia, coastal North Africa, and the south of Europe depicted on the coins. He even found the Indian sub-continent clearly indicated. In other words, the Carthaginians included at the bottom of their coins tiny maps of locations where they enjoyed prosperous ports-of-call. They were publishing their far-flung, mercantile contacts on the face of their own currency, just as today's multinational corporations boast of their international influence in commercial advertising.

After making his original and revealing discovery, McMenamin was more amazed to observe the eastern half of South America depicted on the same coins. Clearly shown are Brazil and Argentina down to Tierra del Fuego, although the tiny map does not include the rest of the continent westward from the Andes. This omission lends credibility to the representation, because it suggests that the Phoenicians had been realistically prevented from further penetration of South America by the formidable mountain range.

In any case, his interpretation of the coin's otherwise-meaningless markings makes a strong case for extensive Phoenician knowledge of not only the continent's Atlantic coastal areas, but about half of its eastern interior up to the Andean foothills, suggesting long familiarity with South America. This numismatic map provides physical proof that the ancient mariners arrived as transoceanic merchants who established regular trade routes to the New World. These trade routes were not generally known outside Phoenician circles, because such prized information—the equivalent of today's industrial secrets—represented what amounted to a trade monopoly. With the thorough destruction of Phoenician Civilization by Roman forces in 146 BCE, knowledge of the Brazilian Antilia and all points west across the Atlantic Ocean was lost.

Reaction to McMenamin's findings from Establishment archaeologists was predictably hostile, "much of it quite harsh at first," he says.[6] But the self-evident appearance of the coin-maps, together with his own academic background, has forced even some skeptics to moderate their opposition. The very *stater* on which he detected a depiction of South America had been minted in Carthage from gold brought back as part of an expedition to West Africa. It was led by Hanno II, since known as "Hanno the Navigator" for his mid-fifth-century-BCE extensive colonization and exploration of Africa's Atlantic coast. His fleet of 60 ships carrying some 30,000 men, women, and children sailed out of the Mediterranean Sea, then steered southward to Morocco. Along its coast, they founded or repopulated seven colonies, including Tangiers, Lixus, and Mogador, where the ruins of a Phoenician harbor wall still stand.

Having discharged his settlers, Hanno ventured around West Africa, into the Gulf of Guinea. After 35 days at sea, and "being out of provisions, we could go no further," he reported in a memorial tablet hung up on his return to Carthage in the temple of Ba'al Hammon, the city's chief sky-god from whom his name—Annôn, Phoenician for "merciful" or "mild"—derived.[7] About 100 years later, the coin on which Dr. McMenamin perceived the tiny representation of South America was minted. The 475 miles separating Brazil from Hanno's passage off Sierra Leone was far less than half of the 1,300 miles he covered from Carthage to Cameroon. Clearly, the lesser distance could have been handily negotiated by Phoenician ships, which were a third as long as a football field and propelled by two and sometimes four banks of oarsmen.

Their even greater achievement preceded Hanno's voyage by 150 years in the first documented circumnavigation of the African continent. Phoenician ships and mixed Punic-Egyptian crews were commissioned by a 26th Dynasty Pharaoh, who sent them to re-discover the lost Lands of Punt (see Chapter 2). By King Nekau II's time, around 600 BCE, previous expeditions associated with such famous monarchs as Queen Hatshepsut or Rameses III had become progressively legendary with the gradual decline of Pharaonic civilization and its accompanying, ever-attenuated maritime skills. But Nekau's attempt proved that at least 2,600 years ago, the Phoenicians possessed the means and know-how to undertake epic, oceanic voyages. That his own Punt expedition included North America is suggested by Barbara Holley Rock, when she and her colleagues saw a contemporaneous Egyptian text in New Mexico.

During April 1991, they examined

> the inscription carved on a gray limestone atop a narrow valley with about a one thousand-foot drop to the valley floor.... Access to this site [its remote location is undisclosed as a preservation measure] is up the west side of the mountain trail cut by wagon tracks, then across the mountain top by foot to a narrow ledge facing west.... All of our symbols [in the nineteen-word text], one hundred percent of them, were found in the

> Egyptian language sources that we consulted. Demotic Egyptian has been the best suggestion to determine a meaning....[8]

Demotic Egyptian hieroglyphs developed around 751 BCE and were in common usage by the 26th Dynasty. The incomplete New Mexican inscription translates into Demotic Egyptian as "Embrace in greeting! Hail, truth! [actually, Maat, the goddess of truth] The village that formerly lived is now as a bare, wooden log. In the space of a month, its authority was broken by an inundation of death. It returned to heaven. In its last days, dual sacrifices were made as a way to live. One's love...."[9]

Although the matter referred to is unclear, the text's ancient authenticity is affirmed by its appearance at a virtually inaccessible location in an obscure New Mexico valley, while coinciding with Pharaoh Nekau's long-distance expedition of mixed Phoenician-Egyptian crews.

Accurately depicted on Dr. McMenamin's Carthaginian coin is the state of Paraíba—South America's prominent protrusion into the Atlantic Ocean, and the most likely region where sea-farers sailing from West Africa would have landed; it is Brazil's closest distance by less than 500 miles from Sierra Leone, familiar to Hanno the Navigator. These observations were borne out in a letter of September 11, 1872, written by Joaquim Alves da Costa, a Brazilian plantation owner, and addressed to *Cândido* José de Araújo Viana, the *Visconde de Sapucahy*, president of *the Instituto Histórico e Geográfico Brasiliero* in Rio de Janeiro.

Da Costa explained:

> As I was having stones carried in my property of Pouso Alto, near the Parahyba [River], my slaves brought me one that they had already broken into four pieces. This stone presented numerous characters that no one understood. I had them copied by my son, who knows a little about draftsmanship, and I was resolved to send this copy to Your Excellency, as President of the Historical and Geographical Institute of

> Brazil, to see if Your Excellency or some other person could determine what these letters mean.[10]

Intrigued, de Araújo Viana passed da Costa's letter and drawing on to Ladislau de Souza Mello Netto, "the most influential Brazilian scientist of his times."[11] Knowledgeable in Punic archaeology, Netto recognized the inscription as Phoenician, but sent a partial copy to his former tutor, Joseph Ernest Renan, a leading expert in Semitic languages, if better remembered today as the author of that classic, non-religious biography, *The Life of Jesus*. Renan found enough grammatical errors in the transcribed text to pronounce it a modern fake, a judgment supported by his European colleagues, epigrapher Christoph Wilhelm Konstantin Schlottmann and orientalist Julius Euting. Undeterred, Netto attempted a translation of the inscription, which told of mariners from the Phoenician city of Sidon, commissioned by their king, Hiram, in the 19th year of his reign, to establish long-distance trade. They left with hundreds of settlers in 10 ships from Ezion-Geber, a Red Sea port on the northern extremity of the Gulf of Aqaba, in the area of modern Aqaba and Eilat. After sailing around the coasts of Africa for two years, at least one vessel somehow separated from the rest of the fleet and landed on Brazilian shores with 15 survivors (12 men and three women).

Netto sent a copy of the inscription, plus his translation of it, to the renowned bibliographer Wilberforce Eames, chief of the American History division at the New York Public Library. Despite the objections of Renan, Schlottmann, and Euting, Netto realized that the modern perpetrator of such a hoax could only have been someone well-versed in Phoenician language and history, qualifications not generally associated with a backwoods plantation owner, but restricted rather to a small circle of fellow scholars. When he attempted to personally track down the source of the inscription, however, Netto was confronted by a bewildering array of several Brazilian locations known as "Pouso Alto." Moreover, some had changed their names over the previous few years. Persistent inquiry failed to find the alleged letter-writer, his plantation, the stone, or the site where it was supposedly found.

Frustrated and worried that the controversy could jeopardize his position as director of Rio de Janeiro's Brazilian National Museum, Netto publicly recanted his former advocacy of the text in a "Letter to M. Ernest Renan concerning the fake Phoenician inscription submitted in 1872 to the Historical, Geographical and Ethnographic Institute of Brazil." He was mortified for having been duped by "foreigners," who must have fabricated the hoax somehow, although the identity of these deceptive aliens could not be determined, nor did anyone profit, in either money or notoriety, from the controversy. Thus dismissed as a failed attempt at archaeological fraud, it would have almost certainly never risen from oblivion, and was, in fact, utterly forgotten for more than 80 years after Netto's apologetic letter to Renan, published in 1885. But the Paraíba Stone was surrounded by a strange fate all its own.

Long after its detractors were dead and mostly forgotten, Jules Piccus was casually strolling through a backyard sale in Providence, Rhode Island, during summer 1967, when the American philologist and professor of romance languages at the University of Massachusetts (Amherst) picked up a curious scrapbook. Inserted among its moldering pages was Ladislau Netto's original correspondence with Wilberforce Eames, together with a copy of the Paraíba inscription. Intrigued, he sent these materials to Cyrus Gordon, at that time head of the department of Mediterranean Studies at Brandeis University, Waltham, Massachusetts. As described in our previous chapter, Professor Gordon was the world's leading authority on ancient Semitic languages. Piccus learned he was then investigating the Metcalf Stone, and assumed his colleague might be interested in a similar challenge.

Gordon found that the harsh judgment Renan, Schlottmann, and Euting passed on the Paraíba text had been over-hasty, because they demanded grammatical perfection from its anonymous author. On the contrary, its syntactical errors lent credence to the inscription's ancient authenticity, Gordon argued, because the body of its text inferred that the unknown writer was not a highly educated person, but rather someone only basically literate.

Moreover, the inscription itself contained elements of Phoenician style unfamiliar to late 19th Century linguists. He then rendered his own translation, which differed somewhat from Netto's, but was more accurately fine-tuned:

> We are Sidonian Canaanites from the city of the Mercantile King. We were cast up on this distant shore, a land of mountains. We sacrificed a youth to the celestial gods and goddesses in the nineteenth year of our mighty King Hiram, and embarked from Ezion-geber into the Red Sea. We voyaged with ten ships, and were at sea together for two years around Africa. Then we were separated by the hand of Baal, and were no longer with our companions. So we have come here, twelve men and three women, into New Shore. Am I, the Admiral, a man who would flee? No! May the celestial gods and goddesses favor us well![12]

Gordon's translation revealed information only a modern forger well-versed in ancient Near Eastern civilization could have known. As mentioned previously, the Phoenicians never referred to themselves as such, but commonly expressed their identity as Canaanites belonging to a particular city-state—here, the city of Sidon. Their religion called for child sacrifice, and Hiram III was a historical king, who reigned between 554 BCE and 533 BCE, about 100 years before Hanno's voyage around West Africa. Ezion-Geber was a real enough place, its ruins excavated at Tell el-Kheleifeh, in Jordan, 60 years after the Paraíba inscription came to light, and dated from the eighth and sixth centuries BCE, with occupation continuing for the next two centuries. Gordon found nothing in the text to contradict its ancient authenticity.

Suggestion of any contact between the Old and New Worlds made before Christopher Columbus elicited a knee-jerk response from mainstream scholars, who loudly reiterated Renan and company's condemnation of the Paraíba inscription, thereby rescuing it from obscurity. Frank Moore Cross, Jr., professor of Hebrew and Other Oriental Languages emeritus at Harvard, showed how the inscription was peppered with spelling and vocabulary errors, "demonstrating conclusively that the text was a modern forgery" for anyone already predisposed to disregard it as fake.[13]

The reignited controversy continued to blaze, and even Netto himself was accused of being the forger. In 1972, Brazilian scholar Geraldo Irenêo Joffily claimed that the distinguished director of Rio de Janeiro's Brazilian National Museum had actually perpetrated the hoax "to further his own career and to ingratiate himself with Emperor Dom Pedro II."[14] Although Joffily's speculation was unfounded, he did cite a little-known, 17th-century colonial administration report that told how Jesuit priests of Minas Gerais found several bronze figurines covered with peculiar inscriptions near the Rio Paraíba in 1641.

Copies were forwarded to the Vatican, in Rome, where antiquarians identified the texts as Phoenician. The bronze figurines and Jesuit correspondence were lost in the more than 300 years since the report was issued, but mere mention of such a find at Paraíba lends some credence to the artifacts discovered there. That credibility was underscored yet again, when Netto's fruitless search for the plantation owner, on whose estate the Paraíba Stone was found, had not gone as far as it should. Even a writer for "Bad Archaeology," an Internet skeptic Website, admits, "[T]here does seem to have been a real Joachim Alves da Costa Freitas, who lived close to Pouso Alto in Minas Gerais province, during the 1870s."[15]

Especially enlightening is archaeology commentator Gerard Michael Burns's explanation that the Paraíba Stone

> is not a "stone," but an isolated instance of apparent petroglyphic writing at a place with much currently known indigenous rock art, in or around a town called Pedra Lavrada ("carved/worked rock"), with a specific grouping known as the Pedra de Retumba [Francisco Soares], Retumba being an engineer who also traced the alleged writing), seeming to be what Netto referred to. The first website I cite by a historian, says this was investigated around

> Netto's time and later by a number of people, who seem to have been fairly qualified, since they recommended placing casts over the writing to preserve it, believing it Phoenician, or at least much different from the rock art, which has since been identified as from three known local cultures and is widespread in the area. A paper (Brito, et al.) from the National University of Santa Catarina says that the portion with the alleged Phoenician text has apparently been covered by silt from flooding of the nearby Canta Galo River, although there is also a danger that it was destroyed for building material.[16]

Indirect evidence from an ancient Old World source not only seems to refer to the story told by the Paraíba text, but provides its happy ending with the return to Europe of at least one of its survivors, who related his account to first-century-BCE Greek geographer Strabo: "Once, while exploring the coast along Libya [Africa], they [crew members of a Phoenician ship] were driven by strong winds for a great distance out into the ocean. After being tossed for many days, they were carried ashore on an island [a term used by Strabo for any overseas territory] of considerable size, situated a great distance to the west of Libya."[17]

Though the Paraíba Stone or petroglyph documented sixth-century-BCE arrivals from the ancient Near East in Brazil, it was the only proof of its kind ever found. They came as castaways, not colonists. Odds are that many shipwreck survivors from numerous lands far across the sea washed up along South American shores long before and since, although no others left behind an account of their accidental landfall. At least some Phoenician sailors, as suggested by Strabo's account, somehow managed a return to Europe or Africa, where their personal experiences sparked serious expeditions to America.

That these actually took place is documented by the same kind of evidence responsible for the Carthaginians' secrecy about overseas sources of precious materials. The single most valuable commodity they possessed was a corner on the purple dye industry, thanks to their monopoly of the purpur murex mollusk shell, as found primarily along North African shores in Mauretania, roughly corresponding to modern Morocco and western parts of Libya. The same purple dye industry was worked by native Brazilians along the Rio de Janeiro coastline.

"This was once fluffed off," writes anthropologist George Carter, "as: The Spanish taught them. But we have C-14 dates for such dyes as early as 200 B.C. Is it a reasonable trade item? It certainly is. Distant trade must rest on light weight, low bulk, high value materials. Dyes fit this perfectly."[18]

The existence of a purple shell industry alone would prompt Phoenician colonization of Atlantic coastal South America and justify classifying the location of its source in Brazil as Carthage's most important trade secret. Evidence of quite a different kind has been recovered from North America: grape vines.

"Historians usually credit 17th Century Europeans with bringing the plant to New England," writes Dr. Gunnar Thompson, "however, French explorers, such as Verrazano, Champlain and Cartier confirmed that abundant grape vines were already growing on the East Coast when they explored the St. Lawrence valley prior to the influx of European settlers."[19]

Dr. Thompson's observation was confirmed by professional vintner John Fitzhugh Millar, who described the Phoenicians' living legacy in Virginia:

> Like many people in the South, we grow *Scuppernong* grapes, making jellies and jams out of them. They also yield a sweet, syrupy wine, and were known to be growing in the same region they now occupy from Virginia to Florida and Texas when the Spanish Conquistadors first saw them, five hundred years ago. Although *Scuppernong* is a Native American name, it is not a native American plant. These grapes are imported from the Middle East,

> which explains why they are called *Muscadine*, meaning, from *Muscat*.
>
> When Jesus drank wine (unless he made it out of water!), he almost certainly drank *Scuppernong*. Cultural isolationists believe that birds must have brought the seeds to North America across the Atlantic Ocean ages ago. But these grapes, which are bronze-colored when ripe, have thick, leathery skins, and birds do not eat them. During the late 1990s, I wondered how the grapes could have possibly reached these shores, and concluded that ancient Phoenician seafarers brought them to our continent....[20]

Unknown to Millar, his conclusion had been supported as long ago as 1524 by Giovanni da Verrazzano, the first European to visit the Atlantic coast between the Carolinas and Newfoundland, including New York Harbor and Narragansett Bay, since Norse settlers in North America around 1000 CE. "We saw in this country many vines growing naturally," wrote the Florentine explorer, "entwining themselves about the trees, climbing as they do in Cisalpine Gaul, which, if they were dressed in the right way of cultivation by husbandmen, they would produce without doubt the best of wines, because often the fruit of that drinking is agreeable and sweet. It is not different from our own."[21]

During the following decade, long before modern European settlement near the St. Lawrence River, French explorer Jacques Cartier reported seeing "great stores of grapes."[22]

While Millar was musing on the Phoenician origins of New England's indigenous grape vines, he

> happened to be having breakfast with an Indiana archaeologist [Dr. James E. Gillihan, former vice president of Yankton College, Illinois]. "Yes, we know about that," he said, and surprised me by agreeing with my thoughts on ancient visitors

> to the New World. He added that a professional team (to which he had not belonged) of fellow archaeologists and linguists made a systematic sweep of the Upper Midwest about 1992, finding conclusive evidence that the Phoenicians had indeed sailed up the Mississippi River on a regular basis. Farmers in Indiana, Ohio, Illinois and Michigan, while clearing their fields in the 1800s, often found rocks inscribed with odd letters in unknown written languages.
>
> Some of these accidental finds survived the course of time, and were examined by team members, who recognized the inscriptions as Punic.... Translations of the inscribed rocks from the Upper Midwest, according to the Indiana archaeologist, usually proclaimed the ancient equivalent of "Joe was here," but at least one specimen carried a different message—"I am the captain (*raz*, the same word for "captain" in modern Arabic), and not feeling well, so I am living in a tent on an island at the mouth of the Great River (the Mississippi). If you want to see me, you have to come down here, because I am not going up to where you are."[23]

Although mainstream scholars keep such revealing discoveries to themselves for fear public disclosure would topple their archaeological apple cart, other finds are too large for concealment. The most recent example was found as recently as 2001, during the demolition of an old house in a western neighborhood of Los Angeles, California. Digging down more than 5 feet into its backyard, workers were surprised to unearth a large, almost perfectly rectangular block of reddish igneous rock weighing 228 pounds. When hoisted out of the ground and placed upright, it stood 3.4 feet tall on a base measuring 1.7 by 1.6 feet. Either side was covered with identical patterns of semi-circles and straight lines, and about two-thirds up the front of the monolith, a human face protruding as far as its ears was sculpted at the center of a series of ridges, suggesting a hairstyle terminating below the head in large, twin curls.

The block was taken to the Natural History Museum of Los Angeles, where examiners observed the effects of having been buried in acidic soil for many years, but were unable to associate it or its sculpted designs with any indigenous peoples or regional archaeology. These carvings resemble nothing similar to indigenous Californian or even North American tribal imagery. They are utterly unlike anything found in Native American art, either prehistoric or contemporary. Indian material culture did not include monumental stone sculpture.

Writing in *Ancient American,* Diane E. Wirth argued that the hairstyle depicted on the Los Angeles monolith most resembled that associated in temple art with a goddess of motherhood venerated throughout the Nile Valley.[24] Beginning in the 18th Dynasty, Hathor merged with their own version introduced by traveling merchants from Tyre around 1550 BCE. Their divine protectoress assumed some features of Egypt's indigenous goddess, particularly her characteristic headdress. Thereafter, Ashtart was usually portrayed wearing the stylized bouffant configuration ending in two, close-fitting curls on either side of the head, wherever the Phoenicians traveled, as evidenced by one of her bronze figures from Carranzo, Spain.

The Los Angeles monolith—its head wearing the Hathor-Ashtart's iconic hairstyle—could portray either conception. Egyptian sacred art never depicted its deities in such a crude manner, whereas Phoenician divinities, on the contrary, were often coarsely portrayed. Still more revealing is the face-forward representation on the California block, diagnostic of Phoenician sculpted art. The monolith also conforms in size and rectangular-cubic shape to a stone altar for the worship of Ashtart, the "Lady of the Sea," an appropriate goddess for transoceanic mariners arriving on the west coast of North America.

Another one—similar in size and dimensions, but different in almost all other respects—was found 200 years earlier, 3,800 miles away, in northern Illinois. Publicly displayed throughout the

20th Century on the main floor of the Chicago Historical Society, the Waubansee Stone has since been warehoused in the basement to make way for less controversial artifacts. On one side is expertly sculpted the face of a man, his eyes closed and mouth open, with a chin-beard. At the top of the stone is a depression, like a small trough. Three interconnecting holes bored through the hard granite linking the trough appear on either side of the artwork and through the parted lips of the face. Incised to a depth of 1.5 inches, the relief sculpture measures 12 inches wide and 17.5 inches high. The top has been hollowed into a depression 4.5 inches deep, 18 inches long by 9 inches wide.

Although the stone was supposedly carved in the likeness of a Pottawatomie Indian chief by an anonymous American soldier, that late-19th-century urban legend has been long since discredited. Chief Waubansee's name, however, still clings to the

Image 4-1 and 4-2: Real-life portrait of Chief Waubansee, courtesy of Wikipedia (left), bears no resemblance to the stone face associated with his name. Photo by author

3,000-pound monolith. Comparison of its sculpted face with his 1840 portrait from life proves they are not related in any respect.

The Waubansee Stone resembles nothing, however, if not a *tophet*, a low altar commonly used by Phoenician priests for ritual infanticide as an offering to their gods for protection. Its depression carved at the top, similar in size to a bassinet, perfectly accommodates the size of a baby's body. Drilled holes would have allowed sacrificial blood to pour out of either side of the stone and through the open mouth of the sculpted face, its eyes shut, suggesting death. This pose recurs in Phoenician art, such as the bronze head of a man with closed eyes from a temple in Ugarit.

Like the sculptor of the Waubansee Stone, Phoenician artists favored frontal, full-face portraiture, as mentioned in our earlier discussion of the Los Angeles monolith. Outstanding examples are the famous Mona Lisa of Nimrud and the ubiquitous, ivory carvings of the so-called "woman in the window" found at Carthage. The face on the Waubansee Stone image wears a chin-beard, a personal grooming detail characteristic of Phoenician priests, but something unknown to beardless Native Americans. During the late 1890s, the Waubansee Stone was removed from its original location on the south bank of the Chicago River, where it opens on Lake Michigan, a meeting-point for seafarers skirting the lakeshore entering or leaving the inland waterway.

Thirty-five miles north, and just 7 miles from Lake Michigan, the Phoenicians left behind another memento of their passage through Illinois. It was unearthed during the early 20th Century from a prehistoric Indian burial mound located on the banks of the Des Plaines River, near the town of Libertyville. Sculpted from a single piece of off-white soapstone, the half-pound statuette portrays a man wrapped in a kind of body-stocking, from which his emerging hands hold a shepherd's crook in the left and a flail in the right. The flail was an agricultural tool used in dynastic times by Nile Valley farmers to separate wheat from chaff by beating stacks of grain on a stone floor for threshing. Pharaohs were commonly depicted in sacred art holding such a device as the emblem of judgment (separating good from bad subjects). The shepherd's crook stood for political guidance over his flock (people).

The Des Plaines River statuette wears a stylized wig behind the ears, together with a long chin-beard. Beginning at the waist and descending to an area corresponding to the ankles are eight lines of hieroglyphic text, with a single, additional line composed of four glyphs running top to bottom from the ankles to the unexposed toes. Other than what is probably some minor erosional damage at the front-left side between the hand holding the flail and the top line of script, the object is in perfect condition. Small accumulations of white material in some of the glyphs, and particularly in between the vertical lines of the wig, are perhaps residues of clay. More puzzling is the appearance of dark orange pigment found mostly on the wig, but also in the eyes of the face, and in some of the glyphs and horizontal lines separating them. The ochre-like coloration may have been caused by an unknown, powdery substance ritually sprinkled on the figure prior to burial, or caused by reaction with the soil after interment.

The artifact's overall workmanship is exceptionally fine. Particularly outstanding are its hieroglyphs, which, for their individually crafted details, betray the hand of a master scribe intimately familiar with his subject. Everything about the object, quite obviously, bespeaks Pharaonic Egypt. So much so, its provenance may be easily traced to a specific dynasty—namely, the 26th, or "Saite," after the Nile Delta city of Sais, where the royal house was founded in 664 BCE, enduring for another 139 years. This era brackets a time frame when such images were portrayed wearing the body-stocking described earlier; numerous, comparative specimens are displayed at Britain's Fitzwilliam College, in Cambridge.

The figure's identification as an *ushabti* is no less apparent. Ushabti were small statuettes placed in ancient Egyptian tombs to act as servants for the soul of the deceased. Imbued with ceremonial magic during his or her funeral, the figures were supposed to come alive after the mummy had been sealed inside its tomb. The term *ushabti* means "the answerer," from the verb *wesheb* ("to answer"). The Libertyville figure's hieroglyphic text appears to repeat lines from Chapter 6 in the Book of the Dead, a collection of sacred texts aimed at guiding the human soul successfully through the terrors of death into the Afterlife; it was likewise interred with the deceased. The object stands 9 inches tall, the same height for most ancient Egyptian ushabti.

What makes its Saite provenance especially cogent was one 26th Dynasty ruler in particular, the same Pharaoh mentioned earlier in this chapter: Nekau II, who commissioned the first known circumnavigation of the African Continent, as documented by the sixth-century Greek historian Herodotus, in his famous *Histories*. The Libertyville item's identifiably Saite configuration, together with King Nekau's contemporary expedition, suggests that the figure is indeed a 26th Dynasty ushabti that probably belonged to an Egyptian sailor aboard one of his hired Phoenician ships, with their mixed Punic-Egyptian crews. The "Indian" burial mound from which the statuette was recovered may instead have been his final resting place.

Some 300 miles north, more evidence of a mixed Phoenician enterprise in the form of a clay tablet was found under the roots of a fallen tree 4 miles outside the town of Newberry, Michigan, in November 1896. Measuring 18 by 25 inches, one side of the 6-inch-thick rectangle was covered with a grid pattern of 1.5-inch squares containing glyphs belonging to no known written language. Images of the object and descriptive articles were published in 1897 issues of *The Marquette Mining Journal*, and a special set of photos taken by the editor of *The Newberry News* was forwarded at his not-inconsiderable, personal expense to the Smithsonian Institution. Curators there never bothered to respond, and promptly "lost" all the photographs he sent them. Other professional archaeologists took the hint by avoiding all mention of the Newberry Tablet, which was allowed to disintegrate through neglect and abuse over subsequent decades, until, around 1960, the last two or three fragments of it were taken to the Fort de Buade Museum, in St. Ignace, Michigan, where they are still preserved.

That its discovery was not a hoax is certain, because no one ever attempted to profit from the object in any way. Although one or two old photographs and the Fort de Buade Museum's small, crumbling pieces are all that are left to modern researchers, Dr. Barry Fell (mentioned in Chapter 2 for the credible connections he made between Algonkian and Egyptian writing systems) found during his 1981 study of the Newberry Tablet's 19th Century images that its glyphs belonged to a Hittite-Minoan syllabary, a set of written characters for a language, each one representing a syllable. Unfortunately, Dr. Fell did not convincingly explain how he came to such a conclusion, other than to add that possibly eight of the Tablet's glyphs resembled Linear A, with variations attributed to Hittite influences. Scrutiny of the glyphs reveals instead that 17 of them are clearly Etruscan, and repeated enough to comprise 66 of the Tablet's 140 characters. The Etruscan P, which appears in no other ancient Old World written language, recurs most often (12 times) on the object, followed by 10 additional Etruscan letters. No less revealing is the appearance of a single Phoenician glyph (W) because it dates the text to circa 900 BCE, making it contemporary with the Archaic Etruscan, nearly half of the characters.

The Etruscans were the descendants of Trojan refugees from the war that burned their fabled city, Ilios, emigrating to western Italy during the mid-13th-century BCE. During the centuries to come, they created a League of Twelve Cities, a loose confederation bound by common culture and race, in which flourished monumental public works projects, the arts, and a bronze technology. Although possessed of all-conquering land armies, the Etruscans owed their real strength and fabulous prosperity to their thalassocracy, or power based on control of the seas. Their ships and sailors were the finest of Early Classical Times, rivaled only by the Phoenicians. After reaching the zenith of civilized glory around 500 BCE, the Etruscans were caught in a self-destructive spiral of materialism, complacency, decline, degeneracy, and ultimate annihilation experienced by other societies, before and since. Once the conquerors of Rome itself, they fell victim to Roman will some two centuries later and were assimilated into extinction.

Despite more than 100 years of effort, scholars are still not able to translate the Etruscan written language, outside of a few place names and pronouns. As such, the Newberry Tablet, though composed in large measure of Etruscan glyphs, cannot be read. Nonetheless, the Etruscans were known for making virtually identical clay tablets likewise divided into grid patterns, a comparison that lends additional credence to the object. As perhaps the only identifiable example of its kind ever found in the Americas, it implies that the Etruscan impact on pre-Columbian America was minimal, at best.

The Tablet does, however, signify a Phoenician relationship, indicated by inclusion of the Punic "W." Though sometimes rivals, the Etruscans and Phoenicians were more often business partners and even allies, as suggested by the appearance of their written languages together on the same Tablet. Its discovery near the shores of Lake Superior in the heart of ancient mining country is especially revealing of a joint copper-trading mission. Although the mines had been shut down two hundred years before the Punic-Etruscan expedition arrived at Michigan's Upper Peninsula, archaeologists have found traces of renewed excavations there on a far less ambitious scale, more off than on, well into the 15th Century CE.

The Etruscans were rather archaic, if serious manufacturers of bronze ware in an age of iron, and would have gone to the ends of the Earth, as they apparently did, for the world's highest-grade copper. But they needed the Phoenicians, who knew its secret location, to take them there. This only explains the presence of a typically Etruscan tablet, with at least one Punic glyph, in the middle of North America's ancient copper mining region. Nor was the Newberry Tablet's mix of Punic with other written languages in any way unusual or unique. As a mosaic people, the Phoenicians absorbed and combined a variety of foreign influences. Often, these cultural combinations reflected close relations Phoenicians enjoyed—however impermanently—with different folk, such as the Etruscans and Greeks, in their mutual Mediterranean commerce.

A North American example is the Blaine Stone, named after the location of its 1969 discovery in a Minneapolis suburb about 10 miles east of the Mississippi River, on old Indian property, and covered with two lines of inscribed Punic and Greek letters. Lance Wonders reported in *Ancient American* that

> the stone was unearthed when tree stumps were being removed from a nearby field to be used for soccer practice by a Christian elementary school housed on the property. The stone sat in some grass near a cluster of trees for probably three years before it was moved for mowing.... The stone was then given over

> to the custody of ACTS Bible College [where Wonders is the Academic Dean].... I am very much convinced that the stone is not a fraud. I can see no purpose served by that, nor how anyone could benefit from it, to say nothing of how difficult (and brilliant!) such an effort would have to be to pull off.[25]

Whereas most characters on the Blaine Stone appear to be Punic, Greek *lambda*, *delta*, *sigma*, *pi*, and *zeta* also appear. Although the bilingual inscription has not been translated, its discovery near a major waterway connecting Upper Michigan's ancient copper mining—like that of the Newberry Tablet, Libertyville statuette, and Waubansee Stone—implies the passage of mixed crews aboard Phoenician vessels engaging in the transport of precious metal.

A remarkable example of how they transformed that natural resource into wealth was found far from the Middle West, in Utah, sometime during the early 20th Century. It measures approximately 6 inches in diameter and appears to have been made from a copper alloy. Circumstances surrounding its discovery are very uncertain, having been allegedly been recovered from 6 feet, 6 inches beneath the surface of the state's geographical center in the Sanpete Valley. An alternative version describes anonymous family members digging a well somewhere along the Sevier River outside Richfield, in south-central Utah, where they accidentally unearthed the object, again, at about 6 feet down. After having been told by a nearby historian that "it must have belonged to local Indians," the unconvinced discoverers passed their find along through three generations and into the possession of a grandchild.

If such paltry background information has robbed the piece of whatever artifactual provenance it may have once owned, it stands on its own as something curiously convincing. Everything about it argues against fakery—from the fine workmanship to its lack of comparison with anything similarly known in the modern world, to say nothing of its truly arcane details. At first glance, it nonetheless seems like an impossible mish-mash of disparate cultures. The typically "Egyptian" figure, hairstyle, profile, eye, necklace, and lotus appear contradicted by uncharacteristic discs on either side of the head and an inscription in cuneiform—not hieroglyphs—at the top.

In truth, the Phoenicians are known for borrowing and incorporating the cultural elements of other folk, particularly the Egyptians. The Phoenicians created their own written language, of course. But, according to *Omniglot*, the online encyclopedia of writing systems and languages, "The Phoenician alphabet developed from the proto-Canaanite alphabet during the 15th Century B.C. Before then, *the Phoenicians wrote with a cuneiform script* [author's emphasis]. The earliest known inscriptions in the Phoenician alphabet come from Byblos [in Lebanon] and date back to 1000 B.C."[26]

Hence, if Phoenicians inscribed the Utah plate with cuneiform, they could only have done so before the 15th century BCE. At that time, they were strictly confined to the Levant, in the Near East, by the predominance of other, more powerful kingdoms. Only with the collapse of these Late Bronze Age civilizations around the turn of the 12th Century BCE were the Phoenicians free to become the far-ranging merchants renowned throughout the Archaic and Early Classical periods. Perhaps the Utah plate was already 500 or more years old and a particularly revered object when it was carried by Phoenicians to our continent's eastern seaboard. They may not have actually reached the location of its modern discovery in the American Southwest, where it could have arrived and been deliberately buried as a precious commercial good handled by aboriginal traders.

In any case, those strange discs at either side of the woman's head identify her Iberian origins. A similar, otherwise-unique accoutrement appears on the so-called "Lady of Elche," the fourth-century-BCE stone bust of a Carthaginian priestess to the Phoenician lunar goddess, Tanit, found outside Valencia. In fact, double-headdress discs depicted on the Utah profile and Spain's Lady of Elche both feature some telltale details in common:

rectangular sets of small, triple knobs running around the edge. As Carthaginians, the Phoenicians built several major cities in Iberia, such as Cartegena and Gadir, today's Cádiz. The Utah image appears related to one of these urban centers. Gadir was founded in 1104 BCE, the earliest possible date for the metallic plate's arrival in North America. Its most recent date would have coincided with the Roman conquest of all Carthaginian cities in Iberia by the early third Century BCE.

Image 4-3 and 4-4: North America's Lady of Utah (left). Photo courtesy of Ancient American *magazine. Spain's Lady of Elche. Photo courtesy of Manuel de Corselas, Wikipedia*

Although insufficiently known circumstances of its discovery obscure the Sevier River object's possible archaeological genuineness, its own beauty, high craftsmanship, and internal details suggest an ancient authenticity beyond the loss of provenance. As such, Utah's embossed plate is potentially powerful evidence for the arrival on our shores of Phoenician visitors from Carthaginian Spain, 2,200 to 3,100 years ago. That they did set foot here is additionally suggested by a particular star seafarers regularly used to help them sail westward from the Phoenician city of Tyre. So vital for navigation was this astral point of reference that they may have designated an entire continent after its name: *La Merika.*

Chapter 5:
Romans

During the early Classical Age, a well-known story illustrating the Carthaginians' determination to keep the whereabouts of their foreign resources hidden from competitors told how a merchantman bound for Antilia—possibly a Phoenician name for Brazil—was sighted by the captain of a Roman freighter just beyond the Straits of Gibraltar, as the merchantman made for the Atlantic Ocean. The Roman followed at a discrete distance in the hope of learning the location of Antilia. When, after several attempted dodges, the Phoenician first officer failed to shake off his pursuer, he scuttled his own ship, rather than reveal a national secret. For this sacrifice of his own vessel, after he and his crew returned to Carthage, they were accorded a heroic welcome and given a new ship, plus monetary gifts, all at state expense. *Ancient American* writers Kingsley S. Craig and Christine Payne-Towler told how "Phoenicians were known to be ready to sink ships and lose lives to protect their trade routes from discovery by competitors from other civilizations."[1]

Such incidents serve to illustrate how the Romans themselves possibly arrived in the New World—namely, by trailing their Punic rivals. Eventually, at least one of these pursuits must have succeeded, and a Latin captain returned to Rome with sailing directions to Antilia. That Roman scholars were well aware of Phoenician incursions far beyond the Mediterranean World is established by Rufus Festus Avienus, whose *Ora Maritima*, or "Sea Coasts," described the Sargasso Sea, in the western North Atlantic, visited, he wrote, by Carthaginian sailors long before his time, in the mid-fourth century AD.[2] Accordingly, the discovery of Brazil's Imperial Roman artifacts logically follows material evidence presented in the previous chapter for Phoenicians in the same country.

They first came to light during 1976, when a Brazilian fisherman sailed into the Bay of Guanabara, about 15 miles outside Rio de Janeiro. Anchoring just off Governor's Island, he lowered his nets near Xareu Rock, named after a local fish that congregates in large numbers around this prodigious boulder sitting atop a submerged hill, its top about 3 feet beneath the surface of the sea. To his surprise and disappointment, the fisherman hauled up less *xareu* than several large, heavy jars. They were about three feet long, barnacle-encrusted, twin-handled, slender, and tapering to their bottom, apparently made of fired clay. More and more appeared in his nets, whenever he pulled them in. He angrily smashed them to pieces with a hammer, then threw the fragments overboard to prevent the presumed "macumba jars"—used in modern voodoo ceremonies—from further tearing his nets.

Later that same year, a local scuba diver, who knew nothing of the fisherman's annoying catch, was searching for lobsters around Xareu Rock, when he found eight similar jars. He sold six of them as curiosities to tourists before the Rio de Janeiro police took him into custody with his two remaining finds and charged him with illegal trafficking in ancient artifacts. University of Brazil archaeologists had identified his "macumba jars" to the authorities as Roman Era amphorae, containers used to store water, grain, salted fish, meat, olives, olive oil, and other foods as part of a ship's cargo about 2,000 years ago. His discovery, arrest, and disclosure attracted moderate attention in the local press, but were soon after forgotten. Six years later, a foremost marine researcher in the United States learned of the unfortunate lobster diver's finds only by chance.

Born 1933 in Pittsburgh, Pennsylvania, Robert F. Marx discovered and investigated literally hundreds of wrecks around the world since 1951, lectured in more than 50 countries, wrote more than 900 popular articles and archaeological reports, and authored 62 published books about sub-surface investigations and maritime history, dozens of which were featured in 55 documentary films for television before international audiences. Having participated in excess of 5,000 dives, Marx is described as "the true father of underwater archaeology," by Edward Lee Spence, himself a recognized pioneer in that field.[3]

During late 1982, Marx traveled to Brazil and dove at the Bay of Guanabara site. There, he found at least dozens of earthen

Image 5-1: A visiting Roman wine merchant trades for native goods with a Maya official in coastal Mexico 2,000 years ago. Illustration by Gunnar Thompson, PhD (www.atlanticconference.org) *from his book* American Discovery.

storage jars scattered within a relatively tight pattern, their loose concentration suggesting a simultaneous deposit via shipwreck. Several intact specimens were retrieved and sent to Dr. Elizabeth Lyding Will, professor of Classical Greek History at the University of Massachusetts (Amherst) and a specialist in ancient Roman

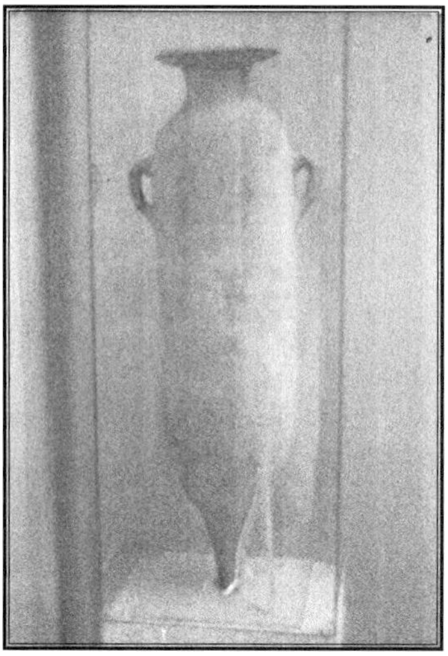

Image 5-2: Roman amphora displayed at Mexico City's Museo Nacional de Antropología, from the sea bottom off the south-central coast of Mexico. Photo courtesy of the author.

containers. Her analysis showed that the Brazilian examples "are, in fact, similar in shape to jars produced in kilns at Kouass, on the west coast of Morocco. The Rio jars look to be late versions of those jars, perhaps datable to the 3rd Century A.D. I have a large piece of one of the Rio jars, but no labs I have consulted have any clay similar in composition."[4]

Twenty-seven miles south of Tangiers, Kouass was a thriving Roman colony and center for amphora-production during the Middle Imperial Period. The seaport from which the ancient freighter sailed to Brazil was Zilis, today's Dchar Jedid, in Morocco.

Historian Gary Fretz told *Free Republic*:

> The Institute of Archaeology at the University of London performed thermo-luminescence testing—which is a more accurate dating process than Carbon 14 dating—and the date of the manufacture [of the sunken jars] was determined to be around 19 B.C. Many more amphorae and some marble objects were recovered, as well as a Roman bronze *fibula*, a clasp device used to fasten a coat or shirt.[5]

Following up on these revelations, Marx engaged Dr. Harold Edgerton from the Massachusetts Institute of Technology (Cambridge), a foremost expert in the application of advanced sonar technologies for underwater archaeological research. Additionally aided by long, metal rods used as probes, they found the remains of a wooden hull perhaps belonging to a Roman freighter lying just beneath the debris field of amphorae. "The ship appears to have been traveling at a high rate of speed when she struck the rock [Xareu]," Fretz stated. "She broke into two pieces, and settled in seventy-five feet of water near the base of the rock."[6]

Word of the ancient wreck struck Brazil like a comet, generating news coverage around the world, while Marx returned to the United States for finalizing salvaging and excavation plans of the 2,000-year-old vessel. In the meantime, initial South American euphoria rapidly soured into bitter controversy. According to Fretz:

> The Italian ambassador to Brazil notified the Brazilian government that, since the Romans were the first to "discover" Brazil, then all Italian immigrants should be granted immediate citizenship. There are a large number of Italian immigrants in Brazil, and the government has created a tedious and costly citizenship application procedure for Italians that does not apply to Portuguese immigrants. The Brazilian government would not give in, and the Italians in Brazil staged demonstrations. In response, the Brazilian government ordered all civilians off the recovery project, and censored further news about the wreck, hoping to diffuse the civil unrest.[7]

Other evil forces contributed to the suppression of politically incorrect evidence. Rio's Catholic bishop declared from his pulpit that Marx had assaulted the sacred history of Brazil, where its official discoverer, a nobleman from Portugal, Pedro Álvares Cabral, and Christopher Columbus have been revered as saints for generations. To suggest they were preceded by "pagans" from pre-Christian Rome is heresy to pious Brazilians. On Marx's return to Rio, he was forbidden to further investigate, much less excavate the sunken vessel.

"The Brazilian Navy were intimidated by the Portuguese raising hell saying that their man Cabral discovered Brazil and not the Romans," he stated. "The [Brazilian] Navy people I worked with told me the Navy had covered up the site to keep it from being plundered. They also said, 'Brazilians don't care about the past. And they don't want to replace Cabral as the discoverer. This thing is causing so much controversy, it's better if you leave.'" Undeterred, Marx dove at the wreck location once more. "I watched the dredge boats covering the wreck over with tons of sediment," he said, "and then dove the site to see how bad things were."[8]

Marx was appalled to observe that it was entirely heaped over with a great mound of silt. When he filed a public protest, he was accused of perpetrating a hoax and defaming Brazil's founding father, and charged with possession of contraband from other, historical shipwrecks in Brazilian waters. Although he had been made a Knight-Commander in the Order of Isabella the Catholic by Spain's government for his re-enactment in the *Niña II* of Christopher Columbus's first voyage of exploration to the New World, Marx was barred from entering Brazil by Rio government officials, who went further by placing "a ban on all underwater exploration," as reported by the *New York Times*.

> All other permits for underwater exploration and digging, a prolific field in Brazil, have been canceled as a result of the Marx controversy, and none will be issued until Congress passes new legislation, Navy officials said. The ban has affected a number of projects in Brazil's harbors and along its forty-six hundred-mile coastline. Mainly foreign diving teams have discovered a panoply of gold and silver objects, but most of the sites, though known, remain unexplored. In Guanabara Bay of Rio de Janeiro, more than one hundred English, French and Portuguese shipwrecks lie unexplored like the pages of an unread, underwater history book.[9]

The high significance of Brazil's ancient shipwreck cannot be overstated, because it is by no means the only evidence for Romans in America. Nor was the site investigated by Marx the first of its kind. "In 1976, Brazilian diver Teixeira found Roman amphoras lying on the seabed near Rio de Janeiro," writes Dr. Gunnar Thompson.[10] The accumulation of so much underwater evidence is supported by "several hundred ancient Roman silver and bronze coins unearthed near Recife, Brazil," according to Fretz.[11] David Hatcher Childress, citing Orville Hope in *Six Thousand Years of Seafaring*, tells how

> a ceramic jar containing several hundred Roman coins, bearing dates ranging from the reign of Augustus [27 BCE to 14 AD] down to 350 A.D. and every intervening period, was found on a beach in Venezuela. This cache is now in the Smithsonian Institution. Experts there have stated that the coins are not a misplaced collection belonging to an ancient numismatist, but probably a Roman sailor's ready cash, either concealed in the sand, or washed ashore from a shipwreck.[12]

Until the late 20th Century, the Romans were regarded by archaeologists as landlubbers. Writes *Ancient American* publisher Wayne May:

> A Roman ship from this era [circa 98 AD] was discovered off the coasts of Marseilles, in the Gulf of Lyons, in 1986. Much of its hull below the gunwales had been almost perfectly preserved in the mud bottom. Thanks to this fortuitous circumstance, experts were afforded a remarkably detailed view of ship construction during the 1st [C]entury. They were surprised by the wreck's modern design features, which would not be rediscovered for another sixteen hundred years. The researchers concluded that the sturdy Roman vessel was certainly capable of transatlantic voyages.[13]

Even before the Marseilles wreck was discovered, scholars were aware that Rome offered regular passenger service to the Near East and Iberia as early as the first century AD aboard liners carrying 600 persons at a time, and 200-foot-long *frumentariae* freighted 1,200 tons of grain each, about 10 times the storage space available to Christopher Columbus aboard his flagship, the *Santa Maria.* There is no reason to believe that these large, well-made vessels could not have successfully completed round-trip, transatlantic voyages. Indeed, their physical evidence is scattered over the bottom of Guanabara Bay.

These revelations seem to bear out a world map Claudius Ptolemy compiled from documents available to him at Egypt's great Library of Alexandria. In 140 CE, he was aided by a fellow Roman, Marianus of Tyre, whose residency there gave him access to some of the old charts still found at that Phoenician city. Their collaborative effort identified a city referred to as Cattigara, 80 degrees east of Asia, a position corresponding to South America, according to Argentine anthropologist Dick Iberra-Grasso.[14]

Based on Ptolemy's version, Bartholomew Colon, the brother of Christopher Columbus, drew up his own map to put Cattigara in western Peru. Unknown to him at the time, his placement of Cattigara coincided with the location of Cajamarca, a pre-Inca city. Obvious phonetic resemblances between the two names are underscored by the founding of Cajamarca, about 2,000 years ago, when Roman seafaring was well under way. Remarkably, Bartholomew Colon's map was completed in 1505, 40 years before the Spaniards knew Cajamarca existed.

Dr. Thompson tells of yet another revealing linguistic parallel: "A name very similar to Peru, *parusta*, shows up on ancient Roman maps of the Antipodes (later South America) depicting a continent laying across the ocean from Africa. In this case, the Latin name refers to the great aridity of the region near the equator: *parusta* is Latin for 'hot, dry, or arid.'"[15]

Substance is therefore lent to the Conquistadors' mid-16th Century quest for *El Ciudad de los Césares,* the "City of the Caesars." Said to have been founded by ancient Roman sailors fleeing civil unrest after Julius Caesar's assassination and later shipwrecked at the Straits of Magellan, the city was supposed to be awash in gold, silver, and diamonds received from grateful Indians for Roman expertise in building the Incas' extensive irrigation network. Interestingly, an Inca aqueduct at Rodadero, Peru, "employs two tiers of rounded, stone arches often referred to as "true arches," according to Dr. Thompson. "This style of architecture was a characteristic of the ancient Mediterranean. Consequently, the Rodadero aqueduct represents a strong argument for Greco-Roman cultural diffusion."[16]

This public works project and the city of Cajamarca do not comprise the only evidence for Roman influences in Peru. No less revealing is an 11.5-inch-high jar with a curving, semi-circular, hollow handle at the back. A tube is connected to and protrudes at an angle from the curved handle, allowing someone to drink or inhale the vessel's contents. Found on the Peruvian coast, the stirrup-spout earthenware is the effigy of a werefox, its chin strapped with a conical helmet, human hands folded above a shield-like disk. A red band running around the disk is punctuated by 15 evenly spaced, cream-colored dots, and surrounds a central, red hooked cross on cream-colored background.

The object belonged to the Moche, a seafaring people, who inhabited the northern coastal plain of Peru. Around 100 CE, they established a thriving trading network that eventually grew into a powerful civilization, thanks in large measure to their fleets of far-ranging, balsa-wood rafts and boats. Although none of these craft survive, they are commonly depicted on contemporaneous pottery.

The Moche were also skilled goldsmiths and potters, creating a broad variety of earthen effigy ware, portraying everything from gods and demons engaging in war, daily tasks, sexual activity, sailing, drunkenness, and human sacrifice. Water management experts on a grand scale, they made the Peruvian Desert bloom with their vast irrigation networks. The centerpiece of their capital city was the Huaca del Sol, the Pyramid of the Sun, composed of more than 130 million adobe bricks to form the largest pre-Columbian structure of its kind built in all the Americas. It originally towered 150 feet over Rio Moche, where it served as a temple for ritual dramas and an imperial residence containing royal burial chambers filled with gold treasures. These were flushed out by 17th-century Spaniards, who diverted the river into the pyramid.

The werefox jar has been dated to the Early Intermediate Period of great outward expansion for the Moche. They were also receptive to outside influences, resulting in a Middle Period (300 to 600 CE) of cultural florescence. It was not to endure, however, and succumbed largely to the effects of a super El Niño. Thirty years of intense rain and flooding were followed by another three decades of drought. Before this calamitous series of events from which the Moche were unable to recover, an Early Intermediate Period of broadening interaction with the outside world saw the creation of their werefox jar. According to Indiana University's Art Museum, "The Moche considered the fox a lunar symbol because of its nocturnal habits."[17]

At the Pyramid of the Sun's smaller, better-preserved companion, the *Huaca de la Luna*, the Pyramid of the Moon, archaeologists found a ceremonial mask of copper-gold alloy configured to mimic a fox head decorated with lunar symbols. This mask was worn by a priest or shaman who personally strove to merge with the animal's identity or soul, thereby taking on its powers. Just when the Moche werefox jar was made, the moon goddess was worshipped in Rome as Diana, divine mistress of the hunt. In Roman art, she was typically portrayed in the company of a fox, usually following the goddess, thereby signifying her "followers"—that is, priests, priestesses, and/or initiates of her lunar cult. But this animal is not the only cogent connection between the ancient Old World and pre-Inca South America.

Diana's brother was Phoebus-Apollo, the sun-god, whose own symbol was a leftward-oriented hooked cross, the Swastika. Its inverse—the rightward-oriented *Sauvastika*—was likewise associated with the sun-god's twin sister, the moon-goddess. Classical Era vase paintings and statues of Diana were typically adorned with the *Sauvastika*. Appearance of this symbol on a Moche effigy jar depicting the same animal identified with an ancient European moon-goddess is emphasized by the 15 dots going around the hooked cross: They correspond to half the number of nights in a lunar month. Moreover, the vessel's manufacture during the Early Intermediate Period occurred between 200 CE and 500 CE, as Roman imperialism expanded to its greatest extent. It was characterized by road-building, irrigation, and military science, civilized virtues likewise chiefly attributed to the Moche.

This is not to argue that they were themselves ancient Romans. They were more probably a native South American people, whose developing society was fundamentally influenced by visitors from the Mediterranean World. Romans impacted not only Moche material culture, but made a lasting impression on Andean metaphysics, as evidenced by the werefox effigy jar. It was almost certainly the original possession of a priest to the moon-goddess, and may have been used as a container for some hallucinogenic potion or drug that enabled him to enter an altered state of consciousness in the performance of his ritual duties.

But evidence for Romans in the New World was not limited to South America. Dr. Thompson writes of a Roman wreck "discovered in 1972 off the coast of Honduras. Scuba divers found a heap of amphoras lying on the bottom of the Caribbean. Scholars identified the amphoras as coming from North African ports, and they applied for a permit to excavate the wreck. Honduran officials denied the request, because they feared further investigation might compromise the glory of Columbus."[18] Thirteen years later, similar finds in the waters off Honduras, at depths of 25 feet, were reported by wreck-diver Archie Eschborn, who later founded Wisconsin's Rock Lake Research Society.

Not all the evidence for Romans in Middle America was found at sea. Writing in London's weekly *New Scientist* magazine (February 9, 2000), anthropologist Roman Hristov, at Southern Methodist University, in Dallas, Texas, announced that a sculpted human head uncovered in Mexico was verified as pre-Columbian. The ceramic representation of a bearded European with a Roman-style haircut was retrieved during excavations of a mound constructed atop an artificial terrace on the slope of Caliviahuaca Hill, near the present-day city of Toluca, 35 miles southwest of Mexico City. Since the figure was found in 1933, unconventional investigators suspected, but could not prove its Roman identity, even though the object's authenticity as a legitimate artifact has never been questioned. Mexican archaeologist Jose Garcia Payon removed it from an undisturbed, 16th Century grave under the pre-Toltec pyramid at Tecaxic-Calixtlahuaca.

The terra-cotta head "was sealed under three floors. It's as close to archaeological certainty as you can get," said David Kelly, an archaeologist at the University of Calgary, in Alberta, Canada.[19] Material drilled from the neck of the carving was sent to Germany's Max Planck Institute of Nuclear Physics at Heidelberg for thermo luminescence testing. Results confirmed that the artifact had been fired 1,800 years ago. According to a related story in the *Boston Globe*, "art experts agree it is Roman and date it to A.D. 200."[20] This date conforms with the figure's headgear, identified by Classical historians as a late 1st Century AD sailor's cap from the important Greek harbor city of Pylos, in the Eastern Mediterranean. Dating from that same period was a wood-and-wax doll still bearing a brief, faded but discernibly Latin text recovered from the depths of Chichen Itza's famous "Cenote of Sacrifice," in Yucatan, during early 2000.[21]

The Roman impact on pre-Columbian America was extensive, and underwater archaeology has revealed much of it. "In 1971," Dr. Thompson writes, "a scuba diver from Maine found two amphoras at a depth of forty feet in Castine Bay. Scholars at the Early Sites Research Society identified the amphoras as Iberic Roman [out of Spain] from the 1st [c]entury. A third amphora was recovered from the Atlantic shore near Jonesboro, Maine."[22]

During July 2012, other scuba divers made their own Roman discoveries just across the northern Wisconsin border from Lake Gogebic, the largest lake in Michigan's Upper Peninsula. While searching for "float copper"—metallic specimens dropped millennia ago by retreating glaciers—Scott Mitchen and his colleagues instead discerned traces of what appeared to be a very old, possibly prehistoric village site, rising partially from under the surface of another, smaller lake, to above water on the shore.

Probing its sunken foundations, they found a cache of copper points and objects resembling ladies' hairpins from Victorian times. The five points were arrow- and spear-heads of exceptionally high quality, but the real identity of the other six pieces was unknown until the following December, when *Ancient American* publisher Wayne May visited Italy's Villa Giulia Museum, in Rome. While examining its rich collection of Classical Era artifacts retrieved from Andalusia, he found himself in front of a mounted display of six Roman items described as *Stli per scrittura su tavolette cerate*, "Writing styluses [sic] for wax tablets." Their physical resemblance to the Wisconsin "hairpins" discovered by Scott Mitchen convinced May that both sets were styli.

A stylus is an instrument made of metal, bone, or some similarly hard material configured to resemble a thin, elongated pencil, and used for writing on a pliable medium. It is pointed at one end for impressing or carving letters or characters into clay or wax. The opposite, flat, and circular end is handy for erasing what has been written. This early form of writing utensil was invented by Iran/Iraq's late-fourth-millennium-BCE Sumerians, who wrote in cuneiform on soft, clay tablets with stiff reeds plucked from a type of tall, grass-like plant that grew profusely throughout Mesopotamia's Fertile Crescent. Egyptians likewise took advantage of reeds flourishing along the banks of the River Nile, but wrote on improved, erasable wax tablets, whereas Minoans preferred bone styli to etch their Linear A script and Cretan hieroglyphs on clay left to dry and harden in direct sunlight.

Stylus derives from the Latin word *stilus*, a pointed "stake," itself derived from the earlier Greek *tsilis* for "pillar." The Greeks introduced metal styli, and both bronze and iron versions were familiar to Roman writers. Erasure handles of the Italian specimens identify them as Roman, examples of a common, inexpensive type owned by students, bureaucrats, accountants, and other record-keepers. The more designed erasure handles of 2012's northern Wisconsin styli indicate that they were produced during the early-to-middle Imperial Era, from the late first century BCE to the turn of the third century AD, when they likely belonged to someone of prominence, being more ornate and costly models than the Villa Giulia finds.

Ancient American purchased one of Mitchen's styli for closer study. It is exactly 4 inches long, weighs .02 ounces, and appears to have been made of bronze, an observation yet to be confirmed by future professional testing. The artifacts' cultural diffusionist significance is revealed by their presence in the Upper Peninsula of the Great Lakes. It was here that the most ambitious mining enterprise in all antiquity occurred, when at least 125,000 tons of the world's highest-grade copper were excavated by unknown persons, mostly between 3000 BCE and 1200 BCE, only to disappear from North America. During subsequent centuries, the pits were occasionally and sporadically reopened and closed, again by unidentified miners, who extracted far less of the metal than quantities removed during previous operations. Native American tribal inhabitants preferred the easier process of simply picking up small nodules of "float copper" whenever and wherever they could be found for personal adornment purposes.

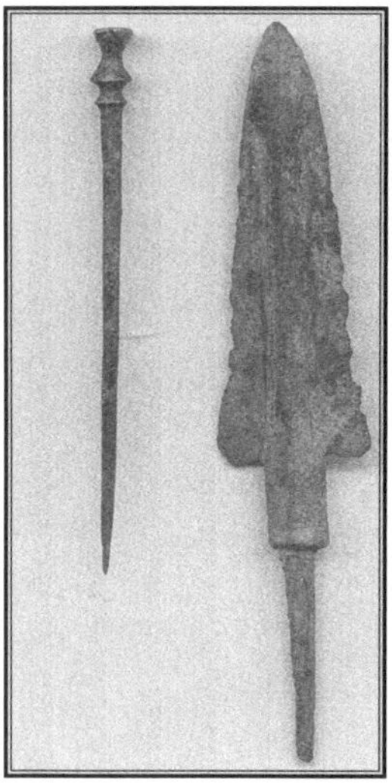

Image 5-3: Wisconsin's Roman stylus with copper spearhead. Photo courtesy of Ancient American.

Unconventional investigators conclude that Upper Peninsula copper was shipped overseas to Europe and the Near East for the production of bronze. If so, the Wisconsin styli may have belonged to Roman accountants, who used them to tally up and record on wax tablets amounts of Great Lakes' copper excavated and loaded aboard freighters for their long, homeward voyage. These possibilities are reinforced by the Michigan-border styli in company with spearheads, which, for their exceptional workmanship and elegant style, are more reminiscent of similar blades in the ancient Old World than cruder counterparts typical of pre-Columbian America.

If Mitchen's discovery were the only one of its kind ever made, it might be dismissed as entirely anomalous, however intriguing. But the objects he found are not unrelated to a ceramic oil lamp that came to light in western Wisconsin. It was unearthed, according to its owner, Robert Freed

> during 1969, in Crawford County, Freeman Township, on a hillside field overlooking the Mississippi River. A farmer's plow got hung up on a root, and when the plow was cleared, the lamp was found face down in the furrow.... I have attended Indian artifact shows seeking help as to its origins.... The insinuation of fake or hoax was a common response. But I knew the fellow I purchased it from, and he did not make the thing. It is genuine.[23]

The Wisconsin oil lamp is 5 inches long, 3.5 inches across, and 1.25 inches thick. Its front, judging by its central hole for the flame, depicts what appears to be the body of a woman between two pairs of other human figures, sitting and engaged in apparent conversation. The back features a central circle—its outer rim studded with 19 knobs—enclosing eight lines. This eight-line symbol recurs six times in the circle around the fire hole, again just beneath it, and once more at the foot of the lamp, bringing its total repetition on the front to eight. To either side of the circle on the back is the representation of a man chasing a four-legged animal. In one version, he bears a knife in his right hand, while the animal looks forward. In the other, the animal looks back at him. Although the object's deliberate symbolism may be elusive, Roman astrologers identified the number eight with Venus, both the planet and the goddess, who may be the female figure portrayed by the oil lamp.

If the 19 knobs going around the perimeter of the backside circle—a common symbol for the Sun—represent years, then the reference here is to a solar eclipse, because "eclipses of the Sun tend to recur in periods of nineteen years," as explained by the *Encyclopaedia Britannica.*[24] This numerical-celestial interpretation of the artifact accords well with its function as a lamp, and, if correct, removes it entirely from any Native American context, a conclusion reaffirmed by its racially alien portrayal of the female figure. "She has long, wavy hair falling down her back," observed art historian, John Friedman, "and is wearing a diadem with cloth attachment, the most common feminine headdress of the Greco-Roman World."[25]

David Pratt writes in *An Ancient History of the North American Indians* how another "1st Century A.D. Roman oil lamp was found at a site on the Coosa River, in Alabama."[26] Related artifacts came to light along the Eastern seaboard, where some Roman arrivals would have made their most likely landfall. South of River Redbank, in New Jersey, a man combing the coast with his metal detector near Beverly found eight Roman coins within a single square yard of the beach. The relatively well-preserved coins were all minted during the fourth century CE, and identified by numismatists as belonging to the reigns of emperors Constantius II (337 to 361), Valentinianus I (364 to 375), Valens (364 to 378), and Gratianus (367 to 383).

According to Dr. Barry Fell:

> As there were fifty-eight emperors of Rome, who issued some three thousand kinds of coins commonly found in Europe, the chances of a single find-site yielding coins of consecutive rulers spanning only four decades can be estimated as roughly one in one hundred thousand. Thus the coins are not being found as a result of accidental losses by collectors, but are strongly correlated with some factor linked to a short time-span of 337 to 383 A.D., and linked also to a single, very restricted find-site. The only reasonable explanation is that these coins are coming from the money-chest of a merchant-ship carrying current coin in use around 375 A.D. Over the past sixteen hundred years, the coins have gradually drifted inshore on the bottom current, and are now being thrown up by waves in heavy weather.[27]

Dr. Thompson told how

> [t]wo Roman coins were found near Fayetteville, Tennessee, in 1819. One was of Antonius Pius (138 to 161 A.D.); the other was of Emperor Commodus (180 to 192 A.D). They were discovered several feet deep beneath trees thought to be several hundred

> years old.... Beachcombers near Beverly, Massachusetts have collected numerous coins embossed with faces of Roman emperors between 337 A.D. and 383 A.D.... Other coins dating between 50 B.C. and 750 A.D. have been found in North Carolina, Ohio, Georgia, and Oklahoma.[28]

"On September 20, 1898," announced Wisconsin's *Glenwood City Tribune* for January 5, 1900, "ex-Alderman Henry Van Ryn struck his pick into the soil under the ledge of sandstone that rises above Sand Creek on his farm north of town. He had previously removed four or five feet of rock some distance from the creek," when he found a curious, bronze coin about the size of a U.S. silver dollar. It "has the profile and name of Emperor Trajan on the obverse, while the reverse is so worn that only the letters, 'S, P, Q, R,' can be readily distinguished."[29]

SPQR are the initials of an official Latin phrase, *Senātus Populusque Rōmānus,* "The Senate and People of Rome." Marcus Ulpius Nerva Traianus Augustus was the emperor of Rome from 98 to 117 CE, a period of vigorous, outward expansion, when the Empire reached its greatest territorial extent. The *Glenwood City Tribune* reporter wondered how a foreign coin issued during the second century could have "found its way under twenty feet of solid rock in a land unknown for more than fifteen hundred years thereafter, and in a region settled by white men only within the last third of a century...."[30]

Trajan's coin at Glenwood City joins Scott Mitchen's styli and Crawford County's oil lamp as credible evidence for Imperial Romans in Wisconsin. Literally hundreds of ancient Roman coins have emerged in the Middle West alone. Writing in *The Lost Worlds of Ancient America*, Pulitzer Prize nominee Lee Pennington observes:

> A revealing picture emerges when all the locations of Roman coins reportedly found in our country are plotted on a map of North America. It shows that virtually all of them were discovered at or near waterways, mostly along the Mississippi and Ohio Rivers, together with their

> watersheds. Six, related finds took place on the eastern seaboard:
>
> In 1950 on Plum Island, Massachusetts; circa 1965 at Long Island Sound, Connecticut; around 1970 at Princeton, New Jersey; about 1960 in Queen Anne's County, Maryland; 1956 in Gloucester County, Virginia; and circa 1970 on St. Simons Island, Georgia. Two other Roman coins were found in the Gulf of Mexico area: around 1970 at Baton Rouge, Louisiana, and about 1970 on St. Joseph Island, Texas. No such coins are reported to have been found west of the Rocky Mountains. Individually, the ancient coins found in North America may be little more than anomalous curiosities. But when seen in the aggregate, they form a recognizable pattern left by visitors from Imperial Rome in those areas of our continent where they passed into prehistory.[31]

Added to these coins and amphorae are Roman era swords, figurines, and oil lamps discovered in the United States, Mexico, Honduras, and Brazil. Altogether, they comprise physical evidence for something more than a few, unlucky vessels occasionally blown off course, accidentally coming to grief on the eastern shores of the Americas. Rather, the shipwreck verified by Robert Marx is part of a much broader impact made on all the Americas by culture-bearers from the Roman Empire. It is an impact that, in the case of the Xareu Rock site, has been, quite literally, covered up by the self-appointed guardians of conventional history. In the 30 years since they personally banned Marx from Brazil and forbade all further study of the underwater location he investigated, no one has followed up on his research of a discovery that would otherwise compel the rewriting of human history in the New World.

Chapter 6:
Kelts

In 57 BCE, Julius Caesar imposed his authority on an Atlantic coastal area of Gaul, at France's Brittany peninsula, known as *Armorica.* Its southern regions, along the Bay of Morbihan, were inhabited by the Venetii, a proud, Keltic people, who bristled at the treaties imposed upon them, and were outraged by the hostages they were forced to give Rome as human tokens of good faith. These coerced agreements did not long endure. The following year, a few Roman officers foraging for food in Armorica were seized by the Venetii, who attempted to bargain these captives for the return of their politically ransomed kinsmen. But an angry Caesar ignored their attempts at negotiation and assembled his warships, which alone could overcome Armorica, defended as it was by a series of apparently impregnable fortresses lining the French coast.

The key to their conquest of Gaul was destruction of the Venetii fleet, an immense collection of vessels superior to those Caesar commanded. Keltic ships, all of them larger than their

Roman counterparts, were more sturdy and structurally sound, because they were made of oak resistant to ramming. These timbers were fastened with exceptionally thick hawsers, oversize pegs, heavy iron chains, and nails as thick as a man's thumb. In contrast to the Romans' Mediterranean sails of woven cloth, which tore in gales, Keltic versions were made of more durable leather, enabling their ships to better withstand the harsher conditions of Atlantic Ocean seafaring, and allowed them to tack against the wind. Caesar related in his *De Bello Gallico* ("Of the Gallic War") how the enemy was able to sail "upon the vast, open sea" (*vasto atque aperto mari*).[1]

Venetii captains, with their intimate knowledge of shores and tides, skillfully maneuvered under sail to restrict boarding by the enemy. Keltic vessels handled better and were more seaworthy, having retained but downsized cumbersome oars for stronger, steeper sides, from which marines showered Roman ships with spears, arrows, and rocks. Nor were the Venetii alone. During their uneasy peace with Rome, they had allied themselves with fellow Keltic tribesmen across the English Channel, the *Pretanians*, from whom the name "Britain" derived. Together, they mustered 220 battleships carrying 66,000 men-at-arms. Caesar was not only out-classed, but outnumbered.

He was fortunate, however, to have one of the greatest admirals in naval history under his command. Decimus Junius Brutus Albinus overcame his disadvantages by using long billhooks to catch and disable enemy halyards, which were fastened out-board. (A halyard is a line of rope used to hoist a yard of sail, from the phrase "to haul yards.") As the Venetii and Pretanian warships swept past, their huge, leathern mainsails suddenly collapsed on deck, hopelessly crippling the vessels, while simultaneously preventing oarsmen from rowing out of harm's way. In the midst of their confusion, the Kelts were boarded and eventually overcome in fierce fighting, until both fleets fell almost entirely into Roman hands.

The decisive Battle of Quiberon Bay allowed Caesar's legions to storm each of the coastal defenses until every stronghold was taken in succession. Defeat meant the dissolution of

Armorica, which had to serve as an object lesson to every other subject people in the Empire. Imperial expediency demanded that the Venetii cease to exist as a people. Most were executed; a few individuals were condemned as slaves, and others escaped in a handful of ships that survived the Battle of Quiberon Bay. History presumes they retreated with their Pretanian allies to Britain. But at least some of them may have gone further. They were, after all, still in possession of ships large and sturdy enough to take them anywhere on Earth.

When, in the early 16th century, newly arrived Spaniards walked ashore at what has since become the nation of Colombia, they were informed by their native hosts that they had arrived in "the Land of Amuraca."[2] Bearing the royal title "Serpent," Amuraca, they said, was a bearded white man, not unlike the Conquistadors themselves. He had long ago appeared after a terrible catastrophe far over the "Sunrise Sea" forced him and his followers to seek refuge. He afterward taught the natives the benefits of agriculture, medicine, and religion, then built the first of several stone cities. Amuraca suggests that the name given to the New World did not derive from a contemporary Italian map-maker, but rather an Indian culture-hero.

European conquerors did not use native names for the land they seized, because they sought to lend greater legitimacy to their New World holdings by re-christening them with Old World versions. Thus, the original Colombian *Amuraca* was changed to the "America" of Amerigo Vespucci for political reasons. Since then, however, many students of history have wondered why both continents would have been christened after the feminized Latin version of "Amerigo" to signify an entire New World, however awkwardly. Supporting an alternative, less dubious provenance for "America," Columbus himself, on his third voyage to the New World, met native peoples who introduced themselves as "Americos." On his second voyage to Hispaniola, Alonso de Ojeda identified the same tribe of Americos.[3]

The "land of perpetual wind"—a Nicaraguan mountain range in the province of Chantoles, between Juigalpa and

Liberdad—was known to the Mayas as *Amerisque*, and recorded as such in the sailing logs of Columbus himself, together with the writings of Vespucci. Martin Waldseemüller produced a world map that indicated how the new continents were to be known by Vespucci's first name. Verifying a notation he wrote on the map, a 1507 book published five years before Vespucci's death in 1512 included one of the Florentine explorer's accounts, long since discredited as a fabrication.

In Chapter 9 in the first part of *Cosmographiae Introductio,* Mathias Ringmann explained that the New World derived its name "from Amerigo, the discoverer...as if it were the land of Americus, thus America," even though Ringmann knew, as did the rest of Europe, that the more famous Christopher Columbus, not Amerigo Vespucci, was "the discoverer."[4] Waldseemüller himself had second thoughts about using Vespucci's first name, and later referred to the New World instead as simply *Terra Incognita* ("unknown land") in his reworking of Ptolemy's atlas. Unfortunately, the first thousand copies of Waldseemüller's world map had already been distributed, and the original suggestion took hold. But if not "Amerigo," then what can account for aboriginal characterizations of their country as Amerisque, Americo, or Amuraca?

We have already leaned, in Chapter 4, how sailors from the Phoenician city of Tyre navigated westward by a star they referred to as "La Merika." These related names from different cultures may be local inflections of *Armorica*, the Venetii homeland obliterated by Julius Caesar. Having lost their tribal identity, survivors would have been assimilated by their British hosts, or progressively marginalized in a world spreading over with Roman imperialism. Given such grim, limited alternatives, transatlantic escape aboard their oceangoing ships was the only option for a people determined to maintain at least a remnant of their folkish existence. Moreover, they were by no means the first of their kind to have crossed the wide sea and made a success of themselves in New Armorica.

They were preceded by other Keltic émigrés nearly one thousand years before arriving as fair-haired, light-complected

Image 6-1: Keltic refugees from their lost war with Julius Caesar make landfall on America's Eastern seaboard. Courtesy of Ancient American.

refugees remembered as the followers of Amuraca by generations of Colombian Indians. Long prior to these calamitous events, Keltic ancestors resided since Neolithic times as prosperous farmers and herdsmen in the Steppes of Central Russia. Then, after the turn of the 12th Century BCE, the grasslands on which their livelihood depended were desiccated by drastic and prolonged climate deterioration. A mass migration of the dispossessed fled westward through Poland and into Bavaria, from which they spread by the start of the first millennium BCE into the Balkans, France, Iberia, and the British Isles. The impetus of such folk wandering carried them across the Atlantic Ocean in their eminently seaworthy ships to the Eastern seaboard of North America.

When their Midwestern earthworks were first identified, archaeologists referred to this pre-Columbian people as the "Adena," named in 1900 after a Chillicothe, Ohio, plantation on which the structures were located. The Adena's sudden appearance in the New World 3,000 years ago took place at the same time the Kelts spread into Western Europe, the first of numerous comparisons. What the Adena mound-builders precisely called themselves is not known, although they are still recalled by Tuscarora elders as the Ron-nong-weto-wanca, or "fair-skinned giant sorcerers," a kind of title for the *Allewegi*, or "People of the Mountains," from which the name "Alleghany" derived. Black Fish, chief of the Shawnees at Chillicothe, described them to Thomas Bullitt, a representative of Colonial Virginia, in 1773, as "a white people from the Eastern Sea."[5]

William Conner wrote in the December 2007 issue of *Ancient American* that George Rogers Clark and two U.S. Army colonels were told by Chief Cornstalk (Hokoleskwa, a Shawnee leader) at Point Pleasant about "a 'race of white or light-skinned people, originally from the East,' who dwelt in large numbers long ago in the Ohio Valley."[6] These foreigners were notable for their tall stature, an oral tradition borne out by archaeological excavation of many Adena earthworks. Burial 54 in West Virginia's Cresap Mound belonged to an Adena man who stood 7 feet, 4 inches tall in life. "All the long bones were heavy," observed Don Dragoo, curator at the Carnegie Museum of Natural History's Section of Man, in Pittsburgh.[7]

The Cresap Mound specimen was not anomalous. Similar finds have been recovered from eastern Ohio's New Benton mound and other Adena earthworks in the Ohio Valley. European Keltic males were also of above-average height. The well-preserved, 5th Century BCE remains of a 6-feet, 6-inch-tall Keltic man found in an Irish bog was no exception. Of the more than a thousand Keltic graves opened by Johann Georg Ramsauer, director of 19th Century excavations at Austria's Hallstatt cemetery, at least a third of the male skeletons were above-average height, with several examples of 7-foot males. The skulls of both Adena and Kelts were brachycephalic—relatively short or broad, with a width 80 percent or more of their length. Contemporaneous Greek and Roman writers described the Kelts as red- or blonde-haired, tall and sturdy, with large heads. The Adena likewise stood out from North America's indigenous populations with larger skulls, higher and broader foreheads, prominent jaws, and more pronounced cheekbones.

These "Fair-skinned Giant Sorcerers" were perhaps the most important people in all pre-Columbian history, because they were its first farmers. Agriculture did not exist above the Rio Grande River before they arrived to grow squash, sunflower, pumpkin, gourds, and possibly corn. Permanent settlements here were unknown until they built the first villages. They introduced metallurgy and built hundreds (at least) of iron smelters throughout the Middle West. They made iron implements—such as a blade found in a 2,000-year-old North Carolina burial pit—and excavated iron mines, like the one in Franklin County, near Leslie, Missouri. The Kelts brought the Iron Age to Western Europe, where they were renowned as skilled metal-workers, particularly in iron. Their bog furnaces—fueled by dried marsh grass and heated to high temperatures by the wind—were identical to those Adena versions still being found throughout the Ohio Valley.

All these cultural attributes were associated with a single people, and appeared simultaneously and suddenly, minus any previous developments, giving every indication that they were imported from outside Amerindian circles. Following their sudden appearance on the eastern coast of North America around 1000 BCE, the Allewegi migrated westward into the Ohio Valley. There, they created a power base, from which their influence would radiate further westward to Indiana, Illinois, and Wisconsin; southward into Kentucky and Tennessee; and eastward across Pennsylvania and West Virginia. After almost one thousand years, the predominant Adena culture began to decline, but it lingered for another eight centuries, until the last of the mound builders fell victim to genocide, as recalled in tribal Indian oral traditions and evidenced by the many thousands of butchered human skeletal remains at Kentucky's Falls of the Ohio and other, contemporaneous killing fields.[8]

In their own, seemingly interminable wars with Rome, the Kelts erected *oppida*, defensive works roughly built of earth, gravel, and mostly uncut stone at the summits of high prominences dominating strategic territories. Referred to by Caesar as a *murus Gallicus*, or "Gallic wall," the layout and even configuration of Germany's Heuneburg hill-fort situated between two tributaries of the Danube is remarkably similar to Tennessee's Old Stone Fort embraced more closely on either side by the Big and Little Duck rivers. Other *oppida* at Zavist in Bohemia, Ireland's Dun Ailinne, Mont Beuvray in France, Portugal's Citania de Sanfins, and Numantia in northeastern Spain are all much the same, and often virtually indistinguishable from their contemporary Adena counterparts. The Keltic *oppida* and look-alike Adena hill-forts represent an exact comparison found nowhere else in ancient history.

Another mirror-image parallel occurs in the sixth-century-BCE *broch*, a type of defended homestead, or squat, single tower, and usually standing about 45 feet high. These dry-stone citadels had walls 15 or more feet thick, with a base diameter averaging approximately 40 feet, and were positioned atop a hill or cliff. More than 500 such structures, most of them in Scotland and Britain's western and northern islands, were counted by Roman military strategists. According to the encyclopedist William Corliss, "the *brochs* are squat, massive, and lacking cement. The thick walls of the *brochs* consist of flattish stone slabs piled atop one another. These walls have to be thick to stand by themselves."[9]

His description exactly matches that of a pre-Columbian tower that dominated part of northern Ohio as late as the mid-19th century. Known to early pioneers as the "Great Stone Stack," it stood near the edge of a hill 10 miles from Newark on a 500-square-foot base tapering upward by 45 feet to share a *broch*'s standard dimensions and configuration. More than 10,000 wagonloads of stone were carried away from the Stack when it was demolished in 1860 to build a dam at West Virginia's Tygart Lake.

It was here, near the Monongahela River, in Marion County, that a prehistoric road ran for at least 12 miles between the Tygart Valley and Little Creek at Catawba. With an average width of 9 feet, construction consisted of macadamized stone and crushed mussel shell. Another 9-foot-wide road, at Corlea in central Ireland, from 148 BCE, suggests a standardization of measurement the Kelts brought to North America, although ancient Irish roads were only made of timbered planks. The Kelts were notable construction engineers, and at least one other pre-Columbian road in Ohio has been attributed to the Adena. Artifacts much smaller than these grand public works projects are nonetheless physical evidence for Kelts in the American Middle West.

Image 6-2: Pre-Columbian Ohio's Great Stone Stack resembled the Shetland Islands' Mousa broch. *Photo courtesy of Wikipedia.*

Walking along the banks of the Wisconsin River in fall 1993, Fred Kingman, a resident from nearby Wisconsin Rapids, located at the center of the Badger State, was hunting antique trinkets when his metal detector "registered a 'halo,' a signal from the surrounding soil attributed to corrosion migrating into the ground over a very long time," according to Dr. James P. Scherz, an archaeo-astronomer and professor of civil engineering at the University of Wisconsin, in Madison[10] Mr. Kingman dug 3 feet down into the riverbank, where his detector indicated a metallic target of some kind to discover a cache of 17 strange coins "grouped together, as though they had been collected into a bag of perishable material that disintegrated over the years since they were buried." All had been manufactured of die-cast copper. "Apparently," Dr. Scherz noticed, "no two were made by the same set of dies. Therefore, seventeen different dies had been required for their production." He observed that the obverse and reverse sides of each coin carried inscriptions of some kind and were illustrated with the finely executed profiles of human, male heads, some crowned and regal.

Close scrutiny of a selected specimen revealed a Latin word, *IMPTETRICUS*, for "Emperor Tetricus." It referred to Gaius Pius Esuvius Tetricus, whose reign was recognized by fellow Kelts throughout Britain and most of Gaul, beginning in 271 CE. It did not endure long. His armies were decimated in what became known as the "Catalaunian Catastrophe," a battle of near-extermination that occurred near Châlons-sur-Marne, in late February 274 CE, as part of Roman Emperor Aurelian's ultimately successful attempt to re-conquer all of his lost, western provinces. The captured Tetricus was paraded through the streets of Rome in chains, but saved his own life by donating seven tons of gold to the city's Temple of the Sun. The purchase included the title of *Corrector Lucaniae et Bruttiorum*, the governorship of a southern region of Italia, where he pensioned out his final years in peace.

His former subjects did not possess the same kind of wealth with which to buy their freedom, but fled the otherwise inevitable prospect of execution or slavery at the hands of a victorious Aurelian aboard their great ships to Terra Incognita, on the other side of the Atlantic Ocean. There, they lost or buried the 17 coins still emblazoned with the profile of their deposed king, Tetricus, last emperor of the *Imperium Galliarum*, the Gallic Empire.

Image 6-3: A Kingman coin emblazoned with the profile of a mustachioed Kelt. Courtesy of Ancient American.

A different Kingman coin depicts the profile of an unidentified man sporting a large, drooping mustache. Keltic men "let the moustache grow until it covers the mouth," according to 1st Century BCE Greek historian Diodorus Siculus.[11] They minted their own coins during the late phase of an epoch known as La Tene, circa 100 BCE, which coincided with another late phase, that of the Adena, whose culture entered its decline just then. Dr. Thompson writes that another Keltic coin dated to roughly the same era was found in Champaign, Illinois.[12] Such finds in the continental United States are not confined to the Middle West, although later Keltic artifacts are mostly unearthed there, just as earlier, related discoveries appear in New England, appropriately enough, because the Kelts first made landfall along the Eastern seaboard, around 1000 BCE, before spreading inland and establishing their seat of power in the Ohio Valley.

Evan Hansen told *Ancient American* readers:

> The Elliott Pendent was retrieved by Mr. Walter Elliott on 18 May 1989, from a two-foot-high, slab-stone mound he discovered in a wooded area of Washington County, Maine. The object lay at the bottom of a small tunnel, accompanied by a large spearhead inscribed with the representation of a human face. Neither find was of interest to archaeologists, because both the pendent and spearhead had been removed without professional supervision.... The Pendent's *BNYW* so closely resembles the name of a Keltic goddess, it seems obvious that *Byanu* is intended here.[13]

The Maine artifact is 4 inches long, with a diameter of 3.5 inches. One side features the crude representation of what appears to be an eye; the other side is a crescent beneath a pair of holes, through which a necklace or string supposedly passed. Under the crescent is an apparent sun face with pairs of rays protruding from either side. Beneath is the seven-glyph name of Byanu, the Keltic mother-goddess.

At a complex of stone chambers—formerly "Mystery Hill," now known as "America's Stonehenge"—spread over 30 acres in Salem, New Hampshire, an inscribed stone found in 1967 was engraved with an Iberic text dedicated to "Bel," the Keltic sun-god. Eight years later, a discovery of another tablet on an adjacent wall at Mystery Hill was found to have been "Dedicated to Bel." While re-erecting a fallen monolith at the site in 1975, workers noticed how a side that had faced into the ground was covered with a Latin inscription reading *XXXVIIII LA*, for "Day 39." During the Roman Era, an annual festival "dedicated to Bel"(Beltane) was celebrated on the 39th day of each year.[14] Not far from the *XXXVIIII LA* stone, another four monoliths standing in a circle of five orthostats are aligned with the Sun's position at the summer and winter solstices. A fifth, referred to as the "North Stone," is a meridian arc measuring the distance between two points with the same longitude. "The antiquity of Mystery Hill inscriptions could now be confidently set at about 800 to 600 B.C.," Dr. Barry Fell concluded, "and it was clear that Goidelic (Gaelic speaking) Kelts were the occupants at that date, and, in all probability, the builders, too."[15]

Even more specific proof of an important Keltic presence in pre-Columbian America was found in Adena burial mounds, which enclosed central, log-frame chambers for the dead surrounded by rough embankments of stone rubble. Keltic earthworks featured exactly the same, otherwise-unique internal arrangement, as exemplified at Vix, Chatillon-sur-Seine, in France, plus Germany's Hochdorf tomb, outside Stuttgart, and Magdalenenberg bei Villingen, Schwarzwald-Baar-Kreis. But what mid-19th Century grave-robbers found inside an Adena burial mound was still more conclusive.

During spring 1838, they dug into the largest conical earthwork in the United States. Nearly 70 feet high, with a base diameter of 295 feet, three million basket-loads of soil, equivalent to some 60,000 tons, went into the construction of West Virginia's Grave Creek Mound, a monumental achievement for its pre-industrial builders in 250 BCE. The gold-seekers shoveled a vertical shaft 20 feet down from its summit until they pierced the roof of a small chamber. It contained a pair of human skeletons surrounded by jewelry, including 1,700 ivory beads, 500 seashells, and five copper bracelets.

Image 6-4: West Virginia's Grave Creek Mound. Photo courtesy of Tim Kaiser, via Wikipedia.

Continuing their vertical excavations in the hope of finding better treasures, the diggers broke into another tomb filled with similar items and the single skeleton of a man who stood around 7 feet tall in life. In his possession was an oval, 1.5-inch-by-2-inch sandstone emblazoned with three lines of an indecipherable text above the profile of a bird. The object was sent to Washington, D.C.'s Smithsonian Institution for interpretation, but curators there promptly "lost" it. Ohio antiquarians had the good foresight to have commissioned several exact replicas of the original artifact, which was predictably condemned as a hoax by orthodox scholars for the rest of the 19th and most of the 20th centuries.

With publication of Professor David Diringer's *The Alphabet*, in 1968, however, Kelto-Iberic was made available for the first time to alternative linguists, who long suspected that the Grave Creek Tablet had been written in the language of the ancient Kelts.[16] Eight years later, Dr. Fell used *The Alphabet* to translate the Grave Creek Stone's three-line text, reading from left to right. In 1991, Donal Buchanan, author of *The Decipherment of Southwest Iberic* and a veteran cryptographer for the Central Intelligence Agency, offered what has come to be regarded as the inscription's authoritative translation: "Tumulus in honor of Tadach. His wife caused this engraved tile to be inscribed."[17]

Although the Grave Creek Tablet had been found 130 years before Professor Diringer made Kelto-Iberian accessible to epigraphers, Buchanan's valid translation was snubbed by mainstream scholars, who never bothered to critique his effort. *Tadach* is an authentic Keltic name, as recorded in the Irish ninth-century *Annals of the Four Masters,* which lamented the death of Ce-Tadach, abbot of Cluain Mic Nois, in 848 CE.[18] *Teth* is likewise Keltic, as in *An Teth Achadh,* "the warm place."

"Teth" is inscribed on another West Virginia stone found in 1931 by a schoolboy beside a tree stump near Triplett Creek, on Braxton County, where it is still preserved at the Department of Archives. Also like its Grave Creek counterpart, the 4 1/8-inch-by-3 3/16-inch micaceous sandstone is covered with three rows of South-Iberic script Dr. Fell was able to translate with the assistance of Diringer's *Alphabet*: "The memorial of Teth. This tile (his) brother caused to be made."[19]

While hiking along the Genessee River bed, near Belfast, New York, in 1975, William Johnson picked up a dense, granular stone measuring 2 inches by 3 inches, because it was inscribed with two lines of mysterious glyphs. Dr. Fell translated its Kelto-Iberic text to read, "Confirmation: I have pledged to pay in full."[20]

The Grave Creek, Braxton, and Genessee inscriptions belong to a rich body of persuasive evidence identifying the Keltic origins of the Adena mound builders—the first villagers, iron-workers, and farmers of what would much later become the continental United States. Perhaps they even gave it the name of their own, forsaken homeland: Armorica.

Chapter 7: Hebrews

In mid-February 1889, John W. Emmert was working on behalf of the Bureau of Ethnology's Mound Survey Project for Washington, D.C.'s famed Smithsonian Institution. His assignment: excavate an undisturbed trio of prehistoric "Indian mounds" standing along the Little Tennessee River, near the mouth of Bat Creek. At 28 feet across and 5 feet high, Mound 3 of the earthworks yielded some wood fragments, plus skeletal remains of nine adult males. Seven were laid out shoulder-to-shoulder in a single row, and one pair had been positioned apart, off-center of the mound, to the west. The head of the easternmost skeleton pointed south; all the rest were aligned to the north.

Emmert noticed that the skull of the lone, southward-oriented figure was resting on something slightly protruding from its jaw. Carefully lifting the cranium, he saw a rectangular stone about 4.5 inches long, 2 inches wide, and 0.39 inches thick. More remarkably, the apparently shaped object had been engraved with five glyphs forming a mysterious inscription. Emmert reported the find to his immediate superior, Cyrus Thomas, not only the Bureau chief, but one of the most politically connected academics of his day. Thomas was unimpressed by Emmert's tablet, dismissing its inscription as "Paleo-Cherokee." This was an early-19th Century attempt by Sequoyah, a Native American silversmith, to develop a Cherokee syllabary, making reading and writing in his native language possible. It signified the only instance in recorded history that a member of a non-literate people independently created an effective writing system. Sequoyah's syllabary was adopted by the Cherokee in 1825.

Thomas forwarded the Bat Creek Stone to the Smithsonian Institution, where it was briefly displayed as a minor curiosity, then shelved and largely forgotten. More than 60 years later, its photograph in a turn-of-the-century history book came to the attention of Dr. Joseph P. Mahan, professor of history and chief curator at Columbus, Georgia's Museum of Arts and Crafts. He recognized at once that the inscription on the Tennessee tablet was not "Paleo-Cherokee," but paleo-Hebrew. In their ignorance of its real identity, Smithsonian officials had first displayed, then photographed and published Emmert's discovery upside-down.

Alarmed, Dr. Mahan contacted Cyrus Gordon, professor of Ancient Languages at New York's Brandeis University. He handily translated the Bat Creek Stone's inscription "for Judah," and dated it to internal linguistic evidence between 70 and 135 CE. These time parameters coincided with the statements of Flavius Josephus, a first-century Romanized Jew. In *The Jewish War* (circa 75 CE), he told how "the Hebrews fled across the sea to a land unknown to them before."[1] The term for the "land" Josephus used was *Epeiros Occidentalis*, or "Western Continent," a self-evident reference to America. This would mean that Hebrew-speaking war refugees from the ancient Old World arrived in eastern Tennessee more than 1,300 years before Christopher Columbus undertook his premier transatlantic voyage.

Following publication of Gordon's findings, the professor was viciously attacked by mainstream academics, who labeled him a "rogue scholar," going so far as to cast aspersions on his sanity, even though he was internationally recognized as the world's leading scholar in Semitic studies. When his vehement skeptics conceded that the Bat Creek Stone was indeed inscribed with paleo-Hebrew, they turned their wrath on its defenseless discoverer.

Having been dead for more than half a century, he was an easy target for orthodox archaeologists, whose careers were quite literally invested in the dominant paradigm, *No Old World Visitors to America Before 1492.* They repeatedly castigated John Emmert as an alcoholic who faked the inscribed stone to win favor from his influential boss, Cyrus Thomas. Although no evidence was ever produced to suggest that Emmert was either an alcoholic or forger, for the next 40 years his invented debauchery and chicanery became part of official positions designed to explain away the Bat Creek inscription as a manufactured hoax.

But during that time, the artifact he found was not entirely without its champions. Among them was Henritte Mertz, a Chicago patent attorney admitted to practice before the United States Supreme Court and a Lieutenant Commander, USNR (Ret.) veteran of World War II, when she was the Special Assistant to the Advisor on Patent Matters, Office of Scientific Research and Development, as a cryptanalyst, breaking Axis military and diplomatic codes for the Allies. Professionally trained in forgery identification, Mertz concluded that the Bat Creek inscription was genuinely ancient. Other supporters were *Ancient American* reporter David Allen Deal, whose close-up inquiry into the tablet re-affirmed Cyrus Gordon's translation, and J. Huston McCulloch, an economics professor at Ohio State University. He won hands down an onoing debate with the artifact's bitter detractors in a series of point-counterpoint articles from 1988 to 2004, published by the *Tennessee Anthropologist.*[2]

Not until 2010, however, was the Bat Creek Stone finally submitted to the kind of scientific testing that would either confirm its pre-Columbian provenance, or finally debunk it as a modern fraud. In charge of the process was Scott F. Wolter, a professional geologist and president of American Petrographic Services, Inc. (St. Paul, Minnesota), an award-winning forensic laboratory equipped with state-of-the-art research technologies. These were applied to the object at the McClurg Museum of the University of Tennessee campus (Knoxville), beginning with the

Olympus SZX 12 *Zoom* microscope, plus a *Spot* digital camera system, on May 28th. Examinations continued into the summer with a scanning electron microscope. After completing analysis and organizing its data, Wolter published his conclusions in *Ancient American*:

> Our geological findings are consistent with the Smithsonian Institution's field report written by John W. Emmert. Complete lack of the orange-colored, silty-clay residue in any of the characters of the inscription is consistent with many hundreds of years of weathering in a wet earth mound comprised of soil and hard, red clay. The inscribed stone and all the other artifacts and remains found in the mound with it can be no younger than when the bodies of the deceased were buried inside the mound. Mr. Emmert's field work and documentation appears to be more than competent by the standards of his time, and should stand on their own merit.[3]

In other words, geological evidence demonstrated that someone engraved the inscription about the same time human remains were entombed with it in the earthen burial mound, somewhat less than 2,000 years ago. This finding roughly coincided with Cyrus Gordon's linguistic dating of the artifact from 70 to 135 AD, thereby confirming the Bat Creek Stone's ancient authenticity beyond reasonable doubt.

Emmert's late 19th Century find was not, however, an anomaly, or pre-Columbian flotsam from some hapless castaway. Neither was it the first or last of its kind. Thirty years earlier, another tablet covered with paleo-Hebrew was found beneath a huge cairn, or prehistoric rock pile, near Newark, Ohio. Known as the Decalogue Stone, a paleo-Hebrew version of the Old Testament's Ten Commandments begins at the front, at the top of an arch above the figure of a robed, bearded man wearing a turban and holding a tablet. Above him reads the name "Moses." The engraved text runs down the left side and continues around all sides, making its way back to the front and up the right side, where the inscription began. A second, related object was found near the Newark Octagon earthworks (see Chapter 2), the so-called "Keystone," covered on all sides with more paleo-Hebrew, reading, respectively, "Holy of Holies," "King of the Earth," "The Law of God," and "The Word of God."

Even though David Wyrick, who unearthed both objects, was a professional surveyor by trade, he was accused of forging and planting them as part of a hoax to support claims for the Lost Tribes of Israel in prehistoric America. Later, local banker David M. Johnson and physician Dr. Nathaniel Roe Bradner uncovered yet another paleo-Hebrew tablet in the immediate vicinity of the same Newark cairn. The Johnson-Bradner Stone has since been lost, but Wyrick's Decalogue Stone is still on display at the Johnson-Humrickhouse Museum, in Coshocton, Ohio.Chief skeptical objection to these items was an untypical style in which the text were composed on the Decalogue, suggesting it had been faked by someone with an imperfect knowledge of post-exilic Hebrew (that is, as it was written after the Jews' last "Babylonian captivity" of 538 BCE).

More than 80 years following the discovery of the "Newark Holy Stones," however, archaeologists uncovered a hitherto-unknown linguistic form since referred to as "box Hebrew." It identically matched the Ohio Decalogue inscription, thereby confirming its ancient provenance.

Another copy of the Ten Commandments in pre-modern Hebrew appears on a boulder outside Los Lunas, "not far from New Mexico's Rio Puerco River, on a small, flat-topped mountain," as described by Hidden Mountain's leading investigator, David Allen Deal.

> On this mountain citadel is also found an astronomical petroglyph that depicts a solar eclipse which occurred at three in the afternoon on September 15th, during the year 107 B.C. There is an equinox observation site on the eastern

slopes of the mountain, and numerous other inscriptions in ancient Hebrew, including a spectacular Ten Commandment inscription near the base of the mountain on its northern face.[4]

Image 7-2: The Los Lunas Ten Commandments' inscription. Courtesy of Ancient American.

The University of New Mexico's Dr. Joseph C. Winter, in charge of state contract archaeology for the area in 1984 stated that the "inscription is the work of pranksters from Socorro, New Mexico School of Mines, done in the early thirties."[5]

His personal belief that the site must have been hoaxed and unsubstantiated rumors concerning the unidentified students constituted the basis for his accusation. Deal's criticism, though directed at official disdain for the Los Lunas text, goes beyond it to expose the canker in modern American archaeology:

Winter's only, and, as he says, his "best evidence" is hearsay and innuendo, none of which would stand in a court of scientific inquiry. It is peculiar that "belief," which is something akin to religious faith, is being used as evidence by a scientist. Belief is not proof, even if it comes from a Doctor of Archaeology. Dr. Winter's system of beliefs apparently disallows such "heretical"

> concepts. He seems to be mixing doctrine (religion) with science, a bad brew, indeed.[6]

That young "pranksters" would have bothered to inscribed nine long lines of some 180 Hebrew letters, each one .25 inches deep, is, according to *Ancient American* writer Lydia Rome, "no small task on basalt, which has a Moh scale rating of six and up."[7]

Dr. Winter's claim that the Los Lunas text could only have been inscribed during the mid-1930s was debunked by a prominent scholar, Frank C. Hibben (professor of archaeology at the University of New Mexico), who documented its earliest known sighting to 1871, although it "has a folk history of sightings and local knowledge from as far back as the early 1800s," according to Deal. He explains:

> The Ten Commandment inscription is written in recognizable paleo-Hebrew. A local resident, Mr. William McCart of Albuquerque, sent a copy of this inscription to the head of the Harvard Semitic Museum, in 1948, a Dr. Robert Pfeiffer, now deceased, who easily translated the work and found it to be an abbreviated form of the Ten Commandments from *Exodus*, not differing in any substantive way. Several critics have pointed out two misspellings and an added vowel, but neither of these presents any problem, as respects the artifact's validity, as viewed from an ancient Hebrew context. The misspellings, however, happen to be grammatically correct, and seem to point to a Hebrew speaker, who paraphrased one section, thus making an argument for authenticity. There is little likelihood that a copyist or modern fraud would have made grammatically correct errors.[8]

After reading Deal's articles about Hidden Mountain in *Ancient American,* subscriber Samuel Oshmier was intrigued enough to personally seek out the site. "Having been to Israel a few years ago," he reported after his visit in 2006, "I was left with a similar impression that I was looking at a scene in the Judean Hills. Photos of these two areas appear identical to the casual observer." Oshmier was particularly impressed by a transition point marking the "Gate," where the Ten Commandments inscription faces roughly north. From here, the trail continues fairly straight for ten or fifteen yards, toward the southwest. Interestingly, this short stretch through the "Gate" is oriented in the direction of the Great Circle Route to Jerusalem (032 degrees; True North, sixty-two hundred twenty nautical miles). In other words, as visitors leave the elevated plateau [at Hidden Mountain] they are literally walking toward Jerusalem.[9]

Image 7-1: The Ohio Decalogue Stone. Photo courtesy of Ancient American.

Professor Hibben was among the very few archaeologists willing to champion the site's pre-Columbian authenticity, and, as Lydia Rome has written, "he thought he had found indisputable proof that the ancient world had visited the new one—a discovery that would change textbooks and draw scholars from all over the world. Instead, it has been largely ignored...."[10]

In 2000, two years before Hibben's death at 91 years of age, even though he donated part of his fortune to build an archaeology research building at UNM, university officials balked at naming the new laboratory after him, citing his unconventional conclusions.[11] But according to Dr. Gunnar Thompson:

> [G]eologist George Morehouse reports that a heavy patina on the stone [inscription at Hidden Mountain] is indicative of an age between five

> hundred and two thousand years,... Dr. Barry Fell identified linguistic peculiarities in the text that are characteristic of 4th Century Hebrew manuscripts, and Cyrus Gordon noted similarities to texts in the Jerusalem Museum, dating between the 3rd and 4th Centuries A.D.[12]

Nor does the Los Lunas site comprise the sole evidence for an ancient Jewish presence in the American Southwest.

Writes Maggid ben Yoseif in *Ancient American*:

> The unique geometric warp and weft weave of the Navajo and earlier some Apache is the same weave found on the breastplate of the high priest in the Jerusalem temple. After searching the world over, Rabbi Chaim Richman of the Jerusalem Temple Institute said the weave described in the Talmud to make the priestly garment on which were attached precious gems representing each tribe, and which also contained the mystical *Urim* and *Thummim* [gems to aid in divination], was found still in use only by Navajo grandmothers.[13]

Corresponding physical evidence appears in the ancient Near East, where, according to anthropologist George Carter, "the Jews that died at the time of the great revolt against Rome (end of the 1st Century A.D.) in part had fled to the desert. In caves, their clothing was preserved so well that even the colors lasted. A study of these dyes showed that one of them was *cochineal* [a scale insect, from which the crimson-colored dye carmine is derived], and *cochineal* is produced by an aphid-like insect that grows on cactus. Cactus is strictly American."[14] Native to tropical and subtropical South America and Mexico, the parasite lives on cacti in the genus *Opuntia*, feeding on plant moisture and nutrients. To deter predation by other insects, it produces carminic acid, typically 17–24 percent of the parasite's weight, which is extracted from its body and eggs, then mixed with calcium salts to make carmine dye, also known as *cochineal*. Although *cochineal* was manufactured by the Aztecs and Maya, Peru is the dye's major source of production.

Native American petroglyphs representing the Hebrew menorah, a seven-branched candelabrum, occur in Arizona, among Michigan's Anishinabe and Sanilac rock art, and in the Catskill Mountains of New York.

Dr. Thompson writes how "Judean shekels dating from the period of the Second Rebellion against Rome (132 to 135 A.D.) have been found in Missouri, Tennessee and Kentucky."[15] He goes on to reproduce five Jewish Bar Kokba period (100 to 200 CE) coins recovered from the southeastern woodlands of North America, together with three paleo-Hebrew inscriptions dated between 1500 BCE and 300 BCE, which surfaced in Brazil. Although the former date may seem extreme for a Jewish presence in America, King Solomon's otherwise-inexplicable wealth suggests as much.

His famous temple, designed and built by King Hyram of Tyre, was not only an entirely Phoenician conception, but the early-first-millennium-BCE's most lavish structure. *Ancient American* writers Kingsley Craig and Christine Payne-Towler calculate:

> The gold in that edifice amounted to twenty-three billion dollars in 1975 terms. And while the bible as a product of religious inspiration should not be confused as a history book, it nonetheless contains numerous historical references professional researchers recognize as valid. A prime example being the bible's report that all the common people in Solomon's domain, even the poor, had gold on their tables. Clearly, ancient Israel was a land of great riches. But where did they come from? Not the mineralogically impoverished lands of the Near East.[16]

Instead, the source for Solomon's phenomenal opulence lay in a place the Old Testament refers to as *Ophir*, or "God's Land." 1 Kings 9:28 asserts

> that one [ship] of his fleet returned with four hundred fifty talents of gold, while another

expedition brought in a monumental seven thousand talents to Ezion-Geber. According to biblical authorities, one talent is equal to seventy-five pounds. All totaled, seven thousand four hundred fifty talents multiplied by seventy-five pounds per talent equals about five hundred sixty-nine thousand, five hundred fifty pounds of solid gold. Divided by two thousand pounds per modern ton, we arrive at the figure of 284.7 tons of gold. No wonder every home in Israel could have gold on the dinner table, while still leaving Solomon the modern equivalent of twenty-three billion dollars to build his temple![17]

Dr. Thompson relates the origins of the Ophir enterprise:

Perhaps the most surprising aspect of the biblical story is that Phoenicians bore the entire cost of mounting the expedition, while the profits of the enterprise went to the Hebrew king. According to Philo of Byblos [a Greek-educated Jew, 64–141 AD, who became a Roman citizen and wrote a mostly lost history of Phoenicia], King Hiram of Tyre sent eight thousand camels loaded with lumber to Ezion-Geber, where Phoenician craftsmen built ten ships for the voyage to Ophir, circa 945 B.C. What did the Hebrews offer as their part of the investment? It seems that their only contribution was a guide who knew the secret location of the secret hoard of gold. German historian, Paul Hartmann, has suggested that King Solomon inherited knowledge of the location of an Egyptian colony called Punt, or "God's Land" from an Egyptian pharaoh. This knowledge of a wealthy, overseas' colony was then bartered in exchange for profits from the first voyage.[18]

The Pharaoh from whom Solomon obtained information about the whereabouts of Ophir was Hor-Pasebakhaenniut II, "Image of the Transformation of Re," better remembered, if at all, by the Greek version of his name, Psusennes II, the seventh and last king of the 21st Dynasty. He ascended the throne in 967 BCE of a politically divisive, militarily diminished, economically attenuated Egypt progressively falling under the looming shadow of Persian ambition. Desperate for a substantial financial transfusion, Psusennes II sold off his country's chief trade secret to the Jews. He had nothing to lose, in any case, because, the Egyptians were no longer capable of undertaking extended commerce, which had slipped entirely into Semitic hands by his time. Thus, in a stroke, former enemies became the inheritors of an enervated Egypt's traditional source of overseas' wealth going back more than 2,000 years before, to the First Dynasty. The formerly sacred sailing directions to the Lands of Punt included a place known as *Khent-on-ofir.*

"The name, 'Ophir,'" Hector Burgos Stone writes in *Ancient American*, is derived from *Khent-on-ofir*, and "the Egyptian *U-per*, or *U-pr*, which was later transformed into *U-fir*. As *U-per,* it signifies 'Great Palace,' or 'far-off, mythical city,' or 'a royal residence.'"[19] These philological connections between Egyptian and Jewish names are underscored by the three years' sailing time (2 Chronicles 8:18) voyages to Punt/Ophir required.

Dr. Thompson continues:

> Diffusionists suggest a New World destination for the land of Ophir because the sailing time of three years seems about right for a round-trip voyage from the Red Sea to Malaysia, and across the Pacific Ocean. Orthodox historians counter that the Americas can be ruled out due to the absence of peacocks, apes and ivory described in the Old Testament account of Solomon's Ophir expedition. However, there is another rationale that provides a reasonable explanation for mention of exotic imports not found in the New World: gold might well have been shipped

> from Peru and other sources in America to a staging area in Malaysia and subsequently exported along with ivory, sandal wood, apes and peacocks back to the Red Sea. In this scenario, Malaysia represents the mysterious Tharsis that was a port of call on the way to Ophir. This second mystery isle came either before or after sailors reached "God's Land." Certainly, ships sailing from the Red Sea towards Peru would have had to stop at these isles along the way in Southeast Asia, in order to re-supply for the trip across the Pacific Ocean.[20]

As pointed out in Chapter 2, similar cargoes of gold, silver, sandalwood, precious stones, rare plants, ivory, apes, peacocks, and other diverse items brought back from Punt or Khent-on-ofir did not originate in a single location, but were obtained en route from various ports at which the expeditions called. Nor were they limited to Peru, but included stop-overs in the Caribbean.

"After Columbus discovered abandoned gold mines on the island of Haiti (Hispaniola)," Childress points out, "he wrote that he had taken into possession for their Spanish Majesties, 'Mount Soporo (Mt. Ophir), which it took King Solomon's ships three years to reach.... *Columbus' own conjecture is the first post-Columbian theory of a pre-Columbian discovery of America* [Childress's italics]."[21]

Observes the erudite Atlantologist Kenneth Caroli:

> Egyptian records consistently refer to the "lands of Punt" and the "countries of Punt." Punt was not one place, but several places. As we noted, the goods brought back to Egypt were from India (panthers, hens), East Africa (pygmies, animal pelts), West Africa (slaves, herbs), the Canary Islands (amber), Mexico (precious minerals), and Peru (gold and narcotics). It would seem that Punt was no, single entrepôt capable of funneling such an impossible diversity of goods.[22]

Known by either the Egyptian or Jewish version, these trading enterprises were themselves named after the chief source of wealth that justified such far-flung undertakings. So, too, Peruvian associations with Ophir are apparent. Dr. Thompson relates how

> Gene Savoy ["one of the premier explorers of Peru in the 1960s ... credited with bringing to light a number of Peru's most important archeological sites, including Vilcabamba, the last refuge of the Incas"[23]] reported finding three stone tablets in Peru that were inscribed with letters similar to writing found in the Sinai peninsula. As the Sinai region was near the port of Ezion-Geber, where ships departed on voyages to Ophir, he believes this discovery supports the theory that the Phoenicians sailed to Peru.[24]

Hector Burgos Stone points out that

> Arias Montano, the scholarly secretary of Phillip II of Spain, identified Ophir with Peru in historical studies. Sebastian Cubero called native Peruvians "Orphic aborigines," and established a relationship between the fatherland of the biblical Ophir and Peru. Fray Gregorio Garcia [author of 1607's *Origin of the Indians of the New World*] quotes the opinions of Génébrard [Gilbert Génébrard, 1535 to 1597, renowned papal scholar and translator of ancient languages] and other writers to the effect that Ophir was identified with Peru.... The truth is that Ophir was what is known today as the territory beginning in the Ecuadoran Province of Esmeraldas (northwest Ecuador), continuing south to the territory of Piura, in modern Peru.[25]

If Solomon's Jews sailed to America for gold, their descendants returned more than one thousand years later, not as wealthy merchantmen, but as impoverished refugees from Imperial Roman hatred of "this most base people."[26]

Chapter 8: Africans

During the early 14th Century AD, Ibn Amir Hajib was returning to his distant kingdom of Mali after completing a sacred pilgrimage, known as a *hajj*, to Mecca. While resting in Egypt, he was interviewed by an Arab scholar from Damascus, then researching a history of West Africa. Chihab al-Umari asked the Sultan,

"How had you become ruler?" He replied:

> "We belong to a family where the son succeeds the father in power. The ruler [*mansa*] who preceded me [Abu Bakr II] did not believe that it was impossible to reach the extremity of the ocean that encircles the earth (meaning Atlantic), and wanted to reach to that (end) and obstinately persisted in the design. So [in 1310 A.D.], he equipped two hundred boats full

> of men, as many others full of gold, water and victuals sufficient enough for several years. He ordered the chief (admiral) not to return until they had reached the extremity of the ocean, or if they had exhausted the provisions and the water. They set out.
>
> "Their absence extended over a long period, and, at last, only one boat returned. On our questioning, the captain said: 'Prince, we have navigated for a long time, until we saw in the midst of the ocean, as if a big river was flowing violently. My boat was the last one; others were ahead of me. As soon as any of them reached this place, it drowned in the whirlpool and never came out. I sailed backwards to escape this current.'
>
> "But the Sultan would not believe him. He ordered two thousand boats to be equipped for him and for his men, and one thousand more for water and victuals. Then he conferred on me the regency during his absence, and departed with his men on the ocean trip, never to return, nor to give a sign of life."[1]

Al-Umari's interview with Ibn Amir Hajib took place about 175 years before Christopher Columbus sailed for the New World. Leading archaeological opinion, however, holds that Abu Bakr II's transatlantic ventures never happened.

"There simply is no material evidence of any Pre-Hispanic contact between the Old World and Mesoamerica before the arrival of the Spanish in the 16th Century," insists University of California-Riverside anthropology professor Karl Taube.[2] He is seconded by official diffusionist deniers Warren Barbour, Gabriel Haslip-Viera, and Bernard Ortiz de Montellano, who are certain "no genuine African artifact has ever been found in a controlled archaeological excavation in the New World."[3]

These gentlemen are apparently unaware of two male skeletons excavated from a grave in the U.S. Virgin Islands by Smithsonian Institution archaeologists during February 1975. Subsequent published reports indicated that the human remains "showed a type of dental mutilation characteristic of African practices," and "soil from the earth layers where the skeletons were recovered dated to circa 1250 A.D.," roughly contemporaneous with Abu Bakr II's oceanic expeditions.[4] But the Virgin Islands' finds were not anomalous.

Previous to his death in 2003, Andrzej Wiercinski, a professor of anthropology and archaeology at Warsaw University, identified skeletons he believed to be of African origin in three, pre-Columbian sites at Mexico's Tlatilco, Cerro de Las Mesas, and Monte Alban. As one of the foremost typologists of the 20th century, his classification of the remains was doubtless correct and has, in any case, never been challenged. Before any of these bones came to light, a French colleague told Barcelona's International Congress of American Anthropologists in 1964 that "the only thing missing in connection with the terra-cottas of ancient America as final proof of an African presence were skeletons of African origin."[5]

The "terra-cottas" to which he referred have been found by archaeologists in abundance across Middle America over the last 500 years, but few scholars have done more to document this expansive collection than Dr. Alexander von Wuthenau, Professor of art history at Berlin University. Typical of the numerous examples he published in his thoroughly researched *Unexpected Faces in Ancient America* is the baked clay representation of the head of a young African man unearthed during a Pre-Classic dig at Tabasco, Mexico, with a high date of 250 CE. A pair of much older (600 BCE to 400 BCE) terra-cotta heads of black men from Olmec Veracruz are displayed at the *Museo de Antropologia de Jalapa*. The smaller specimen is positively identified as West African by facial scarification patterns depicted across cheeks and nose.

According to *Ancient American* writer Paul Baron:

> Ritual scarification is still practiced in many parts of Africa. The Mexican terra-cotta demonstrates a style of tattooing common in southern Sudan, the former, ancient kingdom of Nubia. The same scarification patterns are in use today among the Nuer, Shilluk, and other, ethnic groups in the area.... Various cultural clues and traces unique to Africa can been seen in the faces of these statuettes and terra-cotta heads. For example, the African hairline is clearly visible in a fine stone head from Veracruz. It was carved during the classic period of Olmec Civilization, about 600 to 400 B.C.; it is seventeen centimeters from crown to chin. Another head of about twelve inches not only possesses [African] features, but the hair design is authentically West African. This terra-cotta is on display at the National Museum of Mexico, together with ear-plugs or enlarged earrings, a common feature throughout West Africa.[6]

Portrayals of black Africans are not only found on pre-Columbian terra-cottas. Sir John Erik Sydney Thompson, "one of the foremost mid-20th Century anthropological scholars," stylistically dated a Maya pottery vessel from Chamá, Guatemala, in southern Petén, to circa 800 CE during the Late Classic Period, and was "struck not only by the [black] skin color [of the vase painting], by also by the ... facial features and the beard" of one of the depicted men.[7] "Thompson considered that the figures represented traveling traders," Willard P. Leutze writes in *Ancient American.*[8]

Leutze continues:

> He stated that the god of the merchants was Ek Chuah, and that in modern Yucatec Mayan, "Ek" is the word for "black." Thompson said

> Ek Chuah was also the god of chocolate, and suggests that this is because cocoa beans were the universal currency of the Maya, and consequently associated with merchants. I would add that the Maya, both ancient and modern, are fond of word plays, and to have a dark-skinned man as the god of chocolate would amuse them.[9]

Ek Chuah is likewise depicted as a black man carrying a spear in the Dresden and Madrid Codices. In all three of these different depictions, the Maya artists deliberately rendered the god of chocolate's profile unlike those of any of the other male figures around him. In addition to his black skin and beard—among a beardless population—his jaw is more pronounced; his nose is flat, not aquiline or "bobbed," as are theirs; and the whole cast of his facial features is utterly unique.

Image 8-1: Guatemala's Chamá pottery illustration. Photo courtesy of Ancient American.

During 1931, American archaeologist Ann A. Morris described painted murals inside Chichen Itza's "Temple of the

Warriors," in Yucatan, as "all too typical of the [African] and unlike the Maya to be readily taken for accident."[10] The Temple was abandoned no later than 1224 CE. Abundant archeological evidence for black Africans in pre-Columbian America is no less richly supported by related cultural finds. Early Portuguese colonists in Brazil were surprised to find examples of *Potamochoerus porcus*, or Red River hogs, also known as "Guinea hogs," because they belong to a breed indigenous to Africa.

The first Spanish explorers of Venezuela and Colombia found the plantain, a banana-like fruit native to Africa, already growing on native Venezuelan and Colombian plantations. African jackbeans and *Dioscorea alata* have been recovered from Mesoamerican archaeological sites, and Conquistadors already found the same yams under field cultivation on the island of Trinidad. Agricultural trade was reciprocal, as indicated by 12th-century Nigerian pottery fragments imprinted with the illustrations of American maize. The *Manihot esculenta* is an American *cassava* important as a staple food to the tropical inhabitants of Ghana and Mali long before European colonists arrived in West Africa. (*Cassavas* are American tropical plants used for bread-making.)

Richard A. Fields writes in *Ancient American*:

> Thirty years before the first Columbian expedition to the New World, the Portuguese were supposed to have replanted cotton from their colonies at Guinea in the Cape Verde Islands. But late 20th Century botanists discovered that the genetic composition of the Cape Verde cotton was not indigenous to coastal West Africa. Instead, it was cultivated by Native Americans in the Caribbean. "How did it get to Africa before Columbus?," they marveled.[11]

The manner in which this cotton was put to use by both Native Americans and West Africans further defined their relationship. The Aztecs, Fields continues, wore "vivid, colored mantles of cotton cloth, the colors of which so richly dyed they seemed to copy the iridescent plumage of birds" and designed with "radial wheels of the sun, feathers and stylized shells, the skins of tigers, in the forms of rabbits, snakes, fishes, and butterflies, mingled in a myriad of motifs with triangles, polygons, crosses, squares and crescents. These descriptions closely resemble the cloth and designs manufactured and printed by the Ashanti, Yoruba, Mandingo and other peoples of West Africa."[12] Indeed, Hernan Cortez and his Conquistadors observed how scarves worn by Aztec women were identical to *almayzars* imported to Spain by Moorish traders from Ghana.

Yet more lucrative was the transatlantic trade in gold. The Aztecs worked a copper-silver-gold alloy generally similar to, but markedly distinct from the copper-gold process known to their Musica contemporaries in Colombia as *tumbaga*. The Aztec version was known as *guanín*, but an identical alloy in West Africa was called *guanines*. According to the abstract of Columbus's log made by Bartolomé de las Casas, the purpose of the Admiral's third voyage was to test claims made by the native inhabitants of Hispaniola that "from the south and the southeast had come black people, whose spears were made of a metal called *guanín*...from which it was found that of thirty-two parts: eighteen were gold, six were silver, and eight copper"—"the same gold, silver and copper alloy, as found in spears forged in Africa's Guinea," Fields reports.[13]

Medieval metal-smiths of Ghana and Mali melted gold into characteristically X-shaped ingots, a form that appears to have been repeated throughout Olmec temple art, in which "X" was the symbol for wealth. Olmec connections with West Africans in pre-Columbian America may be the most revealing. *Olmec* derives from a contrived Nahuatl word, *Ōlmēcatl*, for "rubber line," although just how the members of America's earliest recognized civilization called themselves is unknown. They began abruptly building conical pyramids and great urban centers, while writing in a hieroglyphic language, working expertly with jade, and instituting ceremonial ballgames circa 1500 BCE, mostly around the modern-day Mexican states of Veracruz and Tabasco. From the Olmec heartland on the Gulf Coast of Mexico

Image 8-2: Found in San Lorenzo, this 9-foot-tall Olmec colossal stone head is preserved at Mexico's Xalapa's Museum of Anthropology. Photograph courtesy of Wikipedia.

their civilization spread westward to the Pacific coast and southward as far as Nicaragua. After 700 years of cultural splendor, their society slid into gradual decline, finally winking out of existence by 400 BCE.

Their most prominent legacy is a collection of colossal stone heads, the first specimen of which was unearthed during 1858 by peasants in Tres Zapotes. All 17 represent helmeted males sculptured from Cerro Cintepec rock, a coarse-grained basalt named after a nearby volcano. Mudslides carried naturally formed boulders down the mountain slopes, where roughly spherical examples were chosen for their approximation to human head shape by artists. The selected specimens were then removed to ceremonial cities at Tres Zapotes, San Lorenzo, La Venta La Cobata, and Takalik Abaj. How these burdens, weighing many tons, were carried over some 100 miles without the benefit of wheeled transport or beasts of burden is an unsolved mystery. They required, in any case, a workforce of haulers, overseers, tool-makers, construction engineers, carpenters, rope-makers, and sculptors supported by food-providers, housing authorities, medical personnel, and security guards.

The results of these major public works projects were monumental masterpieces ranging in height from nearly 5 to 11 feet, and weighing between six and 50 tons, although the largest specimen remained unfinished not far from the source of its stone. All the faces are naturalistic and realistic, but differently depicted—the true-life portraits of individual men, and the greatest examples of Mesoamerican art. Most of them (10) were unearthed at San Lorenzo, where they were originally arranged in two, roughly parallel lines—five on either side—running north to south, perhaps forming a processional route. None of the 17 were deliberately buried, but had been covered by many centuries of natural deposition that perfectly preserved them until 2009, when members of an evangelical church vandalized four colossal heads and more than 20 other artifacts at Villahermosa's Parque-Museo La Venta, resulting in four-month-long restoration work costing 300,000 pesos (almost U.S. $22,000).

Since the Olmec heads first came to light during the late 19th Century, they have consistently embarrassed conventional archaeologists still clinging to outdated notions of pre-Columbian America's alleged isolation from the outside world, because the monumental faces are obvious portraits of black Africans. Skeptics once argued that noses of the ancient artworks were deliberately flattened by the Olmecs, thereby inadvertently giving the faces a pseudo-African appearance, to avoid damaging them during transportation from the distant Sierra de los Tuxtlas Mountains. But that explanation was contradicted by a few, long-nosed colossal heads. Moreover, their creators would not have risked breaking finished sculpture by dragging them 100 miles over rough terrain, but only began sculpting after the Cerro Cintepec boulders had already been brought to San Lorenzo and other places for final display.

The party line for Establishment scholars reads that the heads' portrayed "physical characteristics correspond to a type that is still common among the inhabitants of Tabasco and Veracruz."[14] If that is true, then they may be mixed descendants of black Africans accurately depicted by the Olmec. DNA testing of these modern-day inhabitants may show how their ancient ancestors were real-life models from Mali or Ghana for the giant heads. Anti-African academic insistence is recent dogma. From the moment the first heads were discovered to the present day, unbiased professional researchers have gone beyond the obvious to confirm the sculptures' all-too-apparent identity.

According to Fields:

> "In 1938, a team of scientists from the Smithsonian Institution, University of California and National Geographic Society traveled to Tres Zapotes for the purpose of retrieving the Olmec stone head. Group leader, Dr. Clarence Welant, told Ivan van Sertima, professor emeritus at Rutgers University, New Jersey, and a specialist in African visitors to pre-Columbian America, "Every one of the members on the team was absolutely convinced beyond a shadow of a doubt that there was an African presence in ancient America, after they excavated the head."[15]

Dr. Welant and his colleagues found that the sculpted face's pronounced features were common characteristics of West Africans. The Tres Zapotes example they examined and others depict supporting, subtle details, such as their distinct peripheral lip ridge particular to inhabitants of Benin, Guinea, Senegal, and the Cape Verde islands. From all the wide variety of stone more readily available for their monumental portrayals, the Olmec sculptors went out of their way to select black basalt, a deliberate choice on behalf of their subjects' skin color, as part of all the other features associated with these portrayals.

"On the back of the head," Fields continues, "generally ignored by investigators, appear seven Ethiopian-style hairbraids virtually identical to the African cornrow mode still worn today by many people of African descent in America and in Africa itself."[16]

Precisely whom the great heads portray is no less controversial. Early observers assumed that they were depictions of slaves, but no one would bother memorializing indentured servants, especially on such a grandiose scale. Modern archaeologists and some cultural diffusionists assume they are the representations of kings or regents, a conclusion implicit in the sculptures' monumentality, and arising from a perceived similarity between headgear worn by the sculptures and tribal crowns from Ghana. After he discovered and excavated the first of the Olmec heads at Tres Zapotes, in 1862, José Melgar overheard local peasants use a term native to themselves: *Yalahau*, for "chief of the blacks."[17]

Four hundred years earlier Spanish explorer Bartholomew Las Casas met a black king in Panama, where geographer Lopez de Gomara independently reported the existence of a black population.[18] In narrating the discovery of the Pacific Ocean to Pedro Martir, historian to the Spanish court, Vasco Núñez de Balboa told how, in 1513, he crossed the Isthmus of Panama, and found large black populations, whom the Spanish believed to have immigrated from Africa and become shipwrecked there. According to Balboa, the Native Americans and Africans often quarrelled with each other.[19]

During 1905, Alfonse Quatrefages, professor of anthropology at the Museum of Natural History in Paris, referred to Panama natives in Darien as "true negroes."[20] The Olmec heads may, therefore, represent royal African figures after all. Or they could be monuments of sportsmen, who were beheaded as a reward for winning sacred ballgames. Such recreation was not mundane entertainment, but deeply religious ritual, in which the Sun's very existence was personified by a large rubber ball. Because a man could never hope to achieve anything greater in life than obtaining victory on the holy ball court, he was sacrificed at its supreme moment of glory, thereby ensuring his soul's direct ascent to heaven's highest level. The disembodied Olmec heads are memorials to these decapitated heroes, as further implied by the headgear they wear, more suggestive of leather helmets than ornate crowns. Both interpretations may not be mutually exclusive, however, because the religious sportsmen might have also been kings.

But if they originated in Ghana, Mali, Benin, Cameroon, et al, why does monumental stonework even remotely resembling the Olmec heads appear nowhere in all of West Africa?

Nor, for that matter, were such highly crafted examples of sculpted art ever repeated anywhere else throughout the long, subsequent history of Mesoamerican Civilization by the Mayas, Zapotecs, Toltecs, Aztecs, or any of the otherwise high cultures that followed. The colossal heads are absolutely unique to the Olmecs, unlike anything seen in pre-Columbian America, before or since, suggesting that they were as foreign to the land as the men they depicted. "The most naturalistic Olmec art is the earliest, appearing suddenly without surviving antecedents."[21]

Numerous broken ceramic vessels and figurines found in association with the colossal heads afforded radio-carbon dating around the beginning of their creation, circa 900 BCE. In addition to Chihab al-Umari's interview with Ibn Amir Hajib cited at the beginning of this chapter, other prominent Arab historians of the 14th Century CE, including Abu-sa'id Uthman ad-Dukkali and Ibn Battuta, wrote that West African oral traditions described transatlantic voyages from Ghana as early as the ninth century BCE. This period additionally coincides with King Solomon's three-year trading expeditions from Israel to the Lands of Ophir, described in Chapter 7.

These enterprises were invariably inter-racial affairs, continuously overseen by Jews, and captained and staffed by Phoenicians, but crewed by various nationalities, which became progressively black, as the commercial fleet put into African ports during its circumnavigation of the continent, and original ships' company from the Near East were replaced by coastal manpower. When King Solomon's armada reached Mexico—specifically, Veracruz, the Olmec birthplace—some of his Nigerian or Senegalese sailors may have jumped ship, or were more likely transferred ashore under a trade agreement arranged by their superior officers to serve in the natives' lethal ballgame. In any case, this scenario is suggested by the existence of other Olmec sculpture, as identifiably Semitic, as the giant heads are West African.

Whenever the former appear in connection with the latter, Africans are generally depicted as servile, such as the image of an African cringing before a standing Jew or Phoenician carved on a sandstone pillar at Alvarado, in Veracruz, dated to around 800 BCE. These are hardly the representations of powerful monarchs, but more reminiscent of Nubian slaves portrayed in dynastic Egyptian art.

Worse, Monte Alban's Danzante figures—some of which are clearly African—are not "dancing," but actually writhing in agony after having just been castrated as sacrificial victims. "The 19th Century notion that they depict dancers is now largely discredited...."[22] Although most of the colossal basalt heads have West African faces, others are unquestionably Amerindian. Moreover, they do not make up a preponderance of Olmec art, which is, as mentioned previously, additionally illustrated with dominant, Semitic personages. As Martin A. Grundy told *Ancient American* readers, "the majority of artifacts available to us suggest that the Olmecs themselves were almost certainly not black."[23]

Production of their colossal heads peaked around 600 BCE, a date corresponding to the Phoenicians' circumnavigation of Africa commissioned by Egypt's Pharaoh Nekau and described in Chapter 4. The last examples were made about 200 years later, another highly significant period, just when a famous Carthaginian expedition under the command of Hanno the Navigator rounded West Africa into Cameroon. These highly civilized Phoenician culture-bearers, not the Native American Olmec or their West African guests, were the artists who carved early Mesoamerica's atypical stone heads. Monumental sculpture was found throughout Phoenicia, to a far less degree in pre-Columbian Middle America, and not at all in sub-Saharan Africa. Although West African influence in Mesoamerica may have begun with King Solomon's Ophir expedition and subsequent Carthaginian enterprises, it did not end in Olmec civilization, but became more expansive during subsequent centuries of contacts that the kingdoms of Mali and other sultanates renewed until the early 14th Century CE.

Transoceanic voyages generally presented no significant challenges to the overseas' desires of these potentates. In his abstract of Christopher Columbus's log, Bartolomé de las Casas quoted the Admiral concerning statements made by King John II of Portugal to the effect that "canoes had been found which set out from the coast of Guinea [West Africa] and sailed [across the Atlantic Ocean] to the west with merchandise."[24] These were actually barges rowed in shifts by 24 oarsmen sitting on benches, port and starboard, with a hut amidships. Early-16th-century Spanish explorers of Venezuela reported seeing exactly the same, so-called "power canoes" plying the Orinoco River, from whence Auaké Indians made regular, round-trip passage to Puerto Rico in open-water voyages of more than 400 miles.

"The shortest distance across the Atlantic is from West Africa to the eastern bulge of South America," explains Leutze. "Any raft or canoe caught by ocean currents off of West Africa will be carried to the Americas."[25] In confirmation, Fields tells how "during 1952, Alain Bombard sailed in a life raft, *L'Heretique*, from Casablanca on the Moroccan coast, via the Canary Islands to Barbados, minus food or water, and equipped with only a small fishing kit. He arrived in perfect health after 65 days at sea, less time than it took Columbus to cover the same stretch of ocean."[26] Thirteenth-century Mombassa merchant vessels known as *booms*, *dhows*, and *mtepes*, carrying 30 ton cargoes as far as Arabia, would have been certainly capable of successfully completing transatlantic voyages to America.

That they in fact did so is affirmed by an abundance of reliable eyewitness reports. Fray Gregoria Garcia, a mid-16th Century priest, saw black inhabitants of an island off Colombia's northern coast. He was seconded by the country's first Spanish explorers, who entered settlements of black people near Cartagena. A copy still exists of the official authorization Miguel de Pasamonte received from the Spanish Crown in 1519 for the capture of native Venezuelan blacks as slaves. Professor Quatrefages specified the locations of indigenous dark-skinned Americans, such as Saint Vincent's Black Caribbees and the Charruas of Brazil, where a tribal people call themselves the Galibis, the identical name by which another tribe is known in Mali. The Brazilian Marabitinas are mirrored by the Marabitine people of the Sudan.

That so many pre-Columbian African correspondences should occur in Brazil, where the Carthaginian Paraíba inscription and other Phoenician trace elements have been found, perfectly complements such evidence for ancient Near Eastern seafarers in South America. Quatrefages also identified pre-Columbian West Africans in North America, including the Jamassi of Florida. Florentine explorer Giovanni da Verrazzano was the first modern European to visit the Atlantic shores of North America in 1524, when his ship was greeted by natives living on the Carolina coast. "The color of these people is black," he was surprised to observe, "not very different from that of Ethiopians." He assumed that they could not possibly be Africans, but had merely painted their bodies, until, near Roanoke Island, some of them "swam out into the surf to rescue a French sailor who had fallen from a dory," Dr. Gunnar Thompson recounts. "Verrazano noted that the natives were still black after wading ashore."[27]

Barton cites a spring 1996 *Freedom Press Newsletter* article about some present-day black Americans claiming descent from West Africans, who allegedly arrived on our continent in pre-Columbian times. He paraphrases the text:

> The Ouachita Nation exists in an area of the southern United States, which includes parts of Louisiana, Arkansas, Oklahoma, Texas, and Mississippi. The name *Ouachita* means "Black Land"...similarities between *Ouachita* and names from Mali and Ghana, such as Ouagadugta city, in the region of Burkina Faso, south of Mali; the term *Ouassei Farmall,* which means "Minister of Property" in the Songhai language; and the word *Wagadu*, which was the actual name for ancient Ghana, all begin with *Ouachita.*[28]

These linguistic commonalities and eyewitness reports by the earliest, Columbian explorers from Europe are complemented by Dhyani Ywahoo, a member of the Eastern Tsalagi, or Cherokees' traditional Etowah band. "Our elders told me that long before the White men made their appearance upon the shores of Turtle Island [North America]," she stated, "other visitors had come. In the great long time ago, the black people came from Africa."[29]

Their experience in pre-Columbian America stands apart from all the other ancient Old World visitors. Once here, West Africans ran the gamut from being worshipped as gods, obeyed as kings, acclaimed as sports heroes and lavished with wealth as export-import merchant seamen to enslavement by Semitic overlords and ritual torture and death as sacrificial victims. Accordingly, the foregoing evidence documenting their extraordinary story must give us pause for reconsideration of Abu Bakr's early 14th Century voyage, which opened this chapter. His disappearance does not necessarily mean he failed to sail the Atlantic Ocean to its other side, where he and his several thousand men may have left some of the enduring clues described in the preceding pages.

Chapter 9: Japanese

The first Americans are believed to be Asians from Siberia who crossed a land-bridge over the Bering Sea into Alaska some 12,000 or more years ago. This commonly accepted theory of mainstream archaeology was apparently proven by Dr. Theodore Schurr of the Southwest Foundation for Biomedical Research in San Antonio, Texas. During the summer of 2008, he presented members of the American Association for the Advancement of Science with new information concerning the earliest peopling of the Americas. The DNA cells in present-day Native Americans revealed their ancestral migration patterns in four major lineages going back to Siberia and northeast Asia, just as orthodox scholars have long argued.

However, Dr. Schurr identified a fifth, previously unknown lineage. This "haplogroup X" is diagnostic of Western Europeans, not Asians, and occurs among most Algonkian-speaking tribes, such as the Ojibwa. "These data imply that haplogroup X was present in the New World long before [modern] Europeans first arrived in the New World," he said, "before Columbus, or the Vikings, or anybody else," about 30,000 years ago.[1]

His research confirmed studies that C. Loring Brace, a University of Michigan professor of anthropology who "influenced a generation of anthropological research into human evolution,"[2] published eight years prior. In February 2000, Brace presented a craniofacial perspective on the origins of today's Native Americans to an annual meeting of the American Association for the Advancement of Science, in Washington, D.C. Brace explained how he used "morphometric comparisons of thousands of ancient and modern skulls, measuring each one as part of a comparative craniometric survey to identify the Old World roots of Native Americans."[3]

For the previous 20 years, he and colleagues from the University of Wyoming, the Chinese Academy of Sciences in Beijing, the Chengdu College of Traditional Chinese Medicine (Sichuan province), and the Mongolian Academy of Sciences, in Ulanbatar, subjected the skulls to a regimen of two dozen measurements apiece, providing each one with a dendrogram (a tree-like figure wherein the distance between its twigs reflects the closeness or distance between any given group from other groups). According to the editors of the University of Michigan's *News Releases,* Professor Brace's "studies show that descendants of the first humans to enter the New World, including natives of Mexico, Peru, and the southern United States, have no obvious ties to any Asian groups."[4]

Instead, the Blackfoot, Iroquois, and other tribes from Minnesota, Michigan, Ontario, and Massachusetts are "descended from the Jōmon. The Inuit appear to be a later branch from that same Jōmon trunk. Tribal groups who lived down the eastern seaboard into Florida share this origin, according to Brace."[5] He told how

> human cranio-facial data were used to assess the similarities and differences between recent and prehistoric Old World samples,

> and between these samples and a similar representation of samples from the New World. The first entrants into the Western Hemisphere of maybe fifteen thousand years ago gave rise to the continuing native inhabitants south of the U.S.-Canadian border. These show no close association with any known mainland Asian population. Instead they show ties to the Ainu of Hokkaido and their Jōmon predecessors in prehistoric Japan and to the Polynesians of remote Oceania.[6]

But who are the Ainu, or Jōmon, and what possible connections could link them to Polynesians and Native Americans, or to Dr. Schurr's Western Europeans in pre-Columbian America?

Jōmon is a term for Japan's Neolithic Age (10,000 BCE to 300 BCE) and derives from the Japanese word for "cord-marked"; early Jōmon pottery was made with cords, which left impressions on the clay. In addition to pottery, the Jōmon folk were skilled in the creation of tools, jewelry, figurines, and lacquer work, their large population concentrated in central and northern Honshu, but spread out all over Japan, from Hokkaido in the north to the Ryukyu Islands in the south. They were not Asians who came from Korea or China, but Caucasians, whose mixed descendants are today's Ainu, a people in residence on the islands when Asians arrived from the mainland during the first millennium BCE. Perhaps 20,000 Ainu reside mostly in Hokkaido, and still exhibit physical traits that set them apart from Japan's majority population.

A renowned linguist and specialist in Ainu culture, Kyōsuke Kindaichi, found that, among the Ainu, "old people who have long desisted from their outdoor work are often perceived to be as white as [Europeans]"[7] Kindaichi also believed that the Ainu's facial features more closely resembled Europeans' than those of the rest of Japan's population.

Anthropologist Arnold Henry Savage Landor more recently described the Ainu as having facial features typical of Europeans. Mitochondrial DNA haplogroup Y in the Ainu also occurs with low frequency among some populations of Europe. This genetic connection was supported and expanded by Professor Brace's comparative craniometric survey, which found that the

> prehistoric Jōmon and the Ainu of Japan are actually closer to the prehistoric and living European groups than to the core populations of continental Asia. The fact that Late Pleistocene populations in northwest Europe and northeast Asia show morphological similarities suggests that there may have been actual genetic ties at one time. Those morphological similarities can still be shown between Europe and the descendants of the aboriginal population of the Japanese archipelago, i.e., the Ainu. This similarity provides some basis for the long-time claim that the Ainu represent an "Indo-European," "Aryan," or "Caucasoid" "type" or "race."...[8]

The Ainu are remnants of a Caucasian race that once spread throughout Oceania and Polynesia, where the last survivors were the victims of genocide at the hands of the Maori as recently as the 18th Century CE. They are remembered as the light-skinned Moriori, builders of irrigation terraces, hill-top fortifications, and monumental walls, including ancient terracing faced with embankments of stone still standing in the district of Pelorus Sound. One hundred years after their extermination and assimilation, Percy Smith, a Christian missionary who lived with the victorious Maori, wondered why

> we find a strain of light-colored people who are not albinos, but have quite light hair and fair complexions. With the Maoris, this strain of-

> ten runs in families for many generations. At other times, it appears as a probable revision to the original type from which this strain was derived. There are also traditions among the Maori of a race of "gods" called *Pakahakeha*, who are said always to live in the sea and are white in complexion—hence the name *Pakeha* they gave to the white man on first becoming acquainted with us in the 18th Century.[9]

In Maori, *Pakahakeha* means "moon-like," or "skin like moonlight." Another 20th Century mythologist specializing in New Zealand prehistory, James Cowan, believed that the infrequency of light-haired individuals among the native inhabitants represented "the remnants of an immeasurably ancient fair-haired people who have left a strain of *uru-kehu*, or blondness, in mostly Maori tribes."[10] The mythic Niwareka, wife of the Maori god, Mataora, belonged to a golden-haired people who introduced weaving and wood-working.

The great Scottish mythologist of the early 20th Century, Lewis Spence, quoted a Maori who remembered traditions of the Iwi Atua, original inhabitants of New Zealand: "In appearance, some of them were very much like the Maori people of today; others resembled the *Paketa* (or Whites). The color of most of them was *kiri puwhero* (ruddy complected), and their hair had the red or golden tinge, which we call *uru-kehu*. Some had black eyes, some blue, like fair-skinned Europeans."[11]

Oral traditions and genetic traces of Polynesia's Caucasian race are not confined to New Zealand. The first native observed by the Dutch discoverers of Easter Island in 1722 was described by Captain Jacob Roggeveen as "a complete white man."[12] So, too, the natives of Male Kula greeted late 18th-century Europeans as "Ambat," the same name applied to an aboriginal race of fair-skinned people in New Hebrides. Hawaiian oral tradition describes Kauai's native people, the Mu, as blondes. Similarly, the Gilbert Islanders of Micronesia have traditions of a blond-haired people, the Matang, who spread across the ocean. Genetic traces of the Matang resurface occasionally among natives of the Solomon Islands, especially in Malaita, where light-haired natives may yet be encountered. Spence hastens to add that these untypical individuals who represent the recurrence of a recessive type, "are indigenous, and not European hybrids."[13]

Much related folk evidence throughout Oceania and Polynesia affirms the former existence of Caucasian islanders known for their maritime abilities. So, too, Jōmon sailors ventured far out at sea, as established by the remains of deep-water catch found at their archaeological sites. But could they have ranged as far as America?

During 1980, six researchers sailed the 43-foot replica of a catamaran depicted in Jōmon rock art from Shimoda, Japan, to Valparaiso, Chile, after just 51 days and through a storm at sea. Covering more than 10,000 miles of open water, the ship, *Yasei-Go*, or "Wild Adventure," proved that Neolithic Japanese mariners were indeed capable of successfully completing transpacific voyages. It also dramatized scientific findings connecting them with pre-Columbian influences. The same mitochondrial DNA haplogroup Y associating the Ainu with some Europeans is likewise found among a few Native American tribes. Studies conducted by renowned geneticist Cavalli-Sforza "suggest that the Jōmon demographic expansion may have reached America along a path following the Pacific coast," while a genetic strain in the indigenous inhabitants of the Pacific Northwest, Professor Brace stated, was a match for the Caucasian Jōmon, who occupied Japan 15,000 and more years ago.[14]

University of Oregon archaeologist Jon Erlandson discovered that the "oldest form of DNA ever recovered from the New World—around 10,300 years old—is common in type to that found in Japan and Tibet,"[15] although he concludes that they arrived along the Pacific coasts almost six millennia earlier, coinciding with Dr. Schurr's independent findings. Erlandson's evidence indicates that "the inhabitants of Honshu set out across the North Pacific more than twenty thousand years ago to Kozushima, an island in the Izu chain, thirty-one miles south of Tokyo, to collect a type of volcanic glass."[16] From there, they sailed northward to the Kuril Islands and beyond to the Kamchatka Peninsula, down the western coasts of North, Middle, and South America.

University of Washington anthropologist Nancy Yaw Davis, PhD, noticed how some Zuni Indians, a tribe residing in western New Mexico, "resemble the Japanese, especially those from the Kyoto region," possibly supporting Erlandson's research showing that transpacific Jōmon seafarers departed from the same area.[17] Pursuing her observations, she found that an exceptionally high incidence of a specific kidney disease unusually common in Japan also occurs among the Zuni.

The genetic trace they left along the western coasts of the Americas paralleled their linguistic traces. Important Native American words—such as *kiva, maize*, and *manoomin*—are spoken identically in Japan and share very close meanings. In the Zuni language, a *kiva* is a "sacred pit house," a circular, subterranean ritual staging area; the same word in Archaic Japanese signifies a "place of meditation." An inter-tribal Indian definition for "corn" is *maize*, very similar to *meshi*, Archaic Japanese for "corn porridge." The Menomonee of the Great Lakes Region derived their name from *manoomin*, or "wild rice," because they were gatherers of the plant. Archaic Japanese for "rice gatherers" is *menominee*. These cognates are neither rare nor accidental, but join dozens of other important words shared identically with the Zuni, such as "man" (*osu*), "woman" (*oka*), leaf" (*ha*), "to be inside of" (*uchi*), "a spherical object" (*mo*), and more.

But the single most dramatic evidence for Jōmon visitors in America emerged on the early afternoon of July 28, 1996, when two spectators walking along the bank of the Columbia River in Kennewick, Washington, discovered a perfectly preserved human skull. They brought it to a local police office, where forensics eventually determined that their find had not belonged to a recent murder victim or missing person, as first assumed, but was actually very old.

The skull was sent to the state archaeologist, who immediately began a search of the Columbia River bank for additional, related material. In short order, he retrieved all major and most of the associated bones, except a few of the hands and feet, together with the sternum, resulting in the most complete ancient skeleton found in North America so far. The remains are those of a 5-foot, 7-inch-tall or 5-foot, 9-inch-tall male of slender build, in late middle age—40 to 55 years old at the time of his death, about 8,500 years ago.

The high-level preservation of his bones and skull with all its teeth further allowed paleo-anthropologists to ascertain his racial identity, which came as a shock that reverberates to this day. Kennewick Man is a Caucasian of the type most related to the Ainu, or, more realistically, the Jōmon, with whom he was a contemporary.

Central to Ainu thought and society is the bear cult, as celebrated in their most important religious ceremony, the *Iomante*, in which the animal is literally "sent off" (i.e., sacrificed). Bears

Image 9-1: Aerial view of the "Marching Bears" at Iowa's Effigy Mounds National Monument. National Park Service photo courtesy of Kenneth A. Block.

were additionally worshipped by Neolithic Europeans (to whom the Ainu have been genetically traced) and Native Americans, but no other peoples, suggesting contacts between them all.

The so-called "Marching Bears" of Iowa's Effigy Mounds National Monument is a line of 10 bioglyphs near the west bank of the Mississippi River, where they were raised by landscape artists belonging to a culture archaeologists refer to as the Hopewell. Its otherwise-anonymous people flourished in the American Middle West from circa 300 BCE to 400 CE, and were, therefore, contemporaries of Japan's Yayoi Period, when similar mound building was under way in both parts of the world. Resemblances between a Hopewell platform mound re-created at Chicago's Field Museum of Natural History and its Yayoi counterpart extend even to their topmost domed structures. Both Hopewell and Yayoi sprinkled their dead with hematite, a blood-red iron oxide, before internment, a burial practice in evidence at Iowa's Marching Bears, some of which are sepulchers.

The parading bruins are accompanied by the image of a flying bird, emphasizing their spiritual significance. Birds are archetypal symbols for the beast's long winter hibernation from which it emerges each spring, a fundamental concept still ritually affirmed by the Ainu. Today, the Algonkian have inherited from their Hopewell predecessors a reverence for the constellations Ursa Major and Ursa Minor as, respectively, the "Big Bear" and "Little Bear," just as these same star clusters were characterized by the Japanese as *Oh-Guma* and *Ko-Guma* ("Big Bear" and "Child Bear").

The small, bronze likeness of a bear was dug up from deep beneath the surface of the Earth by Washington State's first settlers excavating a well near the Puyallup River, on the Pacific Northwest coast, around 1840. Standing only 1 5/8th inches tall, the figurine is erect on its hind legs, grasping a sphere in each forepaw. The underside of the 1.5-inch base on which it stands is emblazoned with designs. Professor Nobuhiro Yoshida, an ancient languages expert and president of the Japan Petrograph Society, in Kita-Kyushu, distinguishes four glyphs on the object in a style known as *Tensho*, which derived from oracle-bone letters and is "an artistic deformation of *Kanji*"—Chinese characters adopted for today's Japanese writing system. Although far older than *Kanji, Tensho* is still "used in engravings, and often preferred, even now," in the making of personal seals.[18]

According to Professor Yoshida, the four *Tensho* glyphs are ordered from left to right in image 9.2: 巫, 平, 雨, and 室. His translation of them reads, "Shrine maiden conquers rain-chamber."[19] He believes the inscription is a prayer for rain, "rain-chamber" having been a poetic analogy for "cloud." As such, the perceived "spheres" held in the bear's outstretched forepaws may be representations of clouds.

Fixing a date to its creation or the time of its arrival in the American Northwest is far more difficult, although the figure's bronze-alloy constitution suggests craftsmanship attributed to the Ainu, characterized as Bronze Age artisans. In any case, the tiny, metal bear's discovery by the first modern settlers of the area from deep underground comprise physical evidence for Japanese visitors to pre-Columbian Washington State. Not far from the artifact's discovery, the Puyallup River leads directly into Commencement Bay in the Pacific Ocean, easy access for visitors arriving by ship.

Image 9-2: Washington State's Puyallup River figure. Photo courtesy of Ancient American.

In fact, Washington State appears to have been a natural port-of-call for early seafarers from Japan. Jutting out into the sea is the Olympic Peninsula, where a Makah Indian fishing village was buried under a mudslide around 1750 CE. Among the numerous, usual items excavated at Ozette were smelted iron blades and bamboo shafts from Japan dating almost 100 years before

Columbus landed in the New World. Although they cannot deny the authenticity of these objects, archaeologists are unwilling to even consider a deliberate transpacific influence, and are content to account for their anomalous presence at Ozette by speculating, without any evidence whatsoever, that the Japanese iron and bamboo must have arrived via accidental shipwreck.

Additional powerful proof they likewise choose to dismiss was also brought to light by one of their own. Even though Emilio Estrada was the Ecuadoran archaeologist who discovered one of his country's earliest cultures in 1956, his outspoken conclusion that Valdivia pottery was indistinguishable from Jōmon ware was dismissed by most of his colleagues. He was, however, supported by Smithsonian Institution archaeologist Betty Meggers, who additionally discovered that Valdivia natives and modern Japanese have low rates of HTLV-1, a virus that does not exist in other populations.

Moreover, Valdivia pottery has been radio-carbon-dated to circa 3000 BCE, contemporaneous with the Middle Jōmon Period. Both sets were identically decorated with chevrons, bone motifs, and stipples. Japanese influence throughout these physical remains is affirmed by Professor Erlandson's genetic research, which showed that Japanese DNA "has been found in American Indians all the way down the west coast of North and South America."[20]

Japanese connections with America are older and more extensive than those established by any other overseas' visitors. Beginning more than 20,000 years ago, they continued, intermittently, until after the start of the same century that later brought Columbus to the New World already known to seafarers from Japan since the Old Stone Age.

Chapter 10: Chinese

New and persuasive evidence for travelers to the New World 70 years before Columbus officially discovered it was presented in London in 2002. Gavin Menzies, a retired Royal Navy lieutenant commander, offered his findings to a large audience of diplomats, scientists, and fellow naval officers at the Royal Geographic Society. His lecture was the result of 14 years' research into an early 15th Century eunuch, Zheng He, who had close connections to Imperial Chinese family members. Entrusted with the command of a huge expeditionary force, Zheng He undertook a series of long-distance voyages aimed at quelling piracy, intimidating foreign kingdoms, establishing commerce, and exploring new lands such as America.

Menzies's quest for information about Zheng He's fleet began in 1988, when he learned how Portuguese sailors possessed a map of the world accurately representing Africa, Australia, and South America almost a century prior to Ferdinand

Magellan's circumnavigation of the globe and 43 years before Christopher Columbus was born. The 1428 map had been based on charts spirited out of Imperial China by a Venetian merchant, Nicolo da Conti, who sailed with Zheng He on part of the Admiral's around-the-world voyage five years earlier. Establishment scholars acknowledge that Zheng He was a historical figure, but claim he sailed no further than East Africa. Their opinion is contradicted by Venetian monk and cartographer Fra Mauro, who annotated his 1459 world map with the description of a huge ship that penetrated 2,000 miles into the Atlantic Ocean during 1420, the same year, in fact, when Zheng He's expedition was underway.

Image 10-1: Zheng He's statue in China's Quanzhou Maritime Museum. Photo courtesy of jonjanego, via Wikipedia.

Advocates of official archaeology attending the Royal Geographic Society presentation were predictably unimpressed. Gillian Hutchinson, curator of cartographic history at England's National Maritime Museum, shrugged it off as "wishful thinking."[1] Other skeptics, such as the *Journal of World History*'s Robert Finlay, concurred with scientists and navigators Su Ming Yang of the United States, Portugal's Jin Guo-Ping, Philip Rivers of Malaysia, and Singapore's Malhão Pereira to oppose Menzies, an honorary professor at China's Yunnan University, in a joint public statement.[2] Unlike them, he conducted his research through 120 countries, investigated more than 900 museums and libraries, and traveled to every major seaport used during the late Middle Ages previous to drawing his heretical conclusions. During service as a submarine captain from 1959 until 1970, he gained knowledge of winds, currents, and sea conditions later applied to his investigations. For all his landlubberly critics' adamant rejection of a documented and footnoted *1421: The Year China Discovered*

America, they offered no facts to debunk its information, but merely cited their own authority as academics. Well-founded propositions are easier to deny, it would appear, than disprove.

More important, Menzies inadvertently prompted the disclosure of a new, reinforcing find. After reading his book for the first time in early 2007, a lawyer in Beijing was encouraged to go public with a 15th Century map obtained several years before from a local antique dealer unaware of its significance. Noticing the date "1418 A.D." inked into an upper corner, Liu Gang traced unmistakable references on the map to coastal California, constituting additional evidence, he believed, for Menzies's work, and held a press conference on January 16, 2007, to go public with his discovery.

Geoff Wade wasted no time in dismissing Gang's purchase as "an 18th Century copy of a European map." The Senior Research Fellow at University of Singapore's Asia Research Institute did not personally examine the map, but felt compelled nevertheless to reject it out of hand, sight unseen, and was enthusiastically seconded by University of Cambridge archaeologist, Sally K. Church, who likewise never saw it. Wade went on to castigate *The Economist*, a prominent British magazine, because its editors ran a balanced, non-committal article, in which arguments both for and against Gang's map were presented. Enraged by such fair play, Wade demanded a full retraction from the periodical. "That your writer has contributed to the Menzies bandwagon and continuing deception of the public is saddening," he lamented. "The support mentioned all comes from Mr. Menzies' band of acolytes, and their claims have no academic support whatsoever. Your writer has been taken in by Mr. Menzies, and you have a social responsibility to rectify this!"[3]

Wade's anger could have been equally directed against China's own Ming Dynasty cartographers for drawing maps of Fu Sang—identified with Japan after the 15th Century, but originally depicted as a great land on the far side of the Pacific Ocean. Confusion arose from an ancient Japanese province called *Fusa-no kuni* ("Country of Fusa") in eastern Honshū, encompassing all of modern Chiba Prefecture, as well as the southwestern part of modern Ibaraki Prefecture. "A 7th Century Chinese astronomer," Dr. Gunnar Thompson writes, "stressed that Fu Sang was 'east' of Japan," and a contemporaneous historical report differentiates Fu Sang from the ancient Japanese kingdom of Wa.[4] Instead, Fu Sang was said to lie 20,000 *li* (about 5,000 miles) from China, just as indicated on Liu Gang's map, which dates to 1418, just when Ming Dynasty geographers were having their own charts of Fu Sang drawn up, and only 10 years earlier than Nicolo da Conti's map based on Zheng He's transpacific voyage.

The earliest reference to Fu Sang appears in the *Shan Hai Jing*, a compilation of ancient geography that reached its final form by the early Han Dynasty (circa 250 BCE), although earlier versions go back before the third century BCE. Whereas scholars regard the "Collection of the Mountains and Seas" as an indeterminate mix of science and myth, they agree that its detailed descriptions of locations, medicines, animals, and geological features seem accurate enough. The *Shan Hai Jing*'s 14th Book describes Fu Sang: "The land is ten thousand *li*, about three thousand miles across."[5] The distance from Washington State's farthest point to the easternmost extremity of Maine is 3,100 miles.

Ancient American author Jack Andrews writes that Fu Sang, according to the "Collection of the Mountains and Seas," is "configured like a mulberry tree. Its branches grow from the trunk (Mexico), upward to the Arctic region...."[6] The Book goes on to mention an immense natural feature "in the southwest corner of Fu Sang's desert" referred to as *Ta Ho shih wei wu ti chi kuh*, or the "Great Canyon," and "tells of a *leang*, or chief, who used *kien*, official writing composed of *wan*, or 'strokes,' while visiting Ta Ho... The leang was said to have ordered royal commands etched into the walls of the canyon, suggesting the petroglyphs which proliferated throughout the Grand Canyon" of Arizona.[7] They have been since mostly effaced by vandals, but others still exist at different locations in the American Southwest.

Greg Nelson, another *Ancient American* writer, describes "Chinese alphabetic figures mixed among the numerous Sinaguan [Indian] pictographs in at least two, separate areas of the [Palatki] ruins," in Sedona, Arizona's Coconino National Forest, dated 1130 to 1280 AD.[8] Dr. Thompson noted "several ancient petroglyphs of the Taoist Yin-Yan" in the vicinity of the Grand Canyon.[9] At least one of them has been positively identified by Professor Nobuhiro Yoshida (see Chapter 9), as a 12th-century Chinese glyph for "king."

The *Shan Hai Jing* relates how the region, in Andrews's words, was inhabited by a people "almost entirely dependent on artificial irrigation, recalling the extensive waterworks of the pre-Columbian Hohokam and Anasazi of Arizona."[10] Modern Hohokam mixed descendants are today's Pima, an Indigenous American tribe that resides in the same area developed so successfully by their ancestors one thousand years ago. "The 14th Book recounts that the land of *Pim-o* lay in the southwest corner of Fu Sang's desert," Andrews points out. "Appropriately, the Native American Pima [language] finds its correspondence in the Chinese *Pi-Mo Kiu* for a level-topped hill. Just such a hilltop was discovered in the Grand Canyon during 1913, comparatively in tact, in the Lower Gila Valley...."[11]

Similar evidence for pre-Columbian visitors from Imperial China occurs far from the American Southwest. "When construction began on a new dam at Safe Harbor at the border of York and Lancaster counties in Pennsylvania," wrote *Fate* magazine's Cliff R. Towner, "the state Historical Commission realized the new facility would eventually inundate the several islands containing the most important petroglyphs,"[12] and, in 1930, appointed the Commission's own archaeologist, Donald A. Cadzow, to study and document them before their loss. He concentrated his efforts at Walnut Island, "about ten miles above Safe Harbor, near the mouth of Costoga Creek. It was home to twenty-one groups of writings that were unquestionably from an entirely different period than those on the islands down river."

After four years of examining the petroglyphs, taking their rubbings and sketching them, the Commission published

Cadzow's report, in which he stated, "the Walnut Island writing was neither Algonkian nor Iroquoian...a very close analogy can be made between the writings of the ancient Chinese and those found on Walnut Island." To support his conclusion, he "called on the services of several distinguished scholars of Asian studies. The scholars were unanimous in identifying nineteen of the twenty-one groups of writing as 'identical' to Chinese pictographs...." Examples of Walnut Island's Chinese glyphs "included symbols for 'well of water,' 'a hill fortress or temporary defense,' 'mountain or fortress,' 'stream,' 'wood or grass,' 'sun,' 'water or lake,' the numerals ten and three, 'heavy rain,' 'high or prominent point,' 'big,' and 'soil.'"[13]

Despite Cadzow's professional background as a university-trained, "respected archaeologist," state officials were horrified by his heretical report, however much independently validated by other scholars in related fields. Cadzow's name is mentioned only fleetingly in passing on the Commission's Website, which refrains from any discussion of the Chinese glyphs he identified on Walnut Island. In any case, their style belongs to a period long after 219 BCE, when Emperor Shi Huangi shipped 3,000 convicts overseas to Fu Sang as human sacrifices in exchange for an "elixir of life," probably a medicinal plant of some kind, from "a volcano god." Though no such deity was ever worshipped by the Chinese, Aztecs in Central Mexico did indeed offer massed human sacrifices to Popocatepetl, "Smoking Mountain," who lent his name to an active, 9,908-foot-high volcano straddling the states of Puebla and Morelos.

A more detailed account of Fu Sang compiled by Yao Silian around 635 CE appears in the *Liang* section of the *Twenty-Four Histories Book*: "In former times, the people of Fu Sang knew nothing of the Buddhist religion, but in the second year of Da Ming of the Song dynasty [485 A.D.], five monks from Kipin [eastern Afghanistan] traveled by ship to that country."[14] One of the missionaries returned 40 years later to the court of Emperor Laing Wu Ti, where Hui-Shen told of his experiences. He said, among other things, that Fu Sang featured a sea of varnish, flying rats and giant birds with white heads; women there married snakes, merchants paid no taxes, and the land was uncommonly rich in copper.[15]

Although his imperial hosts found such information amusing, it was all based on real enough persons, places, and things in North America. Hui-Shen's "sea of varnish" was southern California's La Brea Tar Pits, his "flying rats" were bats, and white-headed giant birds were bald-headed eagles. Women of the Hopi people married tribesmen of the "Snake Clan"; Maya merchants were indeed exempt from taxation; and the Upper Peninsula of the Great Lakes Region has the largest deposits of high-grade copper on Earth.

Admiral Zheng He was undoubtedly acquainted with the earlier, famous voyages to Fu Sang described by Hui-Shen, Emperor Shi Huangi, Yao Silian, and compilers of the *Shan Hai Jing*, all of which rendered his far grander expeditions less voyages of discovery, than trading enterprises. On July 11, 1405, the first of Zheng He's seven such ventures departed from Suzhou with 27,800 crewmen aboard 370 vessels. These were led by eight-oared, 120-foot-long *Zuò Chuán* patrol boats scouting for *Fú Chuán* warships, longer by 45 feet. The fleet was supported by *Shuǐ Chuán* tankers carrying a one month's supply of fresh water for all hands, and 257-foot-long *Liáng Chuán* freighters.

Three 339-foot long *Mǎ Chuán* "equine vessels" carrying horses and repair materials were joined by two 220-foot-long *Bīng Chuán* troop transports for military personnel. At the heart of the fleet were 62 *Bǎo Chuán* "treasure ships," each one 416 feet long, with a beam of 170 feet, and sprouting nine masts. Aboard were navigators, explorers, sailors, astronomers, doctors, and deckhands, along with translators, log-keepers, and troops of armed guards standing watch over tribute goods, much of it gold, jade and precious artwork.

Conventional scholars believe the colossal dimensions of Zheng He's vessels are impossibly exaggerated. But they forget that even his largest "treasure ship" was 9 feet shorter than a battleship built for Ptolemy IV of Egypt, 1,600 years earlier. At

425 feet long and 80 feet high from her waterline to the tip of her sternpost, the *Alexandris* was propelled by 4,000 oarsmen and defended by 2,850 men-at-arms firing catapult batteries. These specifics were cited by Classical writers Callixenus of Rhodes, Athenaeus Deipnosophistae, and Plutarch.

Image 10-2: A scale model of Zheng He's "treasure ship" compares with the Santa Maria *of Christopher Columbus in this display at the China Court of Dubai's Ibn Battuta Mall. Photo courtesy of Lars Plougmann, via Wikipedia.*

The famed Marco Polo and Ibn Battuta—a Moroccan explorer almost as well known for his extensive travels—both documented multi-masted ships carrying 500 to 1,000 passengers apiece in their translated accounts. Zheng He's important foreign contemporary, Niccolò Da Conti, was also an eyewitness of the Admiral's ships as they passed through South East Asia, and claimed to have seen five-masted ships weighing about 2,000 tons each. They were eminently capable of successfully undertaking transoceanic voyages to any place on the planet the Chinese cared to direct them. Always in human history, if men have the means to achieve something, they invariably pursue it. That the ancient Chinese did follow in the traditional wake of much earlier transpacific voyages is confirmed by discoveries in America of a tiny fraction of the riches that burdened their colossal "treasure ships."

Remarkably, at least one piece of their golden cargo appears to have been found, appropriately enough, in northern California. In 1957, while hunting near the Susan River in the southern part of Lassen County, Orval Stokes "stubbed his boot on what appeared to be an automobile hubceap sticking out of the ground," as reported by Arthur D. Palmer in *Ancient American.*[16] Stokes pried out the object, which he recognized as a plate of some kind, and returned home with it. Vigorous scrubbing and the application of "a mild acid solution brought out an unsuspectedly bright sheen of brass, bronze or gold,"[17] but he put the object aside for another 40 years, until a Chinese neighbor, who believed it was a Ming Dynasty artifact, urged Stokes to have the object examined by a specialist in Chinese history at Idaho State University.

Professor Yixian Xu closely studied the plate to find a faint inscription that he was able to translate with little difficulty: "Made in the reign of Tie Xuan of the Ming Dynasty [the same dynasty that oversaw Zheng He's massive fleet].... The artifact's metallurgical composition is uncertain; perhaps a bronze-gold alloy."[18]

Tie Xuan was not the Emperor, as the inscription suggests, but an important official renowned for his heroism in defense of Emperor Zhu Yunwen against usurper Prince Zhu Di. "Although the new emperor presented a charred body as Zhu Yunwen's, rumors circulated for decades that the young emperor had escaped his burning palace in a monk's robe. This rumor is credited by some as having prompted Zheng He's voyages of exploration...."[19] The *Tiěgōng Cí*, or "Ancestral Hall of Lord Tie," still stands as a memorial to Tie Xuan on the northwest shore of

Dà Míng Hú, "Damming Lake," in the city of Jinan, Shandong. The inscription of his name on the Susanville River gold plate helps connect it to the Ming Dynasty's treasure fleet.

Zheng He himself boasted, "We have traversed more than one hundred thousand *li* of immense water spaces," sufficient to encompass the 20,000 *li* from China to the west coast of North America.[20] Mid-18th Century French historian Joseph de Guignes calculated that 20,000 Han-period *li* (206 BCE to 220 CE) from coastal China would locate Fu Sang on the west coast of North America. In 1753, his fellow countryman and contemporary, cartographer Philippe Buache, drew up a map of Fu Sang, which original Chinese source materials helped place in British Columbia.

In the summer of 1882, miners there were working along the Dease Creek, which flows down the Cassiar Mountain Range. Some 24 feet below the mineral-rich sand, they were surprised to find 30 foreign and obviously old coins strung together, but the coins fell apart when one of the men tried to pick them up. Two years after the coins were discovered, they came into the possession of James Deans, a writer for *American Naturalist,* a respected scientific journal of the time. Suspecting their Asian origins, he took the coins to Chu Chong, in Victoria. The professional scholar of Asian studies positively dated them to Chi-Hunang-ti, Emperor of the third-century-BCE Ch'in Dynasty.

David Hatcher Childress relates that Chi-Hunang-ti "sent a huge expedition of thousands of men and women in an armada of ships to the 'Golden Land' in search of the 'magic fungus of immortality.' The expedition failed to return, and lacking the 'magic fungus,' the Emperor died circa 207 B.C. One wonders if this expedition ended up in British Columbia."[21] The Dease Creek cache was not the only such discovery.

Long before, when British Columbia was still a colony, a single copper coin was found in a fresh-water spring not far from the Chilcotin River, and taken to the nearby town of Chillicothe. Ink impressions of the raised characters on both sides of the artifact were made by John W. Willis, then sent to the curator of the Philadelphia Museum in the United States. Resident numismatists compared the Canadian impressions with "four pieces of copper coin procured at different times from China, which are exactly similar to the one found in the spring at Chillicothe."[22]

The Chilcotin River coin came to light during 1801, before any modern Chinese immigrants arrived in British Columbia. That both discoveries, separated by more than 80 years, were made at important river systems helps to validate the authenticity of all the coins. Ancient Chinese travelers penetrating the British Columbian interior from the Pacific coast would have taken advantage of these natural waterways. Lily Chow, a historical writer and teacher at the University of British Columbia, describes an old vase containing Chinese coins discovered in 1885, wrapped by the roots of a 300-year-old tree, likewise in the Cassiar Mountains of British Columbia.[23] Such coins are not the only evidence, however, for Asian impact on the same area.

Childress explains:

> In the 1920s the distinguished folklorist, Marius Barbeau, first noticed the melodic resemblance between traditional funerary songs sung by Buddhists in Asia and those sung by Indians on the reserves along the banks of the Nass and Skeena Rivers, in northern British Columbia. Barbeau noted that the tune scaled a high curve, touched a top note, then dropped over wide intervals to the bottom, where it droned leisurely. He reasoned that the songs came from "a common Asiatic source."[24]

Barbeau's discovery recalls the *Twenty-Four Histories*, which told how five Buddhist monks journeyed across the Pacific Ocean to Fu Sang in 485 CE. A vital component in their spiritual life was green jade. The Chinese of the mid-third millennium BCE regarded the mineral as necessary for the human soul to achieve immortality after physical death. Dynastic funeral practices required the placement of shaped pieces of jade over the eyes, nostrils, ears, and mouth of the deceased. Emperors were put to rest in coffins carved entirely from jade. The ancient Chinese believed jade assisted mothers giving birth, cured disease, brought good luck, and granted long life to anyone who possessed it. A jade cup from the second century BCE bears the inscription "May the sovereign of men have his longevity prolonged!"[25]

Green jade was also used on a large scale for making jars, rings, amulets, discs, sculpture, mirrors, musical instruments, and numerous kinds of ritual objects. As mythologist Donald A. Mackenzie writes, "One's thoughts at once turn to China when mention is made of jade, for in no other country in the world has it been utilized for such a variety of purposes or connected more closely with the social organization and with religious beliefs and ceremonies."[26]

For all its demand in China, natural sources for green jade do not exist there. Actual jadeite was not available to the Chinese until only 300 years ago, when it was imported for the first time from Burma. Until then, white jade (nephrite) was mostly obtained, sparingly, from Lake Baikal, in eastern Siberia, Yarkand (an oasis in the far north, its people defiant of Chinese attempts at conquest until the mid-18th Century CE), and Kashgar (another distant oasis beyond Chinese grasp until 1755).

Book 7 of the *Shan Hai Jing* cited above for its third-century-CE description of the Grand Canyon region also describes "White Jade Mountain," a sacred peak set aside by the gods in a cold and forested land far across the Eastern Sea. White Jade Mountain is indicated on the so-called "Harris Map," an English cartographer's rendering of traditional Chinese folklore. Several lines on the map leading toward the sacred mountain appear to represent the Fraser River in British Columbia. Curiously, several spaces around White Jade Mountain on the Harris Map are labeled "Entrails Country" and "No Entrails Country," which apparently refer to good and bad hunting areas. If so, then this far-off source for nephrite was visited at least from time to time by Chinese miners.

When, in 1986, mineralogist James Brett learned of British Columbia's ancient Chinese coins, he traced them to the original locations of their discovery on modern maps of the Yukon headwaters. While examining his cartographic sources, he was surprised to observe that the area of the Cassiar Mountain Range, where the coins were found, is the largest source of jade in North America and among the richest on Earth.

"And thus," concludes Donald L. Cyr, publisher of *Stonehenge Viewpoint*, "the importance of jade, the location of the Chinese coins at Cassiar, the possibility of water travel up the Yukon from China, and the account of the *Shan Hai Jing* that seems to rename locations and mountains in North America seem to fit together."[27]

The Chinese who voyaged across the broad and hazardous expanses of the Pacific Ocean to British Columbia—their own Fu Sang—were not engaged in an ordinary economic enterprise. They were on a quest for *yu*, the Night Shining Jewel of immortality. The earliest of their coins found in 1801 in a fresh-water spring implies that it had been dropped there deliberately as an offering to the spirit of White Jade Mountain. Such votive gestures were common throughout China until the Communist Revolution of 1949. The exact position of White Jade Mountain is not known, although its location is somewhere among the Cassiar Range. Those summits closest to the Dease Creek, where ancient Chinese coins were discovered in 1882, are its most likely candidates, particularly Dark Mountain, 25 miles due east of Dease Lake, 50 miles southeast from the town of Cassiar. Dease Lake itself is about 40 miles north of Iskut, a small, mostly aboriginal community in northwestern British Columbia.

Archaeological evidence for a major Chinese presence there in pre-Columbian times was independently validated by University of Michigan anthropology professor C. Loring Brace. In 2000, he and his research team announced the findings of their 20-year-long investigation into Amerindian origins using comparative facial and cranial anatomy. According to the editors of the University's *News Releases,* a pre-Columbian group of North American immigrants "originating in China and including the Athabascan-speaking people from the Yukon drainage of Alaska and northwest Canada, spread as far south as Arizona and northern Mexico."[28] Dr. Brace stated that "their craniofacial configuration allies them more closely to the living Chinese than to any other population in either hemisphere."[29]

That Chinese explorers actually sailed to western Canada for the first time at least 2,000 years ago is not as puzzling as how they could have discovered there one of the largest, richest sources of jade in the world. A hardly less remarkable discovery was made Dr. H. Mike Xu, when he detected Chinese glyphs on artifacts crafted by the makers of Middle America's first civilization, the Olmecs: "Comparing the symbols on three of the jadeite 'celts' in Offering Number 4 at La Venta and on a fish-shaped rock from the perspective of Shang writing of ancient China demonstrated similarities too close to be coincidental."[30] The celts he mentions are long, thin, shaped stones resembling chisels.

He told *Ancient American* readers:

> The Shang represented China's first historical dynasty, beginning around 1600 B.C., and produced "the earliest mature writing system in China. Offering No. 4 [in the Olmec collection of doll-like artifacts] consists of sixteen male figures, all except one made of jadeite or serpentine, and six celts of the same materials. Philip Drucker and Robert Heizer, who believed the figures might have depicted an Olmec ritual, excavated them at La Venta, Tabasco, Mexico, in 1955.
>
> Although the context was estimated to date between 1100 and 800 B.C., the excavators suggested because of evidence of damage that 'some of the figures and celts may have been of some antiquity at the time they were deposited.' The sixteen figures were arranged in a semi-circle in front of six, flat, elongated celts measuring 23.7-27.3 centimeters high, 3-4

centimeters wide, and 0.95-2 to 10 centimeters thick. Four of the celts have well-polished surfaces and distinctive coloration of light gray and buff and bluish streaks. All were once covered with bright red cinnabar, a characteristic element in Olmec ritual. The surfaces facing the figurines bear engraved designs arranged in top-down fashion.

During five trips to China, I discussed in detail the symbols I identified with many Chinese scholars specializing in Shang and other ancient Chinese cultures, and compared them with those in the dictionaries of Shang writing.... Subsequent months of matching, comparing, consulting and investigating have revealed close similarities between the characters on the Olmec celts Nos. 4, 5 and 6 and those in Shang writing. In each example, the Shang symbol is more similar to the contemporary Olmec one than it is to the modern Chinese equivalent, which has undergone modification during the ensuing three thousand years.

Another Olmec object with rows of symbols, currently on display in *the Museo Regional de Antropologia Carlos Pellicer*, in Villahermosa, Tobasco, Mexico, was spotted and photographed by Shang experts Zhenzhong Wang and Yuzhou Fan during a recent visit. It is about ninety-one centimeters long by thirty centimeters high, and was carved out of a piece of grey basalt. If it is inverted, it is obviously a fish. A detailed drawing of the markings provided by the museum shows clearly two rows of symbols on the side of the head, one horizontal and the other vertical.

The similarity of the symbols on the La Venta celts is clear, and comparison with Shang writing provides a similar ritual content. The Olmec fish-shaped stone resembles a stone fish from the Neolithic Longshan Culture, Shanxi, China, dating circa 2500 B.C., where these objects, known as Yongs, were

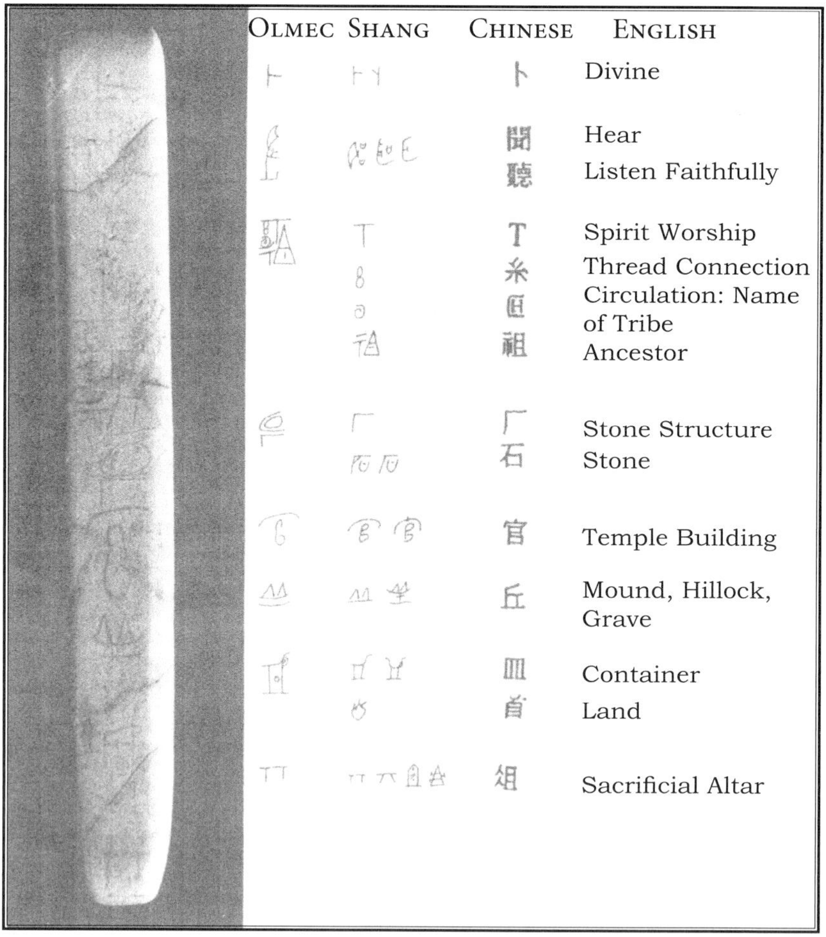

Image 10-3. Photo courtesy of Ancient American.

> suspended to be used as chimes or bells during rituals.
>
> The chronological overlap [between the Chinese Shang and Mexican Olmec], the similarities in religious beliefs and practices, the ritual importance of jadeite, nephrite and cinnabar, the presence of the same, arbitrary features in iconography, and other, shared details enhance the probability of contact.[31]

Citing Dr. Xu's original research and conclusion, Joseph Needham, the renowned British historian, and sinologist known for his research and writing on the history of Chinese science, pointed out that resemblances between the Shang and Olmec glyphs are "so arbitrary, so complicated, so numerous, so spatially and temporally correlatable, in addition to being unique to these two cultures, as to render improbable hypothesis of independent invention."[32]

The "chronological overlap" Dr. Xu mentions is revealing, because the 16 La Venta figures are contemporaneous with the bloody and decisive Battle of Muye, where the Shang Dynasty suffered a staggering mortal blow from which it could not recover. Little imagination is required to envision defeated Shang veterans fleeing in their ships across the Pacific Ocean to escape from revengeful victors. Because there was no turning back, the survivors made a new life for themselves in Mexico, where they contributed to Mesoamerican developments around 1200 BCE. This period coincides with both the Shang Dynasty's collapse and a major cultural surge in pre-Columbian civilization, as evidenced by La Venta's jadeite Offering Number 4. Moreover, the ancient Chinese and Olmecs were the only peoples for whom jade was more highly valued than gold. That connection draws closer still when we learn that craftsmen in both cultures called upon a "jade spirit" whenever searching for the precious mineral.

Dr. Gunnar Thompson tells of a jade statuette excavated in Tuxtla Gutiérrez, Mexico, where he personally "examined the 2nd Century A.D. artifact in 1986, and identified thirteen Chinese characters, including the Taoist Yin-Yang motif."[33] Any remaining doubts concerning a relationship between Asia and Mesoamerica through jade were put to rest when a jade fragment originating in Burma was found set into the burial mask of a Maya warrior, circa 800 CE. More pieces of Burmese jade were recovered nearby in the Yucatan by professional archaeologists, as described by Spencer Bohmmar at the Oriental Institute of the University of Chicago.

That importers from China may have been sailing to Mexico for green jade since the mid-3rd Millennium BCE, or even earlier, was suggested by their Neolithic *yongs*, the same fish-shaped chimes Dr. Xu found among the Olmec. This exceedingly

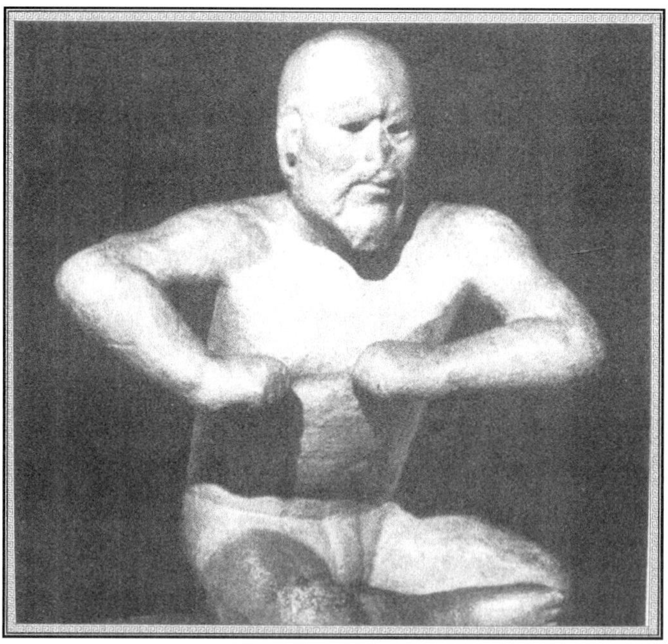

Image 10-4: A decidedly Chinese-looking Olmec statue known as "The Wrestler." Photo courtesy of Ancient American.

remote period received further affirmation by the discovery of peanut shells radio-carbon-dated to circa 2000 BCE from Shanxi's Late Longshan Culture, located, appropriately enough, at Zhejiang, on the East China Sea. Other peanut shells at Jiangsu, likewise a coastal province just north of Zhejiang, were dated about 1,500 years earlier. The peanut is an exclusively native American plant that never grew in prehistoric China, where its appearance within the context of deeply ancient cultures alone proves that transoceanic contact between both sides of the Pacific did transpire, in this case, remarkably, as long ago as the dawn of modern civilization.

These archaeological peanut shells combine with later evidence to show how that connection endured over time. The great mythologist Joseph Campbell compared a Han Dynasty eclipse table of the 1st Century CE with an identical counterpart featured in the Dresden Codex. This oldest book written in the Americas was completed during the 11th or 12th Century by a Yucatecan Maya in Chichén Itzá, although it is a copy of an original text going back 300 or 400 years earlier.

Dr. Thompson explains:

> Both tables predicted twenty-three eclipses during a one hundred thirty-five-month period, when, in fact, only eighteen occur. In other words, the Maya table was not only faulty, it had the same errors as the Chinese version. Because the identical pattern of errors could not have resulted from independent observations by Maya sky-watchers, Campbell concluded that the Maya eclipse table had been adopted from an ancient Chinese version via transoceanic diffusion.[34]

But why do Imperial Chinese records, which otherwise detail Zheng He's expeditions, mention nothing about his voyages to America? Because all documents relating to them were deliberately destroyed by Mandarin bureaucrats aware that the costs of such grandiose undertakings were ruining China's economy. After the Hongxi Emperor forbade further naval enterprises in the early 15th century, the Mandarin bureaucrats hid or destroyed every written reference to Zheng He they could find. All memory of his great fleets was lost for the next 500 years, until a few, surviving scraps of information were painstakingly collected by historian Liang Qihao for his *Biography of Our Homeland's Great Navigator, Zheng He,* in 1904. Since then, the Admiral is once more parting the seas between Imperial China and pre-Columbian America by re-opening their neglected, if deeply ancient, relationship.

Chapter 11:
South East Asians

Otheir only city built of brick. They appear to have deliberately chosen its location—devoid of limestone, with which most other Mesoamerican urban sites were constructed—for a local abundance of brick-making materials. About 40 miles northwest from the modern city of Villahermosa, capital of the Mexican State of Tabasco, the incompletely restored ceremonial center lies some 20 miles from the Gulf Coast of Mexico, to which it was 1,000 and more years ago directly connected by the now-extinct Rio Seco, a former tributary of the Rio Grijalva.

Although Comalcalco fundamentally resembles monumental architecture elsewhere in Middle America, its physical presence strikes observers as distinct, if not odd. It is the only site of its kind missing a ball-court—a startling omission, because such a feature was essential for Maya ritual activity and truly diagnostic of their society. The absence of a ball-court at Comalcalco strongly implies its occupation or, at any rate, its partial residency, if not domination, by a very different people. The site's rectangular north plaza, surrounded by a complex of sacred structures and platforms, is closed on its west side by a temple. It is a pyramidal platform facing west and rising almost 80 feet above the plaza in 10 levels, on top of which stands the main shrine reached via a grand stairway. The foremost construction comprises three other, smaller temples, domiciles, and a residential compound for elite residents composed of a series of structures arranged around open spaces. Referred to as the "palace," this is the single largest part of the Grand Acropolis overlooking the east side of the plaza, above which it stands nearly 30 feet.

Image 11-1: Comalcalco. Photo courtesy of Ancient American.

"If you happened upon this ancient city in the days of its glory," writes Neil Steede, "you may not have realized the pyramids and palace structures were made of brick. The Maya used stucco to cover the tiles, and carved ornate reliefs into the stucco, coloring the walls finally with brilliant earth and sea-tone dyes."[1]

Educated at Iowa's Graceland College, Steede was employed for 11 years as an archaeologist by the Government of Mexico, where he excavated some 200 Mesoamerican sites. He went on to serve in an advisory capacity at excavations in Thailand, Guatemala, Honduras, Peru, and Bolivia. Although best known for his appearance in the NBce Television 1996 documentary "The Mysterious Origins of Man," Steede devoted considerable time at Comalcalco to become its foremost authority. Though the site's singular brickwork initially engaged his attention, he was particularly surprised to observe that it had been fired.

He remarked:

> Although adobe (sun-dried) clay bricks were used in pre-Columbian America, the utilization of fired clay brick is almost without precedent. It is indeed puzzling that kiln-baked brick, otherwise virtually unknown in pre-Columbian America, should emerge in this particular pocket of the Maya area. In fact, it is so unusual that some commentators have not even been aware of its existence. Herbert Krieger [a Smithsonian Institution archaeologist during the late 1930s], in attempting to prove that Amerindian cultures developed entirely independently of any form of transoceanic contact, listed the absence of certain traits in Amerindian cultures which would be expected to appear if some form of contact had occurred. Krieger noted kiln-baked brick amongst other 'trait absences' in Amerindian cultures to prove his point....[2]

Only four other kiln-baked brick sites—all of them cultural satellites of Comalcalco, which they post-date—have been identified in Middle America. Brickwork naturally suggested ancient Roman influences at work, a suspicion that became more likely when Steede began surveying the site. He found:

> Upon measuring one hundred sixty individual bricks, ninety percent fell into an acceptable category of closed Roman inches (within the tolerance of 1/32nd of an inch)...the steps of the central stairway of Temple I conform to Roman inches. Although slump and erosion make precise measurements difficult, as far as can be ascertained, the steps of Temple I measure six Roman inches on the vertical, and eight Roman inches on the horizontal...evidence suggests that the entire site was laid out using Roman feet and inches .... The mortar and stucco mixes at

> Comalcalco are comparable to the 1st Century mixes in the Mediterranean area.... At the site's earliest brick stage, no developmental stage in the mortar has been detected, implying that a near perfect mix suddenly appeared at Comalcalco, only to degenerate later into a less effective mix during the Maya Classic Period.[3]

There were more surprises in store for Steede: The bricks and tiles were covered with strange glyphs and illustrations, but only on one side facing into the construction; they had been mortared into place so as not to be seen.

"In Rome, masons would often place their symbol on the back side of tiles," he learned. "It was common practice for bricks and *tegulae* [building tiles] to be inscribed in various ways before the sun-drying and baking processes. Once the bricks were incorporated into the various structures, the designs on the bricks were theoretically lost to view forever. This is also true of the designs on the Comalcalco bricks," some of which even portray Roman-style clothing.[4]

Steede's research identified eight categories of brick marks made by Roman masons: personal signatures, tally-marks, combing and scoring, roller-printed relief patterns, tile stamps, impression and imprints, graffiti, and Legionnaire and Fleet stamps. All except the Legionnaire and Fleet stamps are reproduced at Comalcalco. Apparent Roman influence extended beyond brickwork to include a drainage system made of underground, fired-clay pipes not found at any other Mesoamerican city. Ancient Romans were world famous for their plumbing. Other unique but Roman architectural features at the site are buttresses, wall niches, and cornice edging.

Steede observes:

> Although arches [at Comalcalco] are corbelled, they deviate from the typical Maya corbelled arch by being slightly curved, in order to strengthen the arch. In fact, an arch at Comalcalco contains the largest span (eighteen feet) known in the

> Maya area. [Professor George F.] Andrews states that "There is no physical evidence for an extended developmental phase for brick vaulting, so it must be assumed that the basic structural concept involved was imported full-blown from elsewhere...."[5]

Andrews assumed that Comalcalco's brick vaulting was inherited from the better-known Maya ceremonial center of Palenque, but the former city actually preceded the latter. Moreover, broken pottery stirred in mortar fill to lighten the load occurred only at Comalcalco and in first-century Rome.

"Although these construction techniques are found in other parts of the world at earlier dates," Steede notes, "they have no known antecedent in Mesoamerica. It would seem that all of the above items appeared for the first time in Mesoamerica at Comalcalco. If confirmed, this finding would imply an amazing leap in construction technology."[6]

That Imperial Romans were responsible for building the Mexican ceremonial center seemed reinforced by radio-carbon dates, Goechron Laboratories in Cambridge, Massachusetts, obtained a median date of 380 CE and low date of 510 CE from the site's original oyster shell mortar. Testing indicated that Comalcalco's first brick floor was laid down around 420 CE. These time parameters generally correlate with archaeological periods for major building phases at Comalcalco between 200 CE and 600 CE. The city flourished into the ninth century, but entered its decline thereafter and was abandoned by 1300 CE. As we learned in Chapter 5, physical evidence confirming Imperial Roman impact on the Americas—from many dozens of amphorae (ancient Roman jars) in the waters off Rio de Janeiro to at least as many coins scattered across the Middle Western United States—is profuse and persuasive. These artifacts are unequivocally Roman.

But if Comalcalco does not entirely resemble a typical Maya building project, neither does it overall suggest an ancient Roman edifice. Nor are observers convinced that it is a synthesis of both cultures. No, something else was at work here. If the site had indeed been built by Romans, they left behind no flanged *tegulae*, flat roof tiles commonly used in Roman architecture, and, more tellingly, no inscriptions in Latin. Nor did they bring the true arch to pre-Columbian Mexico. Among apparently Mediterranean material evidence Steede observed were many objects as non-Maya as they were non-Roman.

"Inside the museum you can also see carved figurines and heads that seem to portray features uncharacteristic to the Maya," he states. "Some of these carvings and masks sport beards and hats, uncommon in the Mayan world."[7] He saw at Comalcalco the sculpted representations of a "human emerging from a lotus-like flower, an animal-headed human with turban, a Shiva-like figure, and a human with bird feet common in India."[8] These images are associated with Asia, not Rome. From a study conducted by archaeologist Paul Tolstoy at the University of Montreal, he learned that of 121 steps used for making bark cloth and paper in South East Asia, 92 had been repeated in Mesoamerica.

"Excavations in the North Plaza at Comalcalco," Steede writes, "also yielded a series of funerary urns (giant clay jars). Inside each of these jars was the body of an individual in a sitting position, accompanied by rich offerings."[9] Very similar urn burials were made about the same time in South East Asia.

Comalcalco's advanced corbelled arch had its counterpart neither elsewhere in Middle America nor in Rome, he discovered, but in contemporaneous Bali. Most revealing was the presence of *Brahmi* script—also known as "shell script," a written language in use throughout Indonesia from the 4th to 8th Centuries—on the underside of many Comalcalco bricks. Of the 44 letter-forms Steede found among them, he identified 24 as *Brahmi* characters. To explain the disparate appearance of Roman and South East Asian cultural elements at Comalcalco, he looked far westward across the entire breadth of the Pacific Ocean to Vietnam's Ca Mau Peninsula.

There, on the Mekong Delta, close to the west coast, and south of a future Saigon, stood the city of Oc-eo. If not founded, it was powerfully influenced by the *Kushana* (also known as the *Yueh-Chih*), a people who migrated from the

Hindu Kush to the lower Ganges, where they developed maritime trade with South East Asia. During their previous Satavahana Dynasty, from 200 BCE to 200 CE, they enjoyed extensive commercial connections with Rome, and these they carried on into Oc-eo. They also introduced the *Brahmi* script into Vietnam, along with horse-trading. Evidence for both occurred in contemporaneous Mesoamerica, where, according to Steede, "horse remains [have been] found in unmistakable pre-Columbian context during Carnegie excavations at Mayapan," and the image of a horse's head was illustrated on a Comalcalco brick.[10]

Between the 2nd and 7th Centuries, Oc-eo was an emporium for Roman ideas, architecture, and import goods, such as cut stones. Even the city's ground plan is similar to that of Comalcalco. In view of these comparisons, Steede concludes that in the early 5th Century—perhaps when Comalcalco's first brick floor was laid around 420 CE—*Kushana* sea-farers from distant Oc-eo arrived with Roman construction skills on the southwest coast of Mexico, where they joined native Maya for building a major trade center with ready access to the sea.

This interpretation of the evidence seems borne out by the city itself. Comalcalco's modern name is not Mayan, but *Nahuatl*, the spoken language of a much later people, the Aztecs. It means "In the House of the Comals." A *comal* is a pan used for preparing tortillas. The site was originally known as "Surrounded Sky," or *Joy Chân*—phonetically far less Mayan than South East Asian.

But Oc-eo comparisons with Comalcalco by no means signify South East Asia's only impact on Mesoamerica.

Journalist Richard Cassaro writes:

> One of the greatest archaeological riddles and grossest academic omissions of our time is the untold story of the parallel ruins left by two, seemingly unrelated civilizations, the ancient Maya on one side of the Pacific Ocean and the ancient Balinese on the other. The

> mysterious and unexplained similarities in their architecture, iconography, and religion are so striking and profound that the Maya and Balinese seem to have been twin civilizations, as if children of the same parent.[11]

His assessment was preceded by an *Americas* magazine interview with Michael D. Coe, among the most important American archaeologists of the 20th century. "There are so many resemblances between mental systems of Bali and Mesoamerica," he said, "it got to the point I could predict what they (the Balinese) were going to do next from my knowledge of the Maya. Truly amazing! ... I'm looking at mental systems, cosmological systems, which are almost identical on both sides of the Pacific."[12]

In a special edition issue of Australia's *New Dawn* magazine, Cassaro enumerated and illustrated "twelve major parallels still visible in the ruins of the ancient Balinese and the ancient Maya."[13] They were not general similarities, but specific points of close relationship beyond coincidental comparisons. Among them are the corbelled arches of central Bali's Ubud religious complex identically reconstructed at Honduras' Late Classic ceremonial center in Copán. The Mayan temple is guarded by the statue of a long-haired deity with bulging eyes and huge teeth. This otherwise-singular representation—even to a torch held in the left hand—likewise appears near the entrances of Balinese sacred sites.

On the 9-foot-tall Honduran stele of Copán's 13th leader, Eighteen Rabbit makes a hand gesture familiar throughout India and South East Asia as a *yoga mudra. Mudras* are symbolic or ritual gestures believed to affect the flow of *prana* ("life energy") in every human body. The Mayan stele's sculpted hand gesture is known as the *Mukula mudra,* signifying a fresh start or the beginning of new enterprises. As such, the *Mukula* is properly expressed by Eighteen Rabbit, because he "is considered the greatest patron of the arts in Copán's history," who initiated more monumental public works projects than any other *ajaw*, or ruler, from 695 to 738 CE.[14]

Cassaro observes that other examples of Balinese temple sculpture include a dot—symbolizing the so-called "third eye" of spiritual enlightenment—at the center of the forehead of portrayed deities. The same dot appears on Maya sacred statuary.

Serpentine balustrades run down the full length of grand staircases at both the Besakih Temple, Bali's "Stairway to Heaven," and at Chichen Itza's famous *El Castillo,* the Pyramid of the Feathered Serpent, in Yucatan. Also known as *Pura Besakih,* the former structure "is the largest, most important [oldest], and holiest pyramidal temple in Bali. One of a series of Balinese temples, it has stepped terraces, resembling a stepped pyramid," virtually a mirror image of *El Castillo,* which additionally shares a common construction period—from the late ninth to early 12th Centuries CE—with Besakih.[15]

An equally close architectural comparison occurs in Central Java, near Suakarta. On the slopes of 3,000-foot-high Mount Lawu is found a stone temple mound known as Candi Sukuh. Its physical resemblance to Mesoamerican counterparts is remarkable, even down to the stele sculpted in relief that stand around its base. "The shape of Candi Sukuh, with its steps leading to the upper part of the temple," reports travel writer, William Dalton, "is strikingly similar to the Maya temples of Yucatan and Guatemala, which were being built at the same time."[16]

A Java government position holds that the monument was completed around 1500 CE. However, this period witnessed not its foundation, but its final abandonment. The official date is nonetheless parroted by most Indonesian handbooks, in spite of a chronogram on the site's western gate inscribed with the Javanese equivalent of 1437 CE. That date actually indicates the year when the area was seized by Majapahit kings, who controlled a vast, thalassocratic, archipelagic empire based on the island of Java. They claimed the temple mound's conquest, not its construction. "It is probable that Candi Sukuh is thousands of years old," states David Hatcher Childress, who personally investigated it, "and may date back to 500 B.C., or even further. No serious excavation or dating of the complex has been done since the Dutch and Indonesian archaeologists turned it into a small state park."[17]

Although Candi Sukuh's true age is uncertain, its resemblance to Mesoamerican monumental architecture is not generalized, but specific to a particular site located in the Petén Basin region of the Guatemalan lowlands. Known today as Uaxactún after its discovery in May 1916 by U.S. archaeologist Sylvanus Morley, he contracted the Mayan words *waxac* and *tun* to coin the name "Eight Stones" for an eight-year-cycle Venusian calendar stele he found there. The site's original name—*Siaan K'aan*, or "Born in Heaven"—was learned after the translation of Mayan hieroglyphs later during the 20th century, although the location is still popularly referred to as Uaxactún and is unique on two counts: The Mayas' earliest examples of their use of Zero on steles 18 and 19 were inscribed in 357 CE. Dated 29 years before, the site's first stele combines with its last set-up in 889 CE to establish Uaxactún as the longest-lived city in Petén. These features define "Born in Heaven" as a distinctly important place, especially for its contemporaneous use of the Zero concept, which was unknown throughout the ancient world, except only in 4th Century India and Mesoamerica.

Other kinds of Indonesian imagery exerted fundamental influences on Middle American civilization, such as their contribution to the so-called "Aztec Calendar Stone," a ritual almanac or calculator for determining astrologically significant days and periods in the Mesoamerican zodiac, which the Aztecs modified and inherited from previous cultures going back to the Maya and probably before to the Olmec.

The monolith's original name was *Cuauhtlixicalli*—"House of the Eagle," or the "Eagle Bowl," but "The Vessel of Time" was closest to its real meaning. The eagle symbolized the Sun, which embodied the passage of time. The Stone's physical beginnings as a 50,000-pound slab hewn from quarries in the mountains south of today's Mexico City were followed by its transportation over 30 miles to the main square of the Aztec capital. It was hoisted more than halfway up the steep steps of the Great Pyramid, then carefully laid flat on a broad landing, where sculptors and artists undertook the complex task of carving and painting the bas-relief masterpiece during the reign of Emperor Axayacatl.

Finally, during the late 15th Century, the 13.5-foot-tall monolith was set up to face out over Tenochtitlán. Less than 40 years later, the 24-ton disk of gray-black basalt was pried from its throne-like cradle on orders of Catholic friars to careen down the grand staircase of the Great Pyramid, where it was buried as a work of the devil. There it remained until accidentally excavated by sewer workers in 1790, when the much-abused "Vessel of Time" was set up against the east wall of the large cathedral in Mexico City's *El Zócalo Plaza Mayor*, until removal to the Stone's present location at the Museo Nacional de Antropología.

Depicted at the center of the disk is the ferocious expression of Tonatiuh, the Aztec sun-god, which perfectly resembles a facial exercise practiced by the followers of *Hatha Yoga* referred to as "the Lion." The yogic calisthenics require extension of the tongue to its muscular limits, the tensing of all facial muscles, widening of the eyes, and stretching of the fingers to resemble lion's claws. Such contortions result in an expression identically displayed by the Eagle Bowl's central figure, including his talons. The *Hatha Yoga* exercise signifies the relief of a tense period, an ending or completion, just as the Calendar Stone's 4-*Olin* marks the end of a tension-filled epoch. The four cardinal directions of 4-Olin allude to an unspecified, if worldwide, catastrophic "movement."

The yogic Lion and Tonatiuh's face are, in fact, physically and symbolically indistinguishable from each other. Though the oldest surviving references to yoga are found in written commentaries compiled around 900 BCE, figures in yoga postures depicted by cylinder seals from the first Indus Valley civilization at Harappa precede the Brāhmanas by nearly 2,000 years. Yoga was a dominant spiritual discipline of Asia, early identified with ancient India, but soon after practiced throughout Indonesia. The appearance of *Hatha Yoga*'s Lion face at the center of the Aztec Calendar Stone is not the Eagle Bowl's only curious connection with ancient

India, however. According to Florida scholar Kenneth Caroli, the Mayas' 5,150-year cycles "certainly fit the traditional Hindu dates for Krishna and the juncture of *Davpara* with the Kali Yugas."[18]

In Hinduism and some branches of Buddhism, the *Kali Yuga* signifies the end of the universe, the last of four *yugas*, just as the Maya knew four Suns. Both sets are "world ages" subject to cycles of creation, destruction, and renewal. The Aztec Calendar Stone's 4-*Ocelotl* ("Jaguar"), 4-*Ehecatl* ("Wind"), 4-*Quihuitl* ("Heavenly Fire"), and 4-*Atl* ("Water") parallel the Hindu *Satya Yuga, Treta Yuga, Dwapara Yuga*, and *Kali Yuga*—all of them world ages defined by catastrophic event horizons. Beginning in 3112 BCE, this ultimate *yuga* is a mere two years difference from the start of the Mayas' Fifth Sun in 3114 BCE. The Maya believed its demise would be brought about by Macuilli-Tonatiuh, the solar god of destruction, portrayed on the Aztec Calendar Stone as the enraged face of a man with his tongue extended in the yogic Lion grimace.

So, too, the Hindu *Kalki Purana* describes Kali, the demon of universal annihilation—as distinguished from the goddess Kali—who terminates the *Kali Yuga* in global upheaval, with a large, lolling tongue. The violent end of both the Mesoamerican Fifth World and the Hindu *Kali Yuga* are presided over by the same god of destruction. As Caroli observes, "clearly, the Maya thought in similar terms to the Hindus and early Buddhists, at least in so far as their scale went."[19] Kali was the tenth avatar, or incarnation of the beneficent deity, Vishnu, just as the Aztec Calendar Stone's Tezcatlipoca was the malevolent twin of Quetzalcoatl.

Other Mesoamerican imagery connecting with the pre-Columbian New World are numerous representations of elephants, which died out in America with the last ice age, 8,000 or more years before the Maya built their first city. The Mayan god of rain was nevertheless sculpted at Uxmal and Copan, the Mayas' outstanding ceremonial centers, as an anthropomorphic pachyderm (a large mammal, usually with thick skin). At the latter city, an extraordinary example appears on the so-called "Stela B," featuring an elephant head surmounted by a man wearing a turban in the self-evident depiction of a *mahout*, or elephant rider in South East Asia and India. Conventional archaeologists insist that such beasts are really meant to signify the Maya rain-god, Chac, not in the form of an elephant, but of a parrot or tapir. Neither of these animals, however, has anything whatsoever to do with rain.

An elephant, on the other hand, characteristically discharges great sprays of water from its trunk, rendering this creature an apt personification of Chac. Moreover, he was typically portrayed in sacred art with dotted circles, symbols for water, running through his trunk.

The unmistakable image of an elephant appears in a famous painted fresco at Bonampak in Yucatan, dated to circa 500 CE. Similar specimens range from elephantine illustrations on contemporaneous terra-cotta plates displayed at Bolivia's Museo Arqueologico, in La Paz, to prehistoric effigy mounds, slates, and pipes found north of the Rio Grande River, in the continental United States. The zoomorphic earthworks were professionally documented for 14 years by surveyor Theodore Hayes Lewis, who covered 54,000 miles, more than 10,000 of them on foot, beginning in 1881.

Lewis concentrated his efforts primarily in Wisconsin, where some 10,000 pre-Columbian mounds were located, but threatened with obliteration by industrial and residential development. Lewis believed he was working against time to preserve their memory, if not their physical existence. Microfilm copies of his meticulous drawings are housed today at St. Paul's Minnesota History Center. The majority of earth-effigies Lewis surveyed were faithful re-creations of animals ancient Americans saw on a daily basis. There were obvious figures of buffalo, deer, birds, fish, spiders, cats, and dogs. But among these common creatures were 10 separate line drawings of elephants at different Upper Midwestern locations in Wisconsin's Rock, Grant, and Vernon counties, with one each in Iowa's Allamakee and Lansing counties. He cited one location in particular as especially noteworthy: "This place is two miles north of the center of Praire du Chien and two-and-one-half miles east of the Mississippi River.... I found the elephants to be the only figures with perfect outlines."[20]

Tragically, none of these effigies escaped the farmer's plow, save perhaps one of the Praire du Chien elephants, which Ho Chunk tribal elders believe still exists in densely overgrown marshland near the east banks of the Mississippi.

During 1885, Charles E. Putnam published a "vindication of the authenticity of the elephant pipes and inscribed tablets in the museum of the Davenport Academy of Natural Sciences [Iowa]."[21] He felt obliged to answer accusations of fraud leveled by Smithsonian Institution directors against two pipes and three slates found between January 1877 and March 1880 in the eastern part of the state, not far from the Mississippi River. Despite the misgivings of skeptics, no one involved with the anomalous objects profited in any way from their discovery. Academy president William H. Pratt was quoted as having said about the disputed artifacts, "No prehistoric relic ever found has better evidence to establish its genuineness than these, and not one suspicious circumstance in connection with them has been pointed out, nor can there be."[22]

The first elephant pipe that came to light was plowed up by an illiterate German immigrant, Peter Mare, on his farm in Louisa County. The sandstone object weighs 6 ounces, and measures 3.5 inches long, 1.5 inches tall at the shoulder, and 1 inch thick. "The artist who made this pipe," writes R.J. Farquharson in *American Antiquarian* magazine, "must have been familiar with the elephant form, either from having seen the living animal, or the delineation by a preceding artist, or from oral tradition in his tribe...."[23]

Both tablets emblazoned with the likenesses of elephants were found within the Davenport city limits. The clay pipes, slate tablets, and landscaped effigies all belonged to the Hopewell culture, which flourished in the Middle West from about 300 BCE to 400 CE. Although similar earthworks and pipes depicting the beast do not occur in Mesoamerica, its representation in Wisconsin and Iowa shares some fundamental commonalities with Maya temple art and sculpture. All, without exception, identify Asian elephants, because they show the characteristically domed cranium, though they lack the larger ears and prominent

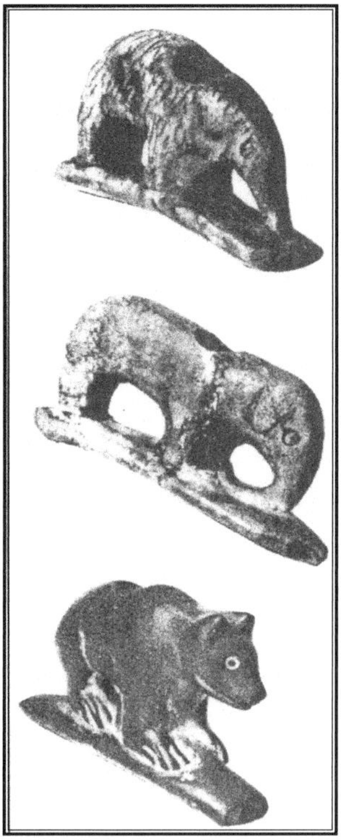

Image 11-2: Upper Midwestern effigy pipes representing (top) an anteater, an animal that lived no closer than southeastern Mexico, more than 1,000 airline-miles from northern Wisconsin; (middle) an unmistakably elephantine figure; and (bottom) a bear, revered equally by the Japanese Ainu and American Hopewell. Photo courtesy of Ancient American.

tusks of their African relatives. Whether among the Upper Middle Western earthworks, slate tablets and pipes, or sculpted variants of Chac and Bonampak frescos, America's pre-Columbian elephant appears mostly without tusks, save in a few instances, where recessive tusks are suggested. They accurately reflect the Asian elephant, female versions of which do not grow prominent tusks; some males sprout tusks (although never as long as those produced by African elephants), but many do not.

G. Eliot Smith wrote in *Nature* magazine:

> The use of the elephant design in these different ways becomes more intelligible when it is recalled that in India and eastern Asia the elephant was frequently represented on temples and *dagobas* [sacred monuments], and special sanctity became attached to it in religious

> architecture. Some of the earliest sculpted representations of the elephant in India, going back to the Asokan period (3rd Century B.C.), are found to have the tusk and ventral surface of the trunk exposed in precisely the same way as the Copán elephants.[24]

Abundant cultural evidence for elephants from Honduras to the Upper Midwest seems to be contradicted by the absence of their bones in pre-Columbian America. To be sure, transporting such large, demanding beasts across the vast Pacific Ocean would have been difficult to impossible. More likely, they were not physically introduced to the Maya or Hopewell, who instead relied entirely on illustrations or verbal descriptions of these animals provided by Hindu or other Asian visitors. They deified the elephant in India and worshipped it throughout South East Asia as Ganesha, the divine Remover of Obstacles and Lord of Beginnings, recalling Eighteen Rabbit's *Mukula* mudra signifying the start of new enterprises at Copán. Patron of arts and sciences, and the *deva*, or spirit of intellect and wisdom, Genesha is the very god of civilization, whose image, like that of Chac in Mesoamerica, adorned numerous temples and religious structures.

Although Ganesha's earliest known religious manifestations go back to the 10th Century BCE, he "appeared in his classic form as a clearly recognizable deity, with well-defined iconographic attributes in the early 4th to 5th Centuries" and "was particularly worshipped by traders and merchants, who went out of India for commercial ventures. Hindus migrated to the Malay Archipelago and took their culture, including Ganesha, with them. Statues of Ganesha are found throughout the Malay Archipelago in great numbers, often beside Shiva sanctuaries. The forms of Ganesha found in Hindu art of Java, Bali, and Borneo show specific regional influences."[25]

From here, the Hindu traders and merchants carried his worship across the Pacific Ocean to the western shores of Mexico, where he was venerated as Chac. Both were envisioned as elephant-headed men and associated with water. Chac, as mentioned, was the Maya rain-god, whereas "an annual festival honors Ganesha for ten days, starting on *Ganesh Chaturthi*, which typically falls in late August or early September.... The festival culminates on the day of *Ananta Chaturdashi*, when idols (*murtis*) of Ganesha are immersed in the most convenient body of water. Some families have a tradition of immersion on the third, fifth, or seventh day."[26]

But elephants are not the only creatures testifying to Mesoamerican contacts with pre-Columbian cultures. Eleven-hundred-year-old bird bones retrieved from Pueblo archaeological digs in Arizona were identified by Texas A&M University's George Carter as the skeletal remains of chickens native to South East Asia. Spurred on by this discovery, his further research revealed that the Hindu name for "chicken" is *karak*; Quechua Indians of the Peruvian Andes refer to the animal as *karaka*. But South East Asians visiting pre-Columbian America received, as well as gave.

Dr. Gunnar Thompson tells how "plant sculptures on temples at Halebid, Mysore, Khajuraho, and Somanthpur are undoubtedly varieties of maize,"[27] which is native to America and never grew in Asia until it was imported. Skeptics argued against the obvious, insisting that the alleged temple depictions of maize were misinterpreted piles of pearls. "That speculative rationale fell apart under the thorough research of Carl Johannessen and Anne Parker from the University of Oregon," states Dr. Thompson.[28]

Dr. Thompson also states:

> Their examination of scores of Hindu sculptures confirmed that the plants depicted in stone carvings had all the characteristics of maize: elongated or conical shapes with rows of kernels; fruit wrapped in leaves; silk strands hang from the top of cobs. Some of the items included hybrid forms of maize with two sizes of grains. Their shapes also conform to the same variety of shapes that are characteristic of maize-bulbous, conical and elongated.... Sculptures on Hoysala temples can be dated by historical accounts

> to the 12th or 13th Century; thus, they are unquestionably of pre-Columbian age. According to [Jaweed] Ashraf, the oldest sculptures of maize at Sanchi, India, date to the 2nd Century A.D.[29]
>
> Dr. Thompson lists pre-modern India's vernacular names for maize in the 16th Century: *juari, jwari, junhari,* and *makka.* Juari Mata was the Hindu goddess for fevers; *juari* (maize) was a medicinal used in the treatment of fevers. Thus, it is only expected that maize ears would be found in temples dedicated to the goddess. The 16th Century Padmvat of Akbar has "juhari" as a royal garden fruit and a food item of the Mogul army.... The 14th Century physician Hakim Diya used a medicine, which he called *makka* or *bhutta.* These Hindi words are still used to refer to maize in some regions of India.
>
> An Arabian traveler from this period, Tahir Maqaddasi, reported that *durah* was used on the west coast of India. This *durah* was synonymous with *khundrus,* a Hindu herb mentioned in a Greco-Arabian medicinal (the *Canons of Avicenna*). *Dura* is a common Arabic word for "maize;" thus, *khundrus* can also be regarded as a name for maize.... Sanskrit lexicons, Puranic texts and palm-leaf manuscripts also mention a plant called *markata* or *makataka,* which is an early version of *makka* (maize). The 5th Century B.C. text, *Apsthamba Sarutasutra,* mentions a plant called *markataka,* the earliest recorded name for maize in India.[30]

It seems clear, then, that the relationship India and South East Asia enjoyed with pre-Columbian America was reciprocal, including architectural and religious ideas for maize. The deep antiquity of that trade is indicated by Dr. Thompson, who told *Ancient American* that "radio-carbon dates for *Zea mays* pollen found in earthen cores from Kashmir fall between the 3rd and 10th Millennium B.C."[31]

Difficult as such a time scale may be to grasp for conventional scholars, the Indus Valley civilization, which began to flourish around the turn of the 4th Millennium BCE, built the city of Lothal, a truly immense seaport on the Indian Ocean for long-distance commerce. But these early overseas' voyages also exported difficulties that nonetheless help prove connections between the ancient Old and New Worlds. During the first decade of the 21st Century, Italian population geneticist Luigi Luca Cavalli-Sforza, professor emeritus at Stanford University, tabulated an extensive study of Human Lymphocyte Antigen distributions of Inca mummies and coprolites (fossilized human excrement). He and his colleagues established the presence of tropical intestinal parasites from South East Asia, including Indonesia's *ancylostoma duodenale,* in ancient Peru and Bolivia.[32]

Such genetic testing combines with numerous, valid cultural comparisons and a wealth of surviving artifacts to confirm the influential and long-term presence of Asian culture-bearers in pre-Columbian America. The Hopewell Culture, with its elephant effigies and pipes, had been immediately preceded by a distinctly different folk referred to by archaeologists as the Adena, after the name of an Ohio plantation first associated with these pre-Columbian iron-workers, who introduced agriculture to North America. From some of their Eastern Woodland earthworks, dated circa 500 BCE, excavators unearthed caches of "money cowery," so-called for their use as common currency throughout South East Asia. These gastropod shells, not otherwise found on the American continent, are native to the Maldive Islands. That specimens of *Cyprea moeta* were deliberately interred by the Allewegi as precious grave goods in their sacred burials constitutes important physical proof for meaningful connections North America's Adena mound builders enjoyed with culture-bearers from the Indian Ocean, some 25 centuries ago.

The same cultural lineage is clearly retraced by comparative metallurgy. Long before the Spaniards arrived, South America's Muisca craftsmen combined copper with molten gold poured into molds for the casting of bowls, cups, pins, statuettes, and other items. The result was a buttery sheen that Indigenous peoples referred to as *tumbaga*. Both the process and name were identically known to metal-workers throughout the Philippines. Across Malaysia, it was familiar as *tembaga, tambaga* among the Indonesians, and *tambaga* in India, where it ultimately derived from the Sanskrit word for "bright gold" (*tamra*) during the 1st Millennium BCE, about the same period the Muisca migrated to Colombia's Altiplano Cundiboyacense.

One of India's great epics, the *Ramayana*, or "Rama's Journey," tells how the title's hero went on a far-flung quest to rescue his wife, who was abducted by a Sri Lankan king. Although its earliest complete manuscripts date to the 11th Century CE, an original version in Sanskrit, the *Valmiki Ramayana*, was compiled during the 5th and 4th Centuries BCE from even older oral traditions. Accretions that later formed its final revision may have been made during the 2nd Century BCE or somewhat later. The epic appears to have been based on an actual, historical figure, a minor chief, who lived in the 8th and 7th Century BCE.

During his travels, Rama encountered "learned architects... they built great cities and palaces...mighty navigators, whose ships passed from the eastern to the western oceans, and from the southern to the northern seas, in ages so remote that the Sun had not yet risen from the horizon."[33] According to the *Ramayana*, these great builders and sailors called themselves the "Maya."

Chapter 12:
Norse

Scholars convinced our continent was hermetically sealed off from the outside world before the arrival of Christopher Columbus have much to reconsider. A map they long branded a hoax, because it indicates European awareness of America prior to 1492, has been found to be genuinely pre-Columbian. In July 2007, world-class experts in document authentication at the Royal Danish Academy of Fine Arts presented the results of their study at Copenhagen's International Conference on the History of Cartography. According to Rene Larsen, rector of the School of Conservation, "We have so far found no reason to believe that the Vinland Map is the result of a modern forgery. All the tests that we have done over the past five years—on the materials and other aspects—do not show any signs of fraud."[1]

The document in question does far more than prove Old World Europeans beat Columbus across the Atlantic Ocean. The Vinland Map was drawn up by the Norse, a mostly agricultural and seafaring people, greatly gifted in woodworking, poetry, and metallurgy, the direct descendants of Scandinavia's Ice Age inhabitants. By the late 8th Century CE, their growing population pressures confined in northern Europe's restricted living space combined with the onset of warmer temperatures to ignite the Viking Age. This was roughly a 200-year period that witnessed extensive overseas raids, conquest, commerce, and exploration throughout Western Europe, the Mediterranean, and Russia, and across the North Atlantic Ocean. *Viking* is derived from the Norse word for "overseas' expedition" (*vik*), and refers to the Northmen as *víkingr*, or "expedition members."

Although usually outnumbered by opponents, their fighting skills, superior weapons, far-better long-ships, and exuberant will-power generally prevailed in battle. Their British enemies eventually realized that the Vikings could only be defeated by converting them to Christianity, which commanded "thou shalt not kill" unless fellow Christians were disobedient to Church authorities. Native folk resistance to such obvious subversion was determined, until Vatican and British princely wealth bought off certain Norse chieftains, who "converted" their subjects by the sword, and cowed them into pacified parishioners. Well into the 14th Century, however, transoceanic "expeditions" were still undertaken on behalf of rich trade goods, such as furs and minerals, and to stake out new, secret territories as places of refuge for Scandinavian royal families threatened by the terrible plagues that ravaged Europe during the Middle Ages.

But in former days of Norse greatness, they braved North Atlantic hazards to establish themselves in a place on the other side of the ocean. Bound in a mid-15th Century history of the Mongols, the so-called "Vinland Map" was re-drawn from a 200-year older compilation of several, earlier maps indicating extensive knowledge of what is now the eastern United States, going back a thousand years ago. The land-mass portrayed farthest to the left, or west, identified as *Vinilanda Insula,* encompasses an area from Maine in the north to the Carolinas in the south; from the Atlantic seaboard to the Susquehanna River in central Pennsylvania.

Although compressed, and directions, as well as some proportions, are skewed, details are less distorted than geographically correct.

An overlay of the Vinland section forms a template for virtually every twist and turn of Maine's northern boundary at the Saint John River, just as the east coast down to Charelston, South Carolina, is clearly defined. Chesapeake Bay, undiscovered until 1586, and Lake Ontario, first visited by Jesuit missionaries 75 years later, are explicitly portrayed. The large region represented here must have been experienced by many Norse explorers over a protracted period of time. No single discoverer could have undertaken such extensive journeys during the course of one lifetime. Moreover, the strange combination of disproportion and accuracy does indeed suggest a later compilation of many maps made by different travelers on separate journeys over time. An anonymous medieval cartographer endeavored to combine them into a single map encompassing all areas of North America explored and known from 1000 CE.

The creation of these individual maps goes on to imply that relations between Scandinavian visitors and Native Americans must not have been as uniformly contentious as some Nordic sagas dramatized them. History records that the Vikings were as adept at commerce as they were at war, and more commonly engaged in trade than pillage. The geographical information that went into the Vinland Map could only have resulted from far-flung travels that absolutely depended on the more or less consistent good will of the indigenous people. The overwhelmingly outnumbered Scandinavians must have sensibly bartered their way across North America.

But what exactly was Vinland? And where was it? The name had been coined by famous Norseman Leif Eriksson in 1001 CE. Seventy-five years later, German geographer Adam of Bremen wrote of Eriksson in *Descriptio insularum Aquilonis* ("Description of the Northern Islands"), "he has also reported one island discovered by many in that ocean, which is called *Winland*, for the reason that grapevines grow there by themselves, producing the best wine."[2]

Two later sources—the Icelandic sagas of Eric the Red and "Of the Greenlanders"—also told of Vinland. Its precise location was unclear until authentication of the Vinland Map, although the sagas already related that it lay south of Helluland ("Flatstone Land," most likely Baffin Island for its abundance of flagstone), and Markland ("Wood Land," an apparent reference to thickly forested Labrador, where, in fact, an early-11th-Century Viking settlement was discovered at L'Anse aux Meadows in 1960, two years after the Vinland Map came to light). "Vinland," then, was not confined to Maine, as some researchers speculated, but only began there, and went on to encompass most of the eastern United States.

Although preoccupied with the Map's depiction of North America, they neglect its additionally provocative features. For example, the entire coastline of Greenland appears in details supposedly unknown until the late 19th Century, when it was officially circumnavigated for the first time. Moreover, Greenland is represented as an island, a fact likewise unappreciated until as recently as 1896, when it was thoroughly surveyed for the first time.

No less surprisingly, the Vinland Map includes two other territories allegedly unknown and unexplored by the outside world in pre-Columbian times. Although their placement and size are only roughly correct, the Atlantic islands of Andros and Puerto Rico are unmistakably portrayed. Andros lies in the Bahamas between Cuba and Florida, about 130 miles southeast of Miami and some 260 miles northeast from Havana. The Vinland Map shows only the larger, northern half of Andros, upside-down. In fact, Andros consists of two islands separated by a 12-mile gap. Beneath it, Puerto Rico appears in a more complete configuration, but improperly oriented north to south from its true, east-west axis. Such topsy-turvy positioning occurred often during the early days of cartography, especially before the advent of latitude and longitude coordinates.

The Vinland Map's verification proves that Norse seafarers had not only explored much of the North American interior from its Eastern seaboard, but had traveled to Andros and Puerto Rico, and circumnavigated Greenland almost a thousand years before modern sailors duplicated the feat. Though the utility of putting in at Puerto Rico can only be surmised, Andros is still valued for its abundance of fresh water deposits, making it a vital port-of-call for any transatlantic sailors, then or now. The Vinland Map shows that its Viking makers, the genuine discoverers of America, traveled much further than anyone imagined in modern times. Testifying to their extensive exploits are two, thin pieces of paper bound in a mid-15th-century book, the *Hystoria Tartarorum*, or "Description of the Tartars" (sometimes referred to as "The Tartar Relation"), composed in 1445.

The map of North America it contains was created for a church council at Basel, Switzerland, five years earlier. The *Hystoria Tartarorum* was acquired by Lawrence C. Witten II, an antiquarian book dealer. In 1957, he offered it for sale to Yale University. Witten's asking price was higher than his alma mater could afford, but another Yale alumnus, wealthy philanthropist Paul Mellon, agreed to purchase the book for his school if the map it contained could be authenticated by independent experts. For three years, it was secretly subjected to the ruthless scrutiny of two curators from London's British Museum and Yale's own head librarian. In 1965, the outside world learned of the Vinland Map for the first time, when they proclaimed its medieval authenticity, and Mellon purchased it for Yale, where it was insured for $25 million, and is still preserved at the University library.

Notwithstanding Yale's academic prestige or the professional credentials of its examiners, America's archaeological establishment questioned the authenticity of the Vinland Map. Their unanimous, vituperative condemnation was based on little or no counter-evidence, but stemmed almost entirely from their unalterable supposition that the Map was, *ipso facto*, a fake, because Columbus was the first and only discoverer of America. They had no less ruthlessly demeaned Helge Ingstad for daring to challenge their sacred paradigm, until the weight of physical evidence he unearthed at Labrador's L'Anse aux Meadows overcame their opposition, which they nonetheless qualified by downplaying his discovery as a botched Norse settlement of no real consequence.

The site is now regarded even by a growing number of mainstream researchers as having been a jumping-off center for the further exploration of Vinland, as documented by the assailed Map. If anything, Ingstad's discovery of the Viking settlement at L'Anse aux Meadows in 1960 verified the authenticity of the Vinland Map, which had been disclosed for the first time three years before.

In answer to the critics, Yale University Press published *The Vinland Map and the Tartar Relation* by Dr. Raleigh Ashlin Skelton, Thomas E. Marston, and George Painter.[3] Although favorably received by cartographers, historians, and document experts around the world, their book only elicited louder howls of outrage, minus any substantial argument, from U.S. archaeologists.

A "Vinland Map Conference" sponsored by the Smithsonian Institution in 1967 stoked the flames of archaeological contempt when most scholars from a broad spectrum of scientific fields reaffirmed the Map's medieval provenance. Five years later, even their majority conclusion was called into question, however, when chemical analysis found titanium dioxide, or anatase, in the Map's ink. Micro-samples retrieved by forensic specialist, Walter McCrone, and his team, were found in a rounded crystalline form manufactured for use in pale pigments since the 1920s. The yellowing of ink on the Map, he concluded, must have been the result of deliberate forgery, not aging. Haters of the Map promptly dismissed it as a proven hoax for the next 15 years. But in 1987, another forensic team led by Dr. Thomas Cahill from the University of California at Davis employed particle-induced X-ray emission to find only trace amounts of titanium dioxide in the ink. The much higher concentrations McCrone found were due to his poor sample selection.

McCrone returned to Yale to re-check his findings with new techniques, taking photo-micrographs at one-micrometer intervals through the thickness of the Map's ink samples. To his surprise, application of *Fourier* transform spectroscopy identified the ink's binder as a gelatin, most likely from animal skin, sending the Map's provenance yet again back into the Middle Ages.

The seesaw struggle over its authenticity took another turn in mid-2002, when a new process (Raman spectroscopy) revealed high levels of 1920s-like anatase. The Map's few remaining traces of black pigment consisted mostly of carbon, which should not have generated the Map lines' yellowish residue, because only pre-modern, iron-based ink leaves such a color when it decays. Most of the Map lines are yellow, whereas the rest of the *Hystoria Tartarorum* was produced entirely in iron-based ink. In Raman spectroscopy, laser light interacts with phonons (vibrations occurring in a rigid crystal lattice, such as the atomic lattice of a solid), shifting their energy up or down to identify particular chemical bonds.

Although this process has been found effective in detecting hidden explosives at airport security checkpoints, or discovering counterfeit narcotics without opening their packaging, it is not entirely reliable under all other circumstances. Smithsonian Institution chemist Jacqueline Olin later reviewed the Raman spectroscopy examination to find it flawed and suggested the ink that went into illustrating the Vinland Map could have been produced during medieval times after all. Although her analysis was supported by many other chemists, skeptics pointed out that she herself did not replicate the supposedly medieval ink.

Beginning in early 2004, Dr. Larsen and his colleagues at the Royal Danish Academy of Fine Arts initiated the longest, most in-depth and broad-based investigation of the Vinland Map so far undertaken. Chemists, cartographers, historians, conservators, and other scientists subjected it to thorough investigation from every conceivable angle. They found that all previous tests of the Map's ink were flawed and missed much of the chemical evidence. For example, the Map's allegedly early-20th-century anatase probably came from sand used to dry the wet ink, because sand was commonly used to dry ink prior to the introduction of blotter paper. "You often find remains of it in old books and manuscripts," Dr. Larsen says.[4]

Kenneth Towe, a retired geologist from the Smithsonian National Museum of Natural History in Washington, D.C., and a long-time opponent of claims for the Vinland Map's authenticity, categorized the Danes' five-year study as "bogus." He explained that "the problem is, if the anatase came out of gneiss or any other natural source, it is going to have a totally different appearance than the anatase that appears on the Vinland map ink," and, according to him, the Vinland Map's ink has small, round, chemically-produced crystals; sand would have larger, fractured crystals that resulted from grinding, along with other minerals, such as quartz.[5]

But Dr. Larsen responded by pointing out that the sand had been washed or cleaned to produce the smallest crystals. Moreover, anatase, even in relatively high levels, has since been found in many, contemporaneous books from the 15th Century and earlier. However, chemical analysis formed only part of his multi-disciplined examination, which found, among other complimentary discoveries, that wormholes in the *Hystoria Tartarorum* caused by wood-beetles were consistent with those in the Vinland Map.

A general consensus of scientific opinion applauds the lengthy, careful research conducted by Dr. Larsen and his team. They proved that the Vikings discovered, explored, and mapped much of North America 500 years before Christopher Columbus set sail for the New World. Confirmation of their impact on North America was apparent to the first Europeans who followed close behind his wake.

"In *Raccolto III* of his *Chronicles* (1556)," writes Dr. Gunnar Thompson, "the French historian, Ramusio recorded a 'Discorso,' or letter sent to the king in 1539 by a *gran Capitano.*"[6] Giovanni Battista Ramusio published *Delle navigationi e viaggi*, a collection of travelers' accounts and biographies, including the accounts of Marco Polo, and the *Descrittione dell' Africa,* a description of Ferdinand Magellan's circumnavigation of the continent. "The letter states that 'the land is called by its people *Nurumbega....* Icelandic historian, Torfaeus [Thormodus Torfaeus, 1636 to 1719, author of *Grœnlandia Antiqua*], assumed the name was derived from the old name for Norway: *Norbegia.*"[7]

The Norse word for "northern settlement," and from which "Norway" itself descended, is *Nordhan-bygda.* The American *Nurumbega* or *Norumbega* was generally applied to New England, with emphasis on an area today comprising its northernmost states, extending still further northward into Atlantic coastal Canada.

Science magazine reported the 1980 discovery of a tiny mollusk shell native to the North Sea present at several middens on the Eastern seaboard. Biologists initially assumed that the *littorina littorea* snails were probably introduced sometime during the 1800s, until the New England stone mounds, in which the shells had been deeply and originally buried, were dated to the early 11th Century.[8] A partial list of Viking Age materials retrieved from this region includes an iron chisel made by Northmen, together with iron boat rivets, found in Newfoundland, plus the discovery of rune stones from Baffin Bay to Byfield, Massachusetts. That state also yielded the foundations of Viking houses and wharves at Watertown, where, in 1889, Boston archaeologists Cornelia and Eben Norton also unearthed a Norse grinding stone at the site of an abandoned mill near the remains of a contemporaneous dam, lock, and canal.

"The people of Watertown erected a statue to commemorate the site," Dr. Thompson reported, "and a Boston firm published the Nortons' field report. Although the Nortons made a valuable contribution to American history, there was little public interest beyond their own community."[9]

In 1950, noted Danish archaeologist Dr. Johannes Brondsted compared several barrows near Sheepscott, Maine—where North Sea *littorina littorea* snail shells would later be found—to stone piles diagnostic of early Norse versions, and urged that these New England counterparts be thoroughly studied with an eye toward medieval Scandinavian influences at work on the Eastern seaboard. His suggestion was ignored. Twelve years after Dr. Brondsted's visit, his observation was supported by physical evidence, when "a dime-sized, Norse silver coin was found in southeastern Maine," reported Col. W.R. Anderson, editor of *Vikingship*, the bulletin of the Leif Eriksson Society in Evanston, Illinois.[10] It was retrieved on August 18, 1957 by a local resident from extensive archeological diggings, collectively known as "the Goddard site," of an old Native American settlement at Naskeag Point, on Penobscot Bay, near the coastal town of Blue Hill, Maine. Among the 30,000 items that emerged from the ancient Indian rubbish heap, the coin was the only non-indigenous artifact.

Generally considered a 12th Century English penny, London numismatists specializing in coinage of the Middle Ages confirmed 21 years later that it was not British, but might be Norse, and had the "Maine penny" forwarded to a leading expert in the field, Kolbjorn Skaare, at the University of Oslo. He positively identified it as having been minted during the reign of Olaf Kyrre in the early 11th Century. Also known as Olaf III, he was King of Norway from 1067 to 1093. Although the Goddard site was dated from 1180 to 1235, coins issued by the monarch were still in circulation during that period, according to Professor Skaare.

The archaeological zone's abundance of cultural materials constituted proof that the location had been at the center of a large native trading network for goods from distant sources. Also found at the Goddard site was a Dorset Eskimo *burin*, with origins in the far north. Conceivably, this lithic flake for carving wood or bone and the Norse penny had been both consecutively handed over trade routes from Labrador or Newfoundland, where the Vikings were known to have established themselves at the time.

Curators at the Maine State Museum, where the penny is preserved, have stated that "the most likely explanation for the coin's presence is that it was obtained by natives somewhere else, perhaps in Newfoundland, where the only known New World Norse settlement has been found at L'Anse aux Meadows, and that it eventually reached the Goddard site through native trade channels."[11] Mainstream archaeologists nonetheless oppose the Museum's position that it is "the only pre-Columbian Norse artifact generally regarded as genuine found within the United States."[12]

Skeptics argue that its alleged discoverer may have perpetrated a sly hoax by only pretending to have made his discovery, although no one suspected its Norse identity for more than 20 years after he found it. Their suspicions concerning Guy Mellgren, who sought neither profit not recognition from the object, are baseless. As Col. Anderson wrote of it, "a priceless rarity, the chances of its having been 'planted' are nil."[13] And although the coin may have found its way to the Goddard site through regular trade channels—an unproved speculation, however plausible—King Olaf's penny was no less probably dropped by a Norseman exploring the coast of Maine, 1,000 years ago.

Olaf Kyrre's predecessor, Olaf II Haraldsson (995–1030), had the prow of his long-ship configured to resemble the head of a bison, perhaps to commemorate, as Col. Anderson writes, "his voyage to America around 1025. No animal similar to a bison can be found in Scandinavia."[14]

The Goddard Penny is not the only physical evidence for medieval Norse visitors in Maine. One of them cut his name into a rocky ledge on the barren island of Manana, approximately three quarters of a mile long and half a mile wide, 10 miles off the south-central coastal mainland. A north-south ledge divided by a shallow dip rises at the center of Manana, from which a ravine descends to the ocean. Halfway up the ravine, on the south face of a rocky outcrop, appears a carved text. It is not a modern hoax, but first noticed as long ago as the early 19th Century by uneducated fishermen, who knew nothing about Vikings. Although the inscription has been severely eroded by centuries of exposure to wind and rain, A.C. Hamlin's illustration drew upon an 1855 plaster cast of the so-called "petroglyph," and subsequently published in Henry Rowe Schoolcraft's authoritative *History of the Indian Tribes of United States.*[15]

Mary and James Gage of the Maine Archaeological Society came to believe "that the Manana Island Petroglyph was carved by Native Americans" after comparing it to vaguely similar designs found on regional Indian pottery.[16] But these simple patterns could have just as likely derived from the more elegant Manana Island specimen, which far more resembles "long-branch" Younger Futhark, a version of the runic alphabet current during the generation of Leif Eriksson. The single line of runes is separated by a short gap that could indicate—approximately—the first and last names of one "Enhyns Lnnlthnilny." An Old Norse name still familiar in Norway and Sweden today is "Enhaynes." That at least this much can be actually translated, or at least closely inferred from the engraving, argues against its alleged Amerindian origins.

The inscription's suspected medieval Scandinavian provenance is additionally stressed by Manana's stone cairn, or circular rock pile of the kind erected by Vikings in coastal Norway as signal beacons. It is still standing, appropriately, at the island's highest elevation, from where its fires would have been visible to fellow sailors out at sea. Also found nearby was a large, finely crafted spear-point made of copper from the far-off Upper Great Lakes Region, where ancient copper mining suggestive of ancient Old World influences took place on a colossal scale.

Vinland is generally associated with Maine, an identification underscored by the Manana runes and their apparently related finds. The Maine Coon Cat first appeared, after all, in the Pine Tree State. DNA tracking of the feline traced its lineage to Norwegian Forest Cats commonly used by Scandinavian seafarers for cleansing their vessels of vermin during extended voyages in the High Middle Ages. When the Norse arrived at Vinland, at least some of their Skogkat (Norwegian Forest Cat) crewmembers jumped ship to mate with a now-extinct American breed. Descendants of these unions are today's Maine Coon Cat, living testimony to the presence of Northern Europeans in Maine, 1,000 years ago.[17]

Despite mounting evidence for medieval Scandinavians in pre-Columbian America, orthodox scholars continue to denigrate the otherwise-authenticated Viking site at L'Anse aux Meadows as an ineffectual outpost, the one and only isolated and fleeting attempt by the Northmen to establish a footing in the New World. That position was demolished in fall 2012 by the discovery of a 700-year-old Norse settlement in Canada.

A research fellow at Scotland's University of Aberdeen, Patricia Sutherland earlier led an investigative team from the Memorial University of Newfoundland (St. John's), where she is adjunct professor of archaeology, to an Atlantic coastal site high above the Arctic Circle. There, they unearthed stone remains closely resembling Viking house foundations more commonly found in Greenland. The roots of her discovery go back to her 1999 visit of Quebec's Canadian Museum of Civilization, in Gatineau, where she noticed two pieces of unusual cord that had come to light during a Baffin Island dig some decades before. Neither strand was made of animal sinew native hunters typically twisted into cordage, but yarn, as characteristically woven by Norse women in medieval Greenland. Following up on this lead, Sutherland initiated her own Tanfield Valley excavation at the extreme southern end of the island in summer 2001.

Over the next 11 years, amid ruins discovered during the mid-20th Century, she and her colleagues retrieved more local wools that had been turned into yarns—a practice unknown to Canadian aboriginals. They also found a whalebone shovel like those fashioned by Greenland Northmen, pelts belonging to Old World rats, and large stones cut and shaped by someone skilled in European masonry techniques; Bafflin Island natives did not work with large or cut stone. Most decisive were whetstones used for sharpening tools and worked according to medieval European traditional methods. When their worn grooves were examined by energy dispersive spectroscopy, Geological Survey of Canada investigators detected microscopic streaks of bronze, brass, and smelted iron—all diagnostic of Viking Age metallurgy.

Carbon-datable materials from Tanfield Valley centered on a mid-to-late-14th Century time frame, although additional, valid periods as much as 400 years earlier were also obtained. These 9th and 10th Century dates have particularly distressed archaeologists convinced the Norse made no lasting impact on the New World, especially as far back as 1,000 years ago. The Baffin Island finds contradict such a conclusion, however, because they prove that not only more than a single Viking settlement occurred in North America, but also that both the Tanfield and L'Anse aux Meadows sites were contemporary and the former continued to function for four centuries. These revelations were heightened by Sutherland's decision to go public with her findings at a meeting of the Council for Northeast Historical Archaeology in St. John's, Canada, before presenting them to her colleagues for peer review. She may have decided to preempt their foreseeable skepticism by announcing her discovery first to the popular press. If so, she had good reason for resorting to such a maneuver.

The same stone ruins where Sutherland's team found the Viking artifacts were first excavated in the 1960s by U.S. archaeologist Moreau Maxwell. He may have held back then from identifying the foundations as Norse for fear of outraging orthodox bias against Old World contacts in pre-Columbian America. To be sure, just when Maxwell began investigating the Tanfield location, that bias was showing its teeth to Helga and Ann Stine Ingstad. They were virtually alone in trying to make their case for a Viking outpost in Newfoundland against the ferocious, personal vindictiveness of fellow archaeologists.

Travel by long-ship from Greenland to Baffin Island took only three days, not much of a navigation achievement by Norse standards. Mainstream shock at Sutherland's discoveries there point up the myopic historical vision of her conventional colleagues, for whom the ocean was not an open highway for traveling to distant lands, but an impassable barrier that remained officially closed until transgressed by Christopher Columbus. In comparison with passage from Greenland, a Tanfield to L'Anse aux Meadows voyage—which the Norse sagas relate took place—is more than 325 miles.

The Vikings used their own alphabet composed of glyphs, or "runes" arranged in groups known as *futhark*, after their first six letters; *th* is formed by a single rune. Across pre-Christian Scandinavia, runic texts were carved into standing stones, usually to memorialize some important person, commemorate a significant event, or designate territorial boundaries. That the Northmen left behind similar monuments in North America long before Columbus set sail for the New World is attested by several surviving specimens. Although all of them are condemned out of hand as "forgeries" by orthodox archaeologists, skeptics are answered by evidence to the contrary. Oklahoma's Heavener Rune Stone, for example, was found by members of a tribal hunting party in the 1830s. At the time, outsiders who might have faked its inscription were forbidden from that part of Indian Territory, which had been ceded to members of the Choctaw removed from Mississippi.

Forty years later, the first men to see the rune stone were three, non-Scandinavian bear hunters, among them Wilson King, whose son, Robert, stated in 1874 that his father and two friends had stumbled upon it by accident. Thereafter, the site was popularly called "Indian Rock," because area residents, oblivious to any Norse connotations, assumed it had been carved by local Native Americans. These earliest known circumstances surrounding the location involved persons who could not have been engaged in the fabrication of an archaeological hoax. Moreover, geological indications speak to the inscription's pre-modern origins.

Image 12-1: Laura Beaudoin's original illustration of the runes envisioned by Wotan, the Germanic god of wisdom. The same chief deity was known as Votan to Middle America's Quiche Mayas, and Vodun among West Africans. Courtesy of Laura Beaudoin.

Gloria Farley, who devoted her life to studying and preserving the Heavener Rune Stone (so named in 1951), writes:

> Although there is no test to determine the antiquity of an inscription on stone, such as the C-14 test on organic matter, the weathering of the edges of carving in relation to the hardness of the stone, and the exposure to the elements, is viewed by the author as an acceptable guide. The site of the Heavener Rune Stone is in a deep ravine, protected from wind on three sides. The stone itself, twelve feet high and sixteen inches thick, is in a vertical position and thus is protected from ice erosion. The eight runes are in a straight line, six to nine inches in height, and

> still one-fourth to three sixteenths of an inch in depth. Weathering is so slow, that a date written in lead pencil on the flat gray lichen on the stone, exposed to rain and snow, was still legible seven years later. And yet the edges of the runes are smooth and rounded by weathering.[18]

Observers have also noted how lichen fills the glyphs punched into the mossy face of fine-grain Savanna sandstone, demonstrating a slow-growth process that precludes their carving in recent centuries. Ignoring these geological facts, mainstream scholars have consistently trashed the rune stone as fraudulent. When Carl F. Kemmerer sent a careful copy of its symbols to Washington, D.C.'s Smithsonian Institution in 1923, its curators simply replied that "whoever made the inscription had a Scandinavian grammar as a guide."[19] No one from the Smithsonian visited the site. Ever since, the Heavener Rune Stone has been ignored by most professional archaeologists.

Farley states:

> Scholars in America and abroad had been stumped, because the runes seemed to be a mixture of two ancient runic alphabets: six from the oldest Germanic (Old Norse) *futhark*, which came into use about 300 A.D., and the second and last runes from a later Scandinavian *futhark* used about 800 A.D. The difficulty of using the Heavener Rune Stone to demonstrate Viking exploration of the area is that the Elder *Futhark* had become obsolete by the 8th Century, long before the Viking expeditions to Greenland and Vinland. Also, only six of the eight characters are correct Elder *Futhark* runes. A transliteration would read G [rough backwards N] O M E D A [backwards L]. A runeologist from Norway transliterated the letters as G N O M E D A L, and suggested it might be a modern name, G. Nomedal. But to do this, he had to consider that

> the second rune was unfinished.

Two other runeologists said it made no sense and had to be a modern fake. None of the three had seen the Heavener Rune Stone, so apparently they failed to appreciate the labor required to carve the runes into the exceedingly hard stone, nor had they considered the weathering of the inscription in its protected location.

In 1967, a translation was offered by Alf Monge, former U.S. Army Cryptographer, born in Norway. He postulated that the Heavener runes did not form an inscription, word, or name, but correspond instead to numbers in both *futhark* versions to encrypt a specific date: 11 November 1012. It followed the founding of Newfoundland's Norse colony in 1008 by only four years.[20]

Monge's conclusion coincided with the founding in 1008 of Newfoundland's Norse colony. L'Anse aux Meadows had never been the "social failure" ascribed to it by their Establishment detractors, but, because of its untypical position very near the sea, was instead "a base camp for further exploration south," in the words of Brigitta Wallace, one of their excavators.[21]

Despite academic hostility, public interest in protecting the Oklahoma oddity had grown by the late 1960s, when the first financial appropriation on its behalf was obtained by State Senator Clem Hamilton, for whom the site's Interpretive Center was later named. Dedicated in October 1970, Heavener Rune Stone State Park is located on Poteau Mountain, where, to the southeast, with another stone with three runes in a triangular pattern was found after World War II.

Later, another stone emblazoned with a runic R and a *bindrune* (a combination of runes) was discovered on the south bank of nearby Morris Creek. Ten miles away, two 13-year-old boys climbing a hill in Le Flore County, near the town of Poteau, made a discovery of their own during 1967. The 15-inch-long Poteau Stone is covered with seven runes, 1.5 to 2 inches high, running in a straight line, and plainly highlighted

> because the bottom of the grooves were in a lighter colored layer of the stone, while the surface was dark. Tool marks in the grooves showed that

> the letters had been made with a punch, like the Heavener Rune Stone. Four of the runes are duplicates of those on the Heavener Rune Stone, and three seemed to be variants of others on it.
>
> In 1986, Richard Neilsen, Ph.D., who obtained his doctorate at the University of Denmark [and later helped authenticate Minnesota's Kensington Rune Stone, as described in Chapter 13], interviewed runeologists at the University of Oslo [to determine that] the Heavener and Poteau Rune Stones both bear a version of the same name, one being a nickname of the other. The Heavener Stone says GLOME ALLW (Alu), which means "Valley owned by GLOME," a boundary marker or land claim.[22]

Yet another rune stone was found during August 1969, this time in central Oklahoma, face down by a small stream, near the town of Shawnee, 1 mile from the North Canadian River, a tributary of the Arkansas River. While hunting serpents along a wooded path, James Estep overturned a 14-inch, oval rock buried about an inch in the soil. Instead of finding a snake, he was surprised to see five strange letters neatly cut into the underside of the stone. Its inscription was identified as Norse by curators at the Robert S. Kerr Museum, in the town of Poteau, where the Shawnee and Poteau Rune Stones are displayed. Both had been broken off a ledge, perhaps from the same ravine where the Heavener Rune Stone was inscribed.

Alone, the Heavener Rune Stone may have seemed too anomalous for belief. But finding four additional, associated texts—three of them uncovered in relative proximity—argues persuasively for their combined credibility. Their discovery anywhere along North America's Eastern seaboard would have rendered them far more convincing artifacts. In fact, however—with the lone exception of Manana Island's engraved runic name—no other, authentically Viking Age runes have come to light on the Atlantic coast of the United States, and the only alleged medieval Norse inscription found there in recent times turned out to be modern.

In 1926, the owner of Noman's Island, a 640-acre island off the coast of Martha's Vineyard (in Massachusetts), spotted a black rock by the water's edge and covered with a long, runic inscription.

Image 12-2: Shawnee Rune Stone. Photo courtesy of Wikipedia.

After its photograph began to circulate the following year, the lettered boulder attracted so much general attention, it was dubbed the "Leif Eriksson Rune Stone." Interestingly, mainstream archaeologists evinced less condemnation than uncertainty, as they were unable to decisively determine whether or not the text did indeed belong to either the 11th or 20th Century. Not until the early 1930s were they informed that the "Leif Eriksson Rune Stone" had been carved before World War I by a visiting Norwegian sailor. Episodes such as these have contributed over the decades to official skepticism whenever pre-Columbian claims are made. Yet, the owner of Noman's Island had not undertaken a hoax, but was only mistaken. And although conventional scholars predetermined against possibilities for the arrival of overseas' visitors from the Old World before 1492 were unsure about the Noman's Island inscription, a staunch cultural diffusionist, Hjalmar Holand, correctly pegged it as modern the moment he laid eyes on it.

Most North American Viking artifacts have not been discovered on the East Coast, as one might expect, but in Minnesota. "More than one hundred distinctly rounded-triangular mooring holes have been found in this state," Col. Anderson observed. "[A] number are 1.22 inches in largest measure, an odd size in both American and metric measure, but almost exactly one-tenth of the medieval Norse 'foot.'"[23]

Minnesota's greatest potential example is a sunken runic inscription found—appropriately enough—at a place called Norway Lake, located less than 90 miles northwest of Minneapolis, approximately 3 miles west of the Shakopee River, about 5 miles east from the town of Sunburg. The Upper Middle West was suffering a severe drought that lowered water levels across Minnesota throughout the summer of 1938. That August, Elmer Roen, a mechanic from nearby Brooten, was fishing beside an algae-coated boulder to which he tied his rowboat near the middle of the lake. Making his way from one end of the boat to the other, he tried to steady himself against the large stone with his right foot when he slipped, pushing off a swath of slime.

To his surprise, the exposed area revealed several inscribed letters in an unknown written language. The stone was flat on its side emblazoned with the inscription, and weighed an estimated 300 pounds. Washing away the rest of the stone face, he was amazed to see that the inscription completely covered the 4-foot-high, 5-foot-long gray granite rock. The letters ran along the stone from top to bottom, going down beneath the surface of the lake. Roen probed along the stone under the cold, turbid water with his fingertips, feeling—not seeing—more incised characters. But he was not the first man to find them.

About 50 years earlier, another drought revealed the same stone to Henry Moen, a Sunburg grocery-store owner. Because he found it a few years before the more famous Kensington Rune Stone came to light, the latter's well-publicized discovery in 1898 could not have inspired Moen to commit a hoax. Moreover, he had a reputation among his fellow townsmen for credibility, but with no interest in history. As an educated man, he nonetheless immediately recognized the inscription as runic, because he had been shown many Norse runes during a previous visit to his native Norway. Minnesota's Norway Lake stone was next glimpsed in 1934 by one "Foxy" Anderson, who hid behind it to ogle the local Qualm sisters exposing themselves to the afternoon sun. He took his eyes off the bathing beauties long enough to notice that the engraved monolith was "tombstone-like."

Two years later, Colonel Anderson (no relation to the voyeuristic Foxy, or Chicago's late-20th Century editor of the *Vikingship* newsletter) was using the boulder as a duck-blind when he observed that flaking-away algae covered what appeared to be "Native American Indian writing." Elmer Roen alone took any real interest in the Norway Lake stone during the late 1930s. Over the next two decades, he sought out one ancient writing system after another—Hebrew, Persian, Greek, Egyptian, Latin, and many more. But none of them matched his eyewitness description of the Norway Lake inscription. Although not university-trained, he was widely known for his inflexible honesty and photographic memory. Finally, by chance, he was shown the contents of a book by a well-known historian of the Norse, *A Holy Mission to Minnesota Six Hundred Years Ago.*[24] In it, author Professor Hjalmar R. Holand—earlier awarded a Guggenheim Fellowship in anthropology and cultural studies and debunker of Massachusetts' "Leif Eriksson Rune Stone"—reproduced a photograph of the Kensington Rune Stone.

Roen recognized the glyphs at once as stylistically identical to those covering the boulder in Norway Lake. He contacted Marion Dahm, head of the Minnesota Viking Society, in Chokio, and told him about the obvious comparison. In 1959, Dahm arranged for them to visit the Kensington Rune Stone preserved in Alexandria, Minnesota. Roen was struck by its resemblance to the Norway Lake script and instantly picked out eight different runes he remembered from the half-sunken boulder. He returned to Alexandria two weeks later, when Dahm asked him to select the same, eight runes from among the several dozen engraved on the Kensington slab. Roen correctly picked them out again without a moment's hesitation.

On July 9, 1972, Dahm led a dozen other scuba divers into Norway Lake's first underwater expedition. But their all-day efforts were frustrated by the murky waters, with sub-surface visibility from 2 feet to 6 inches.

Several other attempts failed to locate the missing rune stone. It was mostly championed by Dahm, a true believer, until his death in 2006. Since then, the inscribed boulder has not been forgotten, but exceptionally poor underwater clarity has so far frustrated all efforts to pinpoint its location. The boulder's re-discovery would be a major find, more significant perhaps than that of the Kensington Rune Stone, just 45 miles to the north. Connection between both sites is easily accessible via a water route down the Chippewa to Shakopee rivers, which were even more navigable six centuries ago than they are today.

The sunken rune stone's existence was underscored by complimentary evidence that surfaced in summer 1908, when a local fisherman found a peculiar axe on a peninsula projecting into the northern section of Norway Lake.

"I picked it up and thought it must have been part of a seeding machine, or some other machinery," recalled Ole Skaalerud, but instead, the axe "was immediately recognized by the staff at several museums in Norway" as a 12th Century blade depicted in contemporaneous Norwegian paintings.[25] It was by no means the only verifiable artifact of its kind found in Minnesota, however. But as more examples came to light—regardless of the unimpeachable circumstances of their discovery or authentication by experts—they were dismissed as modern misconceptions. Skeptic Samuel Eliot Morison tried to explain them all away by stating, "[E]arly Scandinavian battleaxes unearthed in various parts of Minnesota were premiums given to collectors of labels from *Battleaxe Plug,* a popular chewing tobacco."[26]

"This prompted a letter to American Brands, Inc., whose American Tobacco Division had distributed the alleged premium," reported Col. Anderson. "An executive of that company responded, 'The *Battleaxe Plug* tobacco promotion device you inquired about was a tin tag. It was bright red in color, and was approximately one inch in length.'"[27]

Another Norse axe, though in broken condition, was recovered 3 miles south of Erdahl, by Julius Davidson, while pulling stumps on his farm about 100 miles west of Minneapolis. "Beneath one of these stumps," according to his wife, Martha, "he found this heavy axe of strange shape, the like of which he had never seen before."[28] His find was sent to Stockholm, Sweden's Historical Museum, where assistant curator Bengt Thordeman stated that the object "is in type practically identical with the St. Olaf axe (preserved at the Museum) dated to 1468."[29]

A specimen closely resembling the Erdahl find was recovered in 1933 by farmer William H. Williams while harvesting corn 8 miles south of Mora, 47 miles north of Minneapolis. Dr. O.B. Overn, president of Concordia College and the School of Mines at the University of Minnesota, which acquired the object, declared, "It is wrought iron of a composition that has not been used in axes during the last two centuries."[30]

A *halberd*, a long-handled axe with a spike on top, was discovered in 1915 by E.O. Estenson, who told how he "saw the handle of the axe stick out about two feet above the grassy surface of the bank" on the Dakota side of the Red River.[31] Estenson brought it to Charles E. Brown, at the State Historical Society of Wisconsin (Madison). "It looks to me like an ancient Norse weapon," the renowned archaeologist stated, then passed the halberd on to Sigurd Grieg at Oslo's University Museum, who declared, "Without doubt...from the period around 1500."[32]

On the Minnesota side of the same Red Lake River, Ole Jevning was boring holes for fence posts in June 1871 on the bank of a former channel as he unearthed a layer of charcoal and ashes. "When I got about two feet down," he said, "I heard something scrape against the auger, and I pulled it up, thinking I had struck a stone."[33] Instead, it was a U-shaped piece of metal known as a fire-steel, used for striking fires during the 14th Century. According to historian Eivind Engelstad at Oslo's University Museum, "The [Red Lake River] fire-steel...is of exactly the same type as the fire-steels which have been found in Norwegian graves from the Viking Age in great numbers."[34] Another medieval fire-steel later appeared at Cormorant Lake, 75 miles south of the Red Lake River find.

Just 15 miles due north from Norway Lake more confirmation of its lost rune stone was plowed up just west of Brooten in 1943 by Andrew Stene. From a previously unfarmed area of his field emerged a 20-inch-long, badly damaged sword with a zigzag pattern on its grip. Twelve years later, Stene's son, Robert, gave it (minus any details of its discovery) to Professor David J. Mack, chair of the department of metallurgical engineering at the University of Wisconsin. "This structure consists of a high carbon, wrought-iron sword," he concluded, "a most unusual material, which has not been made, to my knowledge, since the introduction of crucible steel, two hundred years ago. This is a material which was used extensively by medieval armorers."[35]

The Brooten Sword closely resembles its counterpart unearthed 120 miles to the northwest, in Clay County, but just 25 miles from Lake Comorant's Medieval fire-steel. Three miles west of the small town of Ulen, the plow of Hans O. Hansen brought up a similar edged weapon during spring 1911. Professor Holand secured notarized statements from Hanson and his neighbors concerning the sword's discovery. Holand affirmed:

> These affidavits brought out the fact that none of them had ever seen the sword before, nor had any knowledge how it had come there.... The bronze handle, including the cross-bar which serves as hilt, is 6.5 inches long, and has spiral ornamentation.... It has a long, shallow, central groove near the point, and two, nearly parallel grooves near the hilt. The quillions [cross-bar] are straight with rounded ends. The surface of the grip is corrugated and in imitation of eagle feathers.... On one side [of the cross-bar] appears a cuirass [an armored breastplate], behind which can be seen two battle-axes and a dagger in crossed

Image 12-3: The Brooten Sword. Photo courtesy of Ancient American.

formation. On the other side is the bearded head of a man surrounded by a helmet."[36]

The Ulen Sword "does vaguely resemble those created in a Romanesque style and carried by U.S. Army personnel in the early 19th Century. Upon examination, however, the Smithsonian Institution [J.E. Graf, associate director, March 4, 1939] stated that the sword was unfamiliar to them. French or English trappers in settlement times would have carried rapiers, not Roman-style swords."[37] Although the anonymous writer for Wikipedia asserts, without proof, that the artifact "is almost certainly a 19th Century French military sword," Holand points out how virtually identical examples of the Ulen Sword were portrayed in the *Historia de gentibus seup septemtrionalibus,* by Archbishop Olaus Magnus, in 1555.[38]

"The sarcophagus in the Uppsala Cathedral shows an identical specimen," Holand continues. "The carved doors of the [early 13th Century] Hyllestad Church in Norway show four swords like the sword from Ulen. Originally, the blade must have been about two feet or more in length, which was the usual length of swords of the Middle Ages. But when it was found, it was only about sixteen inches long."[39]

He speculated that its tip had been deliberately broken off by a local Plains Indian, who transformed it into a hunting knife. "The concave marks from the round head of the supposed tomahawk are still visible for a distance of about 1.5 inches on the remaining stub of the blade, and this has been flattened and widened by the impact of the blows."[40]

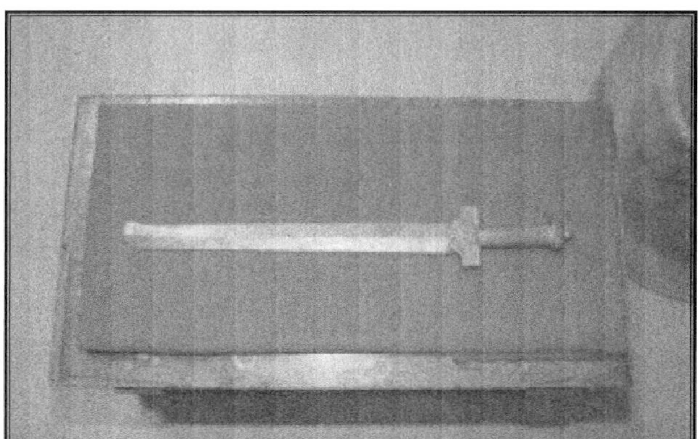

Image 12-4: The Ulen Sword. Photo courtesy of the Viking Sword Museum.

Although the Viking Sword Museum, open since 2007, is dedicated to Hans Hansen's find, the weapon darkly sealed inside its marred, clear-plastic display case is just a replica. Two years later, after he passed away at age 98, the original went to his great-grandson, Scott Hilde, who brings it out of hiding only once each year, at Ulen's mid-August "Turkey Barbecue Day," like some religious icon made public during its annual festival.

Proliferation of verifiably medieval Scandinavian artifacts throughout Minnesota—more than in any other state—indicates Norse settlement of some size across the "Land of Ten Thousand Lakes." The common 12th to 14th Century provenance of these objects likewise coincides with pandemics then ravaging Northern Europe, where Norwegian and Swedish monarchs dispatched far-flung expeditions in search of fresh territories, places of refuge from the disease-plagued Old World. As such, they came to North America's Upper Midwest in search of sanctuary, the same impetus that still inspires millions of immigrants to our continent from around the world.

Chapter 13: Knights Templar

The Kensington Rune Stone is a 202-pound greywacke sandstone stele found by Swedish immigrant farmer Olof Ohman while clearing his land in the largely rural township of Solem, Douglas County, Minnesota, in September 1898. Lying face down and entwined in the roots of a stunted, 30-year-old aspen, the 30-inch by 16-inch by 6-inch slab was covered on its face and one side with some sort of runic writing. Ohman brought it to the nearest town, Kensington, where his find was displayed at the local bank. A badly flawed copy of the inscription was forwarded to the University of Minnesota, where a translation was attempted by Olaus J. Breda. More than 100 years were to pass before scholars, correcting for the imperfect copy, could properly translate the text.

The front face reads "Eight Gotlanders and twenty-two Norwegians on (this) reclaiming/acquisition journey far west from Vinland. We had a camp by two (shelters?) one day's journey north from this stone. We were fishing one day. After we came home, we found ten men red with blood and death. Ave Maria! Save (us) from evil!" Inscribed on the side of the stone are the words, "There are ten men by the sea to look after our ships, fourteen days' journey from this island. Year 1362."[1]

Although a professor of Scandinavian languages and literature, Breda's runic knowledge was limited. But that deficiency did not prevent him from proclaiming Ohman's discovery a transparent hoax. Breda was supported by Norway's leading archaeologist of the late 19th Century, Oluf Rygh, and his colleagues at Northwestern University, in Evanston, Illinois. Their unanimous dismissal of the Minnesota rune stone was based entirely on its error-ridden facsimile, and ruined Ohman's life in an era when a man's word was truly his bond. Olof and his son Edward, who first noticed the runes on the monolith up-rooted by his father, and their neighbor, Nils Flaten, an eyewitness at the time to their discovery, had each sworn affidavits of their memories of the day the object was found, 11 years before.

Olof never tried to profit from the rune stone, often cursed the day he found it, and swore he told the whole truth about its discovery unto the hour of his death on August 27, 1935, at 80 years of age. He came to hate the artifact so much, he threw it into the dirt near his home for use as a back-door step. When Norse scholar Hjalmar Holand offered to purchase the rune stone, Ohman gladly parted with it for a pittance ($25), the only money he ever made off his reluctant discovery. With the family reputation ruined, Olof was shunned and mocked by society to the extent that his daughter, Manda, committed suicide.

Although orthodox archaeologists and linguists continued to brand the Kensington Rune Stone as fraudulent, a geologist at the Minnesota Historical Society, Newton Horace Winchell, undertook a detailed, physical analysis of the object for the first time. His tests immediately underscored Ohman's version of events, as particularly confirmed by weathering on the stone's exterior, which indicated that its inscription was not made during the late 19th Century, but could only have been carved about 500 years before. "There was strong support for an authentic rune stone date of 1362," Winchell concluded, "and little reason to suspect fraud."[2]

But his 1910 report, just one year after Ohman, his son, and his neighbor swore out their affidavit, fell into obscurity beneath the louder denunciations of skeptics, who convinced most of the outside world that the Kensington Rune Stone was a ludicrous forgery. A few amateur researchers had their doubts, however, and wondered if other, local materials might support the rune stone's pre-Columbian authenticity. They cited the inscribed text itself for internal evidence. It describes the location of the rune stone on an "island," even though the object had been found nowhere near water.

Not until 1937, when hydrological surveys were conducted for the State of Minnesota, did investigators learn that the area of discovery was virtually flooded with streams and shallow lakes during the 14th Century, and for at least 500 years before. Increasingly dry conditions beginning in the 16th Century transfigured the regional landscape into swamps and marsh, until it became the rich pasture Olof Ohman settled in the late 1800s. The hill on which he and his son found the rune stone was indeed an island, although neither he nor anyone else at the time knew it had been surrounded by water back in 1362, the inscribed date.

Researchers also pointed out several, unusual triangular holes cut into boulders, apparently very long ago, occurring along riverways leading toward Ohman's farm; 14th Century Norse seafarers, contrary to early American settlers, favored triangular mooring holes.

Not far north, and 27 years before the Kensington Rune Stone came to light, an old fire-steel identical to medieval Norse specimens at Oslo's University Museum emerged from deep beneath the bank of the Red River, near Climax, Minnesota. Compelling considerations such as these prompted investigators to seek out professional help of their own in 2000. They contacted the St. Paul–based American Petrographic Services, a firm specializing in the analysis of construction materials to determine suitability, conformance to specifications, or causes of failure. It was and is owned and headed by Scott F. Wolter, a university-trained, certified geologist, who proved that Tennessee's Bat Creek Stone had been inscribed 18 centuries ago. Now, he would be applying the same scientific criteria to the Kensington Rune Stone for its first, detailed analysis since Winchell's investigation, nearly 90 years before.

With no preconceived notions and indifferent to the outcome of his research, Wolter began using photography with a reflected light microscope, core sampling, and examination via a scanning electron microscope. During November, he presented his preliminary findings: the alleged artifact exhibited unmistakable signs of a sub-surface erosional process requiring a minimum of 200 years. In other words, the Kensington Rune Stone was buried for at least a century before Olof Ohman excavated it. Wolter's conclusion was based on the complete breakdown of mica crystals on the inscribed surface of the stone, compared to his collected samples of slate gravestones from Maine; these showed that biotite mica began to mechanically flake off their surfaces after 197 years. Skeptics endeavored to fault his determination by arguing that standards for mica degradation do not exist.

He responded:

> It is true that there is no standard for the mica degradation work I performed on the Kensington Rune Stone. The reason is, to my knowledge, I am the first to perform this type of relative dating study. Because the biotite mica began to weather off the manmade surfaces of the slate tombstones after approximately two hundred years, the Kensington Rune Stone inscription must be older than two hundred years (prior to 1898, when it was pulled from the ground), since all the mica had weathered away from the manmade surfaces.[3]

Intrigued, Wolter went on to examine each individual rune through a scanning electron microscope, which revealed some remarkable characteristics. Also noticed was a hitherto-unseen series of dots engraved inside three R-runes. This discovery was highly significant, because such dotted runes occur only on the headstones of 14th Century graves in church cemeteries at the island of Gotland, off the coast of Sweden. The Kensington Rune Stone's text dates itself to the same century and mentions eight crewmen from Gotland.

Wolter then studied and replicated the rune stone's first, long-neglected geologic report, released in 1910. Early 21st Century technology confirmed Professor Winchell's conclusion that the artifact was authentically pre-Columbian. But the proverbial "smoking gun" was discovery of a single runic letter. As Wolter explained, "the rare, medieval rune, called 'the dotted R,' was not known to modern scholars until 1935. Yet, it is found on the Kensington Rune Stone, unearthed in 1898. Interpretation: the presence of 'the dotted R' indicated the Kensington Rune Stone inscription could only have been carved during medieval times."[4]

Unequivocal verification of the Kensington Rune Stone's 14th Century identity was a true scientific triumph, establishing beyond doubt that Scandinavian seafarers arrived in the heartland of North America 130 years before Christopher Columbus left Spain in search of the New World. But Wolter expanded his research to reveal much more. He discovered that the Kensington Rune Stone was not just some pre-Columbian anomaly proving only that some Norse sailors beat the Spaniards to America. He competently defined it as a land-claim marker. In other words, the men who set it up did so to declare what later became west-central Minnesota for themselves. The inscription's date of 1362, Wolter demonstrated, was additionally encoded in the runic text itself, because its Arabic numerals were vulnerable to alteration by interlopers.

After carving, the Kensington Rune Stone was deliberately buried, and triangular-shaped holes were drilled into glacial boulders not far away; these were used to triangulate and relocate the precise position of the buried monolith. The directional marker holes are no speculation, but were recently found, and do indeed still indicate the original location of the Kensington Rune Stone's discovery by Olof Ohman. Wolter went still further in his quest for information about the artifact to learn the identity of the man who carved its inscription: a Cistercian monk from Gotland, the same Swedish island cited in the runic text.

Cistercians were the first Knights Templar, who survived the latter's immolation during the early 14th Century by migrating from France to other parts of Europe, including Gotland. Templars still resided on the island at the same time the Kensington Rune Stone was carved in 1362. One hundred forty-four years earlier, Bernard de Clairvaux—better known after his death in 1153 as Saint Bernard—selected nine Cistercian monks from his monastic order to serve as the Knights of the Poor Fellow Soldiers of Christ. He dispatched them to Palestine, where they were supposed to protect travelers on pilgrimage to the Holy Land. Welcomed by the Latin king of Jerusalem, Baudoin II, they were allowed to establish their headquarters at the site of Solomon's Temple, on the city's Temple Mount, from which the name Templar derived. Over the next 200 years, their numbers and wealth grew to such political and economic influence that they emerged as a state within a state, with its own church buildings, armies, and banks spread over all Christendom.

By the close of the 12th Century, the Knights Templar had become the first pan-European organization, its members and officers drawn equally from all over the continent, regardless of nationality, but less devoted to any particular country than to a their own theology, more Gnostic than mainstream Christian. Gnosticism emphasizes direct experience of God through mystical experience, which does not require priestly mediation. This heretical concept combined with royal greed during the early 14th Century to bring about the sudden demise of the Knights Templar.

In October 1307, King Philip IV of France issued warrants for their arrest and seized all their holdings, while Pope Clement V disbanded the Order throughout Europe. Warned in advance, Templar Jean de Châlon "heard people talking that [Gerard de Villiers, the Templar Master of France, had] put to sea with eighteen galleys, and the brother Hugues de Châlon fled with the whole treasury of the brother Hugues de Pairaud," in charge of the Order's French assets."[5] De Châlon's statement gave rise to modern theories that a "Templar fleet" loaded with riches escaped to somewhere in the Americas.

But as historian Helen Nicholson pointed out:

> [T]hey did not have more than four galleys (warships) and few other ships, and if they needed more, they hired them.... This was not a fleet in any modern sense...those would have been transport vessels, rather than warships...too shallow in draught and sailing too low in the water to be able to withstand the heavy waves and winds of the open Atlantic, and suited for use only in the relatively shallow waters of the continental shelf. What was more, they could not carry enough water to be at sea for long periods.[6]

Nicholson's correct characterization of de Villiers's forces as numerically insignificant is misleading, because they comprised only part of a combined Knights Templar fleet then concentrated in the Mediterranean Sea. With papal proscription, its vessels fled through the Straits of Gibraltar, into the Atlantic Ocean for Portugal, where they were temporarily safe from the French king and Roman pope. Re-supplied, ships and crews were joined by de Villiers's galleys on their passage to Argyll, in Scotland. In just seven years, they made themselves invaluable by turning the tide at 1314's Battle of Bannockburn, enabling Robert the Bruce to become the first king of an independent Scotland. Eighty-four years later, Henry I Sinclair, Earl of Orkney, accompanied by fellow Templars, financed and mounted a transatlantic expedition of 12 ships.

Fitchburg, Massachusetts, historian Michael Kaulback wondered why "Henry Sinclair set off with twelve ships and over three hundred men, a rather large force for an exploitative mission, across the sea? The Prince may have been looking for a place to start a colony far away from the suppression of the Templars that still raged in Europe."[7] In any case, theirs was not entirely a voyage of discovery, because Henry was supposedly informed by the survivor of four fishing boats blown across the sea to Newfoundland. From there, after 20 years, the lone castaway eventually fashioned his own makeshift craft, which carried him back to Scotland, where he died just before the Earl's expedition was about to get underway.

"It is possible that Sinclair already knew of lands west of Greenland," writes researcher Steven Sora. "The Sinclair family had Norse connections through marriage, and they were aware of the Norse settlements in the western isles."[8]

Years previous to his voyage, Henry had conferred with Nicolo Zeno, who had been put in charge of designing and outfitting the Scottish vessels. Italy's foremost cartographer and navigator later penned a detailed account that left no doubt the expedition arrived at the appropriately named Nova Scotia, "New Scotland." In 1981, directors of Nova Scotia's Ministry of Culture asked Michael Bradley, an expert on the life of Henry Sinclair, to examine the ruins of a stone structure atop a hill at the middle of the peninsula. Bradley closed his two-year investigation of the site after concluding that the remains resembled rubblework construction consistent with Scottish fortifications, as they appeared in the late 14th Century.

Kaulback described the early 20th Century discovery, off Nova Scotia, of "a cannon of the same kind displayed at the Naval Museum in Venice, and typical of the ordinance aboard Zeno's ships. The Nova Scotia cannon is presently housed in the fortress of Louisberg, on Cape Breton Island. Such artillery was obsolete by the end of the 14th Century, so the American find dates to the period of Prince Henry's expedition."[9]

Skeptics deny that he was a Templar, nor that any existed by 1398, when the Earl set sail for North America, because the Order had been officially abolished 90 years before. But they forget that Henry was also the Baron of Rosslyn, where his Chapel features an engraving portraying a Knights Templar holding his sword over the head of an initiate, to protect the secrets of the Order from being disclosed.

"Earl William St. Clair (Sinclair), the last Earl of Orkney," Kaulback writes, "was the Grand Master of Craftmasons in 1439. He was also the Grand Prior of the Scottish Knights Templar..."[10]

Rosslyn Chapel is also adorned with the carved representations of aloe cacti and ears of corn—plants native only to the eastern United States at a time when the New World was as yet officially unknown. Overlooking the obvious, deniers prefer to see instead the stylized depictions of common European wheat and strawberries, although no one has been able to point out any comparable depictions in Scotland or anywhere else throughout Europe before Christopher Columbus returned with news of his 1492 discovery. Few impartial investigators doubt that Rosslyn Chapel enshrines a lost history. Its very name, according to Rosslyn experts Tim Wallace-Murphy and Marilyn Hopkins, "translates from Scottish Gaelic as 'ancient knowledge passed down the generations.'"[11]

A key unlocking this "ancient knowledge" is the mysterious "hooked X," which not only appears on the Kensington Rune Stone, but among several other runic texts in Europe and pre-Columbian North America. As Wolter explains:

> [T]he hooked X is an important encoded runic symbol likely created by Cistercian monks. The "X" is symbolic of the allegorical representation of the duality and balance of man and woman, and heaven and earth. The "hook" in the X is symbolic of the child or offspring, representative of the continuation and perpetuation of the "goddess" ideology through common blood lines and thought.[12]

His interpretation is substantiated by medieval scholars long aware of the proto-Templar Cistercians' unusual brand of theology. Appropriately, "the hooked X appears on dated inscriptions from two exploration parties during a forty-year period," inclusive of the Kensington Rune Stone text's creation.[13] This peculiar glyph is especially helpful in authenticating a runic inscription, because it is highly unlikely to have been known to a hoaxer, appears on few artifacts, and has been credibly dated to the Middle Ages, thereby helping to establish not only

Image 13-1: Rhode Island's Newport Tower. Photo courtesy of Ancient American.

the authenticity, but the time parameters of a particular object. Accordingly, Wolter places the Kensington Rune Stone within the context of other, related finds. Among the better known is Rhode Island's Newport Tower.

Ordained by conventional archaeologists as nothing more than the ruin of a 17th-Century mill supposedly owned by the family of none other than Benedict Arnold, Wolter instead demonstrates that the stone structure in Touro Park

> was built using architecture that is not consistent with pre-Colonial construction practices before the first known recording in Benedict Arnold's will in 1677 [this was an ancestor of the later, infamous traitor of the same name].... Since the standard unit of measurement used in construction throughout New England in the 17th Century was the English foot, the Newport Tower was not built by 17th-Century colonists.[14]

Here is a first clue to the structure's real identity, whose builders, according to Kaulback

> employed a unit of measurement remembered as the "Scottish *ell.*" Known in England until Shakespeare's time, ells were based on Norse fathoms; hence, the understandable misidentification by modern Viking enthusiasts who regard the Newport Tower as the work of Northmen. It really more resembles Templar and even 14th Century Scottish counterparts, and is similar to round churches built in the Holy Land, examples being the Church of the Holy Sepulcher and the Dome of the Rock, in Jerusalem. Interestingly, it was mentioned in documents of London's public record house dating back to 1632, seven years before Rhode Island was founded.[15]

Wolter cited dating procedures applied in 1997 to the building by Danish geologist Professor Andre J. Bethune, whose carbon-14 analysis indicated that, in Bethune's words, "the Newport Tower was standing in the years 1440 to 1480."[16]

Wolter showed that its close resemblance to sacred buildings in medieval Europe and the Near East, such as Scotland's mid-12th-century Eynhallow Church in Orkney or Jerusalem's *Templum Domini*, defines the Newport Tower as a baptistery additionally employed for land-based navigational purposes.

He quoted a prominent researcher, James Whittal, who pointed out that

> the tool marks created in the dressing out of the stonework [on the Newport Tower] can directly be related to tools before 1400. These marks are unique and unknown when compared to tool marks noted in Colonial stonework.... The single and double-splay windows have prototypes in medieval Europe and in the northern isles of Scotland, in the 1300s, in churches and the bishop's palace in Orkney.... The walls were covered with a plaster stucco finish, both interior and exterior. Stucco finishing started in the 1200s, and is a feature known in Orkney and Shetland.... There is no archaeological parallel in Colonial New England for the Newport Tower and its specific architectural features.[17]

Just 8 miles across the mouth of Narragansett Bay from the Newport Tower, a mostly buried inscription was found during December 1984 by a clam-digger probing mud flats in North Kingstown, near Pojac Point. According to Janet Freedman, coastal geologist with Rhode Island's Coastal Resource Management Council, who investigated the Narragansett Rune Stone in 2012, it "had been buried and was slowly unearthed from tidal surges over the decades."[18] By the early 21st Century, the 8-foot-by-5-foot, 2-ton sandstone stood out in the water, "about twenty feet from the extreme low tide," she explained. "In 1939, that location was on the upland.... The elevation of the site at that time was lower than ten feet above mean high tide.... The inscribed boulder...is currently about thirty-five feet seaward of the shoreline structure.... By 1975, the boulder location was on the inter-tidal beach near the high water line.... It is seen on the 1988 aerial photograph in the water just offshore...."[19]

Within little more than three decades, a rapidly eroding shoreline had transferred the stone from terrestrial to marine surroundings, where the glyphs carved into the top of the boulder just protruded above the surface of the sea, subjecting them to constant wave action. They were approximately 2 inches long and cut .5 inch deep, six on one line and two just below. The uppermost line was translated by Donal Buchanan, the same epigrapher who mastered West Virginia's Grave Creek inscription, to read: "Registered Boundary Line." The two characters underneath are initials of "the owner."[20] Buchanan determined that the Narragansett runes were engraved in Vulgar Latin, a conclusion that dovetailed with Wolter's identification of a version of H dated to the late Middle Ages. This suspected period was confirmed when he located a telltale "hooked X" on the Rhode Island stone.

Wolter already demonstrated that Minnesota's Kensington Rune Stone had been aligned with additional lithic markers, as part of a land claim. The same orientation appears to have been set up to similarly affirm the Narragansett Stone's self-proclaimed purpose as a Registered Boundary Line. "Other features on the landscape were several rows of boulders that seem to align with the inscribed rock," Freedman observed. "After the photo analyses, it is clear that they were placed along earlier shorelines...."[21] The Rhode Island rune stone's position at New England's largest estuary, which functions as an expansive natural harbor, suggests that this site served visiting seafarers as an ideal headquarters location for further exploration.

Other "hooked X" specimens were uncovered far from the Narragansett Stone in 1971. They were found shallowly buried along the shores of Spirit Pond, near Popham Beach, not far from the coast of Maine. Like other accidental discoveries unfortunate enough to have been made by unaccredited persons, the three Spirit Pond stones were automatically deemed fraudulent by orthodox opinion and tossed into the Maine State Museum at

Hallowell, where Wolter took some 1,700 photographs of them from 2006 to 2007.

His examinations showed that one of the stones, apparently illustrated with a map, was strangely oriented with east at the top and north to the left, something a forger would have been unlikely to do. Yet, until 1500, medieval maps were identically oriented to place Jerusalem, in the east, at the top, something generally unknown outside academic circles. His colleague, linguist Richard Nielsen, had already determined an internal date of "1401" from the Maine artifacts' runic texts.

Only later, just 300 yards from Spirit Pond, did archaeologists uncover the remains of a Norse-style, sod-roofed building, and radio-carbon-dated its floorboards to circa 1405 CE. Wolter was likewise impressed by the convincing antiquity of a very large granite boulder illustrated with the outlines of surrounding topography and located in a town near the Merrimac River, as it flows through the northwest section of Middlesex County, Massachusetts. Known as the Tyngsboro Map Stone, it is an amazingly accurate representation of the local Merrimac River-Lake Winnipesaukee watershed.

"I was struck by the advanced stage of weathering of the manmade lines," Wolter recalled after having seen the object. "I peeled back some of the lichen, and there was virtually no difference between the cut lines and the glacial surfaces. The weathering actually surprised me. Whoever carved this did it a long time ago."[22]

Not far from the Tyngsboro Map Stone, in the same county, a better-known Massachusetts site he investigated is the Westford Knight allegedly illustrated on glacially striated, mica-schist bedrock. The image had been familiar to generations of Westford residents before it was mentioned in 1883 by Reverend Edwin Hodgeman: "Rude outlines of the human face have been traced upon it, and the figure is said to be the work of Indians."[23]

Shortly after World War II, the Westford Knight image was described at greater length in *The Ruins of Greater Ireland and*

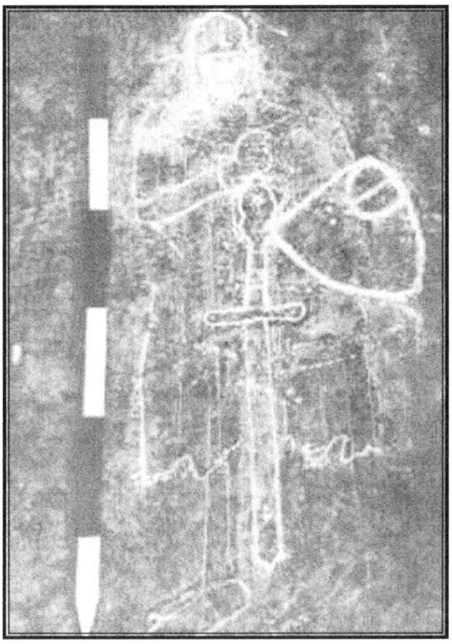

Image 13-2: The Wexford Knight was still barely discernible in 1954, when investigator Frank Glynn deftly and faithfully chalked its surviving highlights. His photograph is courtesy of Cindy Glynn.

New England. To protect the site, author W.B. Goodwin never revealed its precise whereabouts. Some years after his death, however, a determined reader, Frank Glynn, eventually tracked down the image, which had been created by many hundreds of punch-holes made with a hammer.

"Careful cleaning revealed what appeared to be the memorial effigy of a helmeted man-at-arms," writes Kaulback, "complete with sword and shield.... At its bottom was a galley; a star and crescent appeared at top-right....The image is weather-beaten, badly faded, yet barely perceptible."[24]

By the time Wolter examined it in 2006, he was unable to make out anything resembling a human figure, perhaps because it eroded away in the decades of exposure to the elements after moss covering the illustration was removed. In any case, he did clearly discern the pecked outline of a broadsword, which, according to Kaulback, "was identified by British antiquarians as a large 'hand-and-a-half wheel-pommel blade' of the 13th or 14th Century."[25] Such a weapon would make the image contemporary with Minnesota's Kensington Rune Stone.

Cultural diffusionist author Frederick Pohl commissioned an accurate impression of the Westford Stone and sent it in 1954 for evaluation to the same Thomas Charles Lethbridge, who earlier identified a Byzantine oil lamp found during the 1930s by Brant Welge, in Clinton, Connecticut. Lethbridge's research showed how the illustrated figure was wearing a "basinet" helmet of a kind in use from the 1360s to the early 15th Century. He also learned how similarly pecked effigies in the western British Isles were made at sites where knights had been killed in battle as memorials. Following two years of study, Lethbridge informed Glynn that the Massachusetts boulder clearly depicted "the arms of some maternal relation of the Sinclairs," a conclusion supported in 1973 by one of England's foremost authorities on heraldry, Sir Ian Moncreiffe.[26] The stone's portrayed "shield and coat-of-arms belonged to a branch of the Sinclair group," explains Steven Sora, "the clan of Gunn, and to a knight that was Henry Sinclair's principal lieutenant, Sir James Gunn."[27]

A short walking distance from the Westford Knight, the J.V. Fletcher Library displays a 300-pound glacial granite boulder depicting a sailing vessel in the company of an arrow and three glyphs. Wolter writes:

> All had been made using a pecking technique similar to the Westford Sword. The stone had been found only a couple of miles from the library in 1932 by a landowner named William Wyman. He moved the "boat stone" into a shed and kept it in his possession until one of his descendants gave it to the library in the early 1960s. The fact that the pecking technique was similar to the Westford Knight did not mean that the carver was the same person, but it could be an indication of the particular period when they were made. I was certain that the weathering of both the Westford Boat Stone and the Westford Knight were not made in the past several decades, and could very well be many hundreds of years old.[28]

These artifacts have become invaluable for confirming their pre-Columbian provenance, thanks to an accredited scientist, a professional geologist. As such, he has removed them from the uncertain speculation of amateur theorists. More importantly, Scott Wolter has demonstrated that they are pieces of a puzzle far greater than its individual parts. Others include Templar artifacts "discovered in the Province of Quebec and elsewhere in the Maritime Provinces of Canada," writes Gerard Leduc in *Ancient American.* A Templar breastplate

> was found in the early 1950s by a farmer on the shores of Lake Memphremagog, which crosses into Vermont. It was purchased by Mr. Jacues Boisvert from Magog, Quebec. The surface of the metal appears free from corrosion, which suggests it was tin-plated. It has a reinforced rim all around its exterior, and the surface is incised with fine etchings illustrating various male and female figures,[29]

features characteristic of neo-Templar craftsmanship of the late 14th Century. This was the same period that Prince Henry Sinclair appears to have arrived in New England.

Leduc continues:

> A related discovery was made during the early 19th Century, in Irasburg, Vermont, not far from Lake Memphremagog, when another farmer found chain armor under a large tree stump while plowing his field. The chain-mail was made of rings about an eighth of an inch connecting a collar made of closely interwoven brass rings, all consistent with Templar armor. The object was given to surveying engineers, who happened to be in the area at that time. It was supposedly taken to New York City, as reported in an 1826 edition of *The Vermont Patriot.*[30]

On a mid-summer day in 2000, diver Nelson E. Jecas was hunting seashells along the Atlantic shores of New Jersey, near

Bernardsville, when his attention was attracted by an unusual, circular stone. One side was embossed with a Knights Templar cross; a small hole had been drilled near the edge. The 3-inch granite object impressed him as a kind of ornament or badge, its image partially water-eroded by wave action over the course of what must have been a very long time.

The very nature of the Knights Templar was secrecy. They nonetheless left behind sufficient clues to establish their singular impact on America before the arrival of Christopher Columbus, whose own father-in-law, Bartolomeu Perestrello, was, after all, head of the Order in Portugal. As such, the Admiral's arrival on the shores of our continent in 1492 may not have been the first time that the Templar cross, hugely emblazoned on the sails of his ships, appeared in the New World.

Chapter 14: Christians

During fall 2004, John Hudnall was digging up the front yard of his Lawrence County home near Southpoint, Ohio to replace a broken sewer line. About 6 feet beneath the surface of the ground, his shovel unearthed a 4-inch long, baked-clay oil lamp emblazoned with an inscrutable text.

He brought his find to Andrews University, in Berrien Springs, Michigan, where Institute of Archaeology Assistant Director David Merling dated the object from 400 to 800 CE, with origins in either the Eastern Mediterranean or Near East. He translated its faint words etched on one side to read "The light of Christ shines for all."[1]

After lending the lamp to the Huntington Museum of Art in West Virginia for public display, Hudnall donated it permanently to Andrews University for preservation and further study. His accidental discovery not only joined a growing collection of authentic, Christian artifacts left behind in pre-Columbian

America, but roughly defined a period that coincided with the arrival of a Welsh prince in what would much later become the state of Kentucky.

The mid-16th Century *Cronica Walliae* tells how "the Lord Madoc, sonne to Owen Gwynned, Prince of Gwynedd, led a Colonie and inhabited in Terra Florida or thereabouts," in 1170.[2] Fleeing the interminable squabbles of his royal family, Madoc and his brother, Rhirid, took ship from Rhos-on-Sea, in coastal north Wales, westward across the Atlantic Ocean in a small fleet of *curraughs*. Thin strips of wood lashed to a frame of steamed and bent saplings covered by double layers of rawhide soaked in lard gave these vessels a strength and resilience to capably ride out Atlantic swells and resist battering waves. After arriving on the southeastern shores ("Terra Florida") of North America, 100 men under Rhirid's command were disembarked to found a colony, while Madoc, accompanied by a few sailors, returned to Wales. There, he recruited enough male and female settlers to outfit 10 ships, which the Prince led back over the sea, never to return.

The account has been dismissed by conventional scholars as a British ploy to assert the prior discovery, and hence legal possession, of North America by the Kingdom of England. As proof, they assert that the story attained its greatest prominence during the Elizabethan era, and point out how the earliest surviving full account of Madoc's voyage (the *Cronica Walliae* previously cited), as the first to make the claim that Madoc had come to America, was written by the Elizabethan map-maker Humphrey Llwyd in 1559, 57 years after the first voyage of Christopher Columbus to the New World.

The *Cronica Walliae* was no diffusionist fantasy, but a serious history that drew information from and was an extension of the *Brut y Tywysogion,* one of the most important primary sources for original records documenting Welsh history. This "Chronicle of the Princes" dated to the mid-14th Century, a hundred years before Columbus was born. Humphrey Llwyd was himself a prominent cartographer, whose large personal library formed the basis of the Royal Collection of books that later became Britain's first public library. He was a colleague and student of Abraham Ortelius, creator of the first modern atlas, the *Theatrum Orbis Terrarum,* or "Theatre of the World." As the first scientist to suggest that the continents had been joined together before drifting to their present positions, the Flemish genius precipitated the discovery of continental drift by 300 years. Honored with a stipend from the Crown to create the first printed map of Wales in 1567, Llwyd was an unlikely propagandist for Queen Elizabeth II. His motto, *Hwy pery klod na golyd* ("Fame lasts longer than wealth"), could have reflected Llwyd's interest in documenting the transatlantic voyages of Madoc.

They were actually described long before the *Cronica Walliae* was written—or Columbus was born—by the Welsh poet, Maredudd ap Rhys of Powys, around 1250. About that same time, Willem, the obscure author of a Middle Dutch poem, "Van den vos Reynaerde" ("Concerning Reynard the Fox"), mentioned in passing that he had previously written a work—since lost—called simply *Madoc,* an adaptation of the Welsh story. These earlier references clearly debunk skeptical opinion maligning Humphrey Llwyd as its inventor for ulterior political purposes.

Everything known about the Prince has been authenticated, even though orthodox scholars biased against any notion of pre-Columbian contacts with the Old World stop short of affirming the undertaking of his foreign expeditions. For example, Modoc's father was a verified historical figure, widely regarded as one of Wales' greatest rulers during the Middle Ages. Toward the end of Owain Gwynedd's life, incessant battles with fellow Welsh princes and against Henry II of England preoccupied him until his death in 1170. It was followed by a predictably acrimonious dispute between his sons and daughters for possession of the vacant throne. Madoc and Rhirid were, in fact, listed in late-12th Century royal annals among their father's 15 or so contentious off-spring.

Although sufficient Welsh and English evidence exists to affirm Madoc's overseas' colonization of "Terra Florida," none of it was known to the early explorers or frontiersmen who were amazed to find the singular language of Wales spoken among various Native American tribes. During 1608, Welsh members of

Captain Christopher Newport's visit to aboriginal villages located above the falls of the James River, in Virginia, found that the Eastern Siouan Monacan Indians spoke Welsh so thoroughly, they asked one of Newport's expedition members, the Welshman Peter Wynne, to act as an interpreter. In a November 26th letter, Wynne himself wrote, as a revealing aside to his friend John Egerton, how the Algonquians commonly referred to the Monacan as *Mandoag*, reminiscent of "Madoc." *Madogwys* was the suggestive name of another New England tribe. The Modoc Indians originally occupied an area in northeastern California and central Southern Oregon.

Sixty-one years after Wynne penned his personal account, Reverend Morgan Jones was taken prisoner in Virginia by Doeg Indians. They were about to kill him when their chief overheard the captive exclaim in his native Welch, which the chief understood, and spared his life. Jones lived among the Doeg for several months, preaching the Gospel to them in Welsh, before being allowed to return home. He related his ordeal to Thomas Lloyd, William Penn's deputy to the British Colonies, in 1686.

Similar encounters were reported for the remainder of the 17th, throughout the 18th, and well into the 19th Centuries, most famously by George Catlin. The renowned frontier artist was convinced the Mandan Indians he portrayed were part Welch, given their sometimes physical resemblance to Welsh men and women he had known, in addition to apparent linguistic similarities. His Welsh-American contemporary, Llewellyn Harris, was a Mormon missionary who visited the Zuni, a pueblo people residing along a tributary of the Little Colorado River, in western New Mexico, 34 miles south of Gallup. In 1878, Harris wrote that their language contained many Welsh words.

Long before Catlin was born, Piere Gautier deVarennes was intrigued by some fair-skinned Mandans he met near Bismarck, North Dakota, during 1738. The French explorer was more astonished to hear the Mandans speaking Welsh and see them worshipping an ancestral spirit they worshipped as *Madoc Maho*. Twenty-six years later, Maurice Griffin, a trader from Wales, after visiting the Mandans, referred to them as "white men in Red Man's dress, who understand Welsh."[3] A chief of the Asguawa Indians, who resided 800 miles southwest of Philadelphia, engaged in prolonged discussion with Joseph Roberts in the U.S. Army lieutenant's native Welsh, as reported in a May 1819 issue of the *Louisville Advertiser.*

In the mid-19th Century, James Girty, captured as a boy and later adopted by the Shawnee, served as their "runner" to the British and other Indian tribes with vital information in their joint hostilities against the American colonists, because he was naturally gifted with multi-lingual skills. By the time he met Francis Lewis, after the Revolutionary War, he could converse fluently with the Welsh signer of the Declaration of Independence in his native tongue, a knowledge that served Girty well when he later administered to the Shawnees' Mandan prisoners. While learning their language from them firsthand, he could not help but notice that their words were often very similar or identical to Welsh, so many that he compiled a *Welsh-Indian Vocabulary* of more than 350 terms, phrases, and short sentences.

His close comparisons clearly define an intimate relationship between the two languages. Girty found that such diverse, singular words as "he" (*efo*), "bread" (*bara*), "estuary" (*aber*), "river" (*nant*), "old" (*hen*), "valley" (*koom*), "blue" (*glas*), "bridge" (*pont*), and "to cross" (*croesi*)—among a great deal more—were expressed identically in Mandan and Welsh, far too many for coincidental comparisons of any kind. It goes without saying that the undereducated Girty never heard of Prince Modoc or Humphrey Llwyd's *Cronica Walliae,* but rather composed *Welsh-Indian Vocabulary* exclusively from his own, personal encounters with the Mandan. Prior to the emergence of these linguistic parallels, an early expedition into the territory west of the Great Lakes, and the first to visit the Mandan, made a cogent discovery.

During 1738, Pierre Gaultier de Varennes et de La Vérendrye found an inscribed tablet atop an upright stone, possibly a cairn, along the banks of the Missouri River, at a location near present-day Minot, North Dakota. Nearly 13 inches long, and between 4 and 5 inches wide, the text was engraved in a written language unknown to the French Canadian explorer. The Mandan told him both tablet and monolith had always been together, as far as they knew, and laid no claim to either, but told him nothing further about them. Vérendrye removed the tablet and sent it to Quebec, where Jesuit priests concluded that the inscription was "Tatarian." They forwarded it to the French Secretary of State, the Comte de Maurepas, who included it among a collection of other American artifacts for shipment to France. All were cataloged and stored in an archaeological warehouse attached to Rouen Cathedral, until World War II Allied bombers reduced the building to rubble, from which the tablet was never recovered.

Because Vérendrye is still regarded by scholars as a great explorer, whose find was validated by an equally revered, contemporaneous Swedish scientist, Pehr Kalm, researchers at the Minnesota Historical Society, in St. Paul, offered a thousand-dollar reward for the tablet's rediscovery, so far without success. Some Viking enthusiasts speculate that it was engraved with Norse runes, which faintly resemble Kazan Tatar, a Turkic language written with stick-like characters during the Kazan Khanate. But the presence of Tartars from west-central Russia in 15th Century North Dakota—or anywhere else in the New World—is as unattested as it is improbable. Moreover, Jesuit priests commonly deferred to any unfamiliar script as "Tartarian." Given the tablet's location among the Mandans, and their numerous Welsh affinities, it was more likely associated somehow with colonists led by Prince Madoc. Vérendrye's discovery was not the only lithic indication of their influence on the Mandans, however.

In 1782, John Sevier, who would later become the first governor of Tennessee, heard a venerable account of medieval foreigners in Native America firsthand from Oconostota. The revered Principal Chief of the Cherokee related how hilltop forts found in ruinous condition along the Alabama River had been built long ago by a people called the "Welsh." They raised the stone walls, he said, as protection against Oconostota's ancestors, who eventually drove the white-skinned foreigners from the region. The best-known location of these fortresses is the Devil's

Backbone, a rock formation and peninsula formed by the flow of Fourteen Mile Creek into the Ohio River, near Charlestown, Indiana, and across the Ohio River from Louisville, Kentucky. It was upon this bedrock ridge that the followers of Prince Madoc supposedly erected their defenses.

No one has done more to identify the remains of Welsh hill-forts in North America than Rick Osmon, author of *The Graves of the Golden Bear: Ancient Fortresses and Monuments of the Ohio Valley.* Using colonial-era maps, satellite imaging technology, historical accounts, official documents, archeological reports, and collaboration with several other researchers, he found the sites of more than 45 such locations. "The use of satellite imagery," Osmon explains, "allows comparison of the strategic placement of the Ohio Valley fortresses and other ancient structures to those of the British Isles."[4] A careful investigator, he found an Indiana location meeting his strict criteria for medieval military structures "in Lawrence County, very near Fishing Creek, and within half a mile of the East Fork of the White River. From here, the 12th Century Welshmen surveyed a wild landscape they dreamed of incorporating into their royal realm."[5]

A plaque at Georgia's Fort Mountain State Park repeats Oconostota's statement to Governor Sevier that the structure had been built by the Welsh to repel Indian attacks. Another plaque reading, "In memory of Prince Madoc, a Welsh explorer, who landed in 1170, and left behind, with the Indians, the Welsh language," stood on the shores of Mobile Bay, Alabama. Although erected during 1953 by the Daughters of the American Revolution, the Alabama Parks Department removed it in the early 1990s under pressure from intolerant archaeologists.

In 1792, Sevier wrote about the unearthing, near Jefferson, Missouri, of half a dozen male, human skeletons with brass armor bearing a mermaid-and-harp insignia, the Welsh coat-of-arms. Accompanying them was a stone tablet engraved with an inscription in Latin that read, "Virtuous deeds meet their just reward." Seven years later, another six skeletons in armor, similarly emblazoned with Welsh heraldry, were excavated near Jeffersonville, Indiana, on the Ohio River. Their discovery was described in an 1824 letter to John S. Williams, editor of *The American Pioneer*, from Thomas Spottswood Hinde, a noted historian and biographer. Also during the early 19th century, more armor breastplates bearing mermaid-and-harp imagery were uncovered outside Louisville, Kentucky, together with a severely weathered tombstone, its text entirely effaced by erosion, save for the date 1186 CE. Sevier described his Chief Oconostota interview in 1810 correspondence with his friend Major Amos Stoddard.

A particularly interesting discovery associated with 12th Century Welsh colonists in North America was made during autumn 1912 by farmer Craig Crecelius as he was working his field near the Ohio River in Paradise Bottoms, just west of Battletown, Meade County, in northern Kentucky. The thing that caught his attention was a flat, 27-inch-long limestone fragment inscribed on one side with a line of 24 inscrutable glyphs. For the next 53 years, he took the stone to various fairs in the hope he might meet someone who could offer a credible explanation of his find. In 1965, it came into the possession of the Meade County Library at the town of Brandenburg, where the object has since become known as the Brandenburg Stone.

Eight years later, a professional geologist who examined them declared that "the markings are of a natural, geologic origin, and not artifacts."[6] His pronouncement discouraged any further consideration by archaeologists, and the stone was removed from public view to a back room of the library, where it lay in virtual obscurity until April 1995. James Michael, president of the Ancient Kentucke Historical Association, succeeded in having the stone removed to the Falls of the Ohio Interpretive Center, in Clarksville, Indiana, for re-evaluation by Alan Wilson and Barram Blackett, amateur historians with the Arthurian Research Foundation, from Cardiff, Wales. Their expertise in Coelbren, the ancient Welsh alphabet, and Cumry, the ancient through medieval Welsh language, enabled them to translate the Brandenburg Stone inscription for the first time: "Toward strength (to promote unity), divide the land we are spread over, pure (or justly) between offspring and wisdom."[7]

Though the meaning of these words is open to interpretation, their translation into the Welsh language, as it was spoken during the Middle Ages, comprises part of the material evidence for visitors from Wales in pre-Columbian Kentucky.

A more revealing, related discovery that took Madoc's story beyond Llwyd's mid-16th Century *Cronica Walliae* was not made in North America, however, but in the East Midlands of England, near the Welsh border. During 1972, workers there were renovating the interior of a medieval church dedicated to Saint Andrew at Stoke Dry, a village with just 14 homes and a population, in 2007, of 39 residents. While carefully stripping old whitewash from a wall, the restorers were surprised by the gradual emergence of a painting depicting a royal figure, his hands behind his back, flanked on either side by representations of what appear to be Native American Indians, both of them shooting 10 arrows apiece into his body from the shoulders down to his hips.

This previously unknown illustration led James Michael and his colleagues to wonder if it was originally intended to graphically portray the fate of Prince Madoc, who disappeared from Welsh history after his second voyage across the Atlantic Ocean. At least some of his colonists who witnessed his death may have returned to Wales and told their story, which was commemorated inside Stoke Dry's church. In any case, the painting is unmistakably medieval, as revealed by its diagnostic style, a remarkable fact, because it seems to show characteristically featured indigenous Americans before such people were supposedly known to Western Europeans. Such a conclusion is supported by the name, as it was spoken in a local dialect during the High Middle Ages, for the little village. In Old British, Stoke Dry means "Evil Bow," a clear reference to the wall's illustration, its existence unsuspected by the residents prior to discovery. "Some scholars claim the scene actually depicts the martyrdom of King (later Saint) Edmund the Martyr, on 20 November 869," writes Osmon, "by followers of Ivar the Boneless [Inn Beinlausi, in Old Norse; real name,

Ivar Ragnarsson, a Viking chief]."[8] But the Norse never wore the kind of feathered headdresses portrayed at Stoke Dry.

Despite the unremitting hostility of mainstream scholars to any factual consideration of medieval Welsh arrivals in North America, the township of Madoc, Ontario, and the nearby village of Madoc are both named in the prince's memory. However, his transatlantic expeditions were not medieval voyages of discovery, but preceded by the monastic exploits of Naomh Breandán, or Bréanainn of Clonfer, better remembered as Saint Brendan, "the Navigator." His founding of numerous missions throughout the British Isles had already taken him by sea from Ireland through the Hebrides, to Wales, and up the coast to Scotland. Although these travels are historically well attested, scholars offended by implications of Old World visitors in pre-Columbian America insist his overseas' journey did not take place.

Among his 60 crewmembers was Saint Malo, which dates the seven-year, round-trip voyage from Ireland to the Land of Promise between 512 and 530 CE. The *Vita Brendani* and *Navigatio sancti Brendani abbatis* overlay an original, lost account with episodes of fantasy, which are nonetheless transparent to real encounters just beneath the surface. Included is a "coagulated sea," suggestive of an area in the North Atlantic Ocean, 700 statute miles wide by 2,000 statute miles long, floating with masses of the *genus Sargassum,* which gave its name to the Sargasso Sea. Brendan and company also experienced the eruption of a volcanic island, reminiscent of fiery Surtsey, off the coast of Ireland. Finally arriving at the Land of Promise, they find grape vines—recalling Virginia's Phoenician grapes, as described in Chapter 4—growing in profusion not far from shore.

Although the earliest, surviving records of Brendan's voyage are no older than the end of the 12th Century, Saint Aengus the Culdee cited his successful round-trip in a late 8th Century litany. Contrary to Establishment archaeologists, Brendan's transatlantic achievement has been recognized by the United States Naval Academy in Annapolis, Maryland, where a large stained-glass window commemorates his voyage. There are statues to the Navigator at Ireland's Fenit Harbour, Tralee, and the

Square Bantry, in County Cork. Numerous place-names and landmarks along the Irish coast (Brandon Hill, Brandon Point, Mount Brendan, Brandon Well, Brandon Bay, Brandon Head, etc.) memorialize his journey. Not without cause.

The *Vita Brendani* relates how he found three "choirs of anchorites" already established in the Land of Promise. A church for one of these pre-Brendan congregations has been uncovered in the southern Connecticut's Cockaponset State Forest, near the town of Guilford. John Gallager, epigrapher consultant for New Hampshire's American Institute of Archaeological Research, tells how

> a pattern of holes drilled into the rock face of an apparent altar spells out the ancient Greek Christian ICXCOYC, an acrostic for *Iesous Christos Theos Yios Soter,* or "Jesus Christ, Son of God, Savior." [An *acrostic* is a form of writing in which the first letter, syllable or word of each line or paragraph in the text spells out a word or a message.]...
>
> Appropriately, it is in the shape of a fish, an early Christian symbol for "Jesus" and "baptism".... The flame-shaped baptismal font is carved into a large rock outcrop which also contains the letters, FPBce, probably an abbreviated form for the Latin words, *Fons Pro Baptisimus Catechumen,* or "Font for the Baptism of Catechumens."
>
> A beautifully crafted carving representing overflowing water and fishes protruding from the waters lies nearby. It is symbolic of the newly baptized Christians (who were known as "little fishes") emerging from the waters of eternal life after being baptized...a *cathedra*, or throne, candelabras and an altar have been found at the site. The items indicate that it was a place of worship, an early

> Christian church.... An inscription, carved in two, different written languages [ancient Greek, as spoken in Cyrene, Libya, and Micmac; see Chapter 2], has also been recovered from the site ... A Roman Catholic priest of New York City, Father John O'Connor, has identified the Guilford inscription as a paraphrase of the Epistle of Saint Paul to the Romans (Chapter 8, Verses 14–17, and Verse 34). The writing style is 5th Century Greek, just when the Vandals invaded North Africa, where Libyan Cyrene was one of the oldest Christian bishoprics.[9]

Their violent conquest occurred during the early 5th Century, just when the Guilford church was founded, according to the linguistic evidence identified by Father O'Connor, a time frame supported by respected cultural diffusionist Frederick J. Pohl, who dated the site to circa 480 BCE.

Contemporaneous Irish Christians wrote less in Latin, however, than in *Ogam*. It consisted of an alphabet comprising long and short lines, some of them slanted, appearing above and below a single, horizontal line connecting them into spaced groups. *Ogam* was the preferred choice of Ireland's monastery scholars during the Middle Ages. Examples of this singular "grooved writing" may be seen at Monhegan Island, off the coast of Maine, and in South Woodstock, Vermont, to name only a few such sites. Before its deliberate destruction by chisel-wielding cultural criminals in the early 1990s, an *Ogam* inscription at the Laurel Branch of Goose Creek, in Clay County, Kentucky, in the southeastern part of the Bluegrass State, dated to Brendan's arrival in North America's "Land of Promise" between 512 and 530 CE. Writing for *The Kentucky Explorer* magazine, M.C. Edwards wrote how "Professor Robert Meyer, an authority on Old Irish dialects, and Professor of Celtic Studies at the Catholic University of America [Washington, D.C.], confirmed in an interview with

West Virginia Public Television that the Kentucky *Ogam* was the work of Irish monks in the 6th Century."[10]

Ogam specimens have been found as far west as Ardmore and the so-called "Anubis Cave," both locations in Oklahoma, and along the Smokey Hill River, near the small town of Kanopolis, in north-central Kansas. About 100 feet from the inscription, a *Chi Rho* has been incised into the rock face. A *Chi Rho* is a fusion of the Greek letters Chi (X) and Rho (P). Their combination makes up a monogram for the name CHRISTOS, or "Christ," widely known as a symbol referred to as the *labarum*—an Imperial Roman army standard—Christians used during the Middle Ages to identify themselves. The appearance of this sign as a petroglyph in such a remote, seldom (if ever) visited location, and the slow-growing lichen that fills the *Chi Rho*'s grooves, argue persuasively for its pre-Columbian authenticity.

The lengthiest *Ogam* example found in either North America or Ireland is West Virginian, discovered at Boone County's Horse Creek. Although attempts at its translation by Dr. Barry Fell and other epigraphers remain controversial, the inscription itself is unquestionably medieval. The same conclusion was reached by Robert L. Pyle, a teacher of archaeology at the Smithsonian Institution (Washington, D.C.), Carnegie Mellon University (a private research university at Pittsburgh, Pennsylvania), and Waynesburg College (Pennsylvania). He found that another West Virginia example of "grooved writing"—the Cook petroglyph in Wyoming County—joined with Kentucky's Goose Creek inscription mentioned above to make a particularly strong case for the existence of *Ogam* in North America.

Pyle declared:

> Resemblances were so comparable to this old script, the West Virginia and Kentucky specimens could be identified with a specific variation of *Ogam*, known as "stem type," familiar in early Christian Ireland.... In support of a conjectured relationship, the West Virginia and Kentucky petroglyphs were examined

> by university-trained scholars in Celtic linguistics. Dr. William Grant, from Edinburgh University, Scotland, and Dr. John Grant, of Oakland, Maryland, confirmed that the Wyoming County petroglyphs were indeed authentic Ogam. In 1998, and again in 2000, I was in Ireland to compare European *Ogam* scripts with their possible American counterparts. Dr. William Grant was kind enough at the time to invite my participation in research investigating the earliest known Irish *Ogam* panel. It is located in the remote and rugged mountains of southern Ireland. There, I learned that *Ogam* is commonly found on the corner edges of tombstones, not on rock formations. To my surprise, the Irish *Ogam* panel, although larger (eight feet high and twenty feet long) and more complex than its North American versions, comprised many characters virtually identical to the West Virginia and Kentucky petroglyphs.[11]

At a rock shelter near the former inscription a partial human skeleton was found in 1989. "It comprised the brachycephalic skull of an adult male," Pyle said.

> Brachycephalic, or "round headed" cranial forms suggest possible European origins. More certain was the skull's pre-Columbian provenance. Just how old it was could not be determined, however, until DNA and radio-carbon testing could be brought into play to determine its specific age and racial origins.... Mitochondrial DNA was extracted from the skull's teeth and compared to previously catalogued DNA sequences from ethnic groups around the world. No association was found among North American groups. The closest

> DNA matches were European, complimenting the skull's brachycephalic type. Radio-carbon dating established its age at 1,292 years old (+/- forty years), or 710 A.D. (+/- forty years).[12]

Discovery of an early 8th Century skull in close proximity to a written inscription of the kind common in Ireland at the same time validates both finds. They suggest that transatlantic missions from Ireland were still being undertaken 200 years after Saint Brendan's voyage to the Land of Promise.

A cogent North American artifact from his time came to light during the late 19th Century, and once more in the Mountain State. On January 19, 1897, Dr. J.P. Hale, president of the West Virginia Historical and Antiquarian Society, told how 15-year-old Frank F. McConahay found a strange figure in the Kanawha Valley. He and three, younger boys were climbing a high mountain behind Lewiston, present-day Chelyard, on Cabin Creek, more than 12 miles above Charleston.

Nancy Clark writes in *Wonderful West Virginia* Magazine:

> In the nearly inaccessible, dry crevice of a forty-foot high cliff, they discovered an unusual, doll-like object concealed beneath a large, flat four-inch-thick stone. The stone was a different color and texture from the other rocks in the cave. McConahay carried the mysterious article down from the face of the cliff, and took it home. Dr. Hale, who later visited the site, observed that the crevice from which the image was retrieved could not be seen from above or below the cliff or on either side, and found nothing else of significance in the location.[13]

However, some 20 miles above the location where the wood figure was found in Kanawha County, Dr. Hale spoke of "an ancient, extensive and unique stonework" on Armstrong Mountain, near Mount Carbon, Fayette County, up the river, on its south bank: "On the Well-marked, natural bench of a high ridge which runs back from the Kanawha River, nearly at right angles, between Armstrong and Loop Creeks, about one thousand to twelve hundred feet above river level, was built a rough, stone wall of undressed and unjointed stones, without cement or mortar...."[14]

The wall originally stood 6 to 7 feet high, and was nearly as wide at its base. Within the enclosure, Hale found a small stream with remnants of two, round towers, twenty feet high and twenty feet in diameter. Ancient burial mounds hugged the base of the mountain along the river, while a pile of stones covered each grave. Hale observed that "the mode of burial was peculiar and entirely different from that of the white settlers, Indians or mound builders. The bodies were deposited about four feet underground, horizontal from the hips down, and at an angle of about thirty degrees from the waist up, and all facing the east. This is a significant fact...."[15]

Image 14-1: The Kanawha Madonna. Photo courtesy of Ancient American.

Perhaps because the deceased had been oriented to face the direction from which they came to the Land of Promise. Dr. Hale did not discover the Armstrong Mountain stone works, which were familiar to early 19th Century settlers in the area. One of them, Paddy Huddleston, "who lived across the river from the stone walls, recalled that in the mid-1800s, when he was a boy, some native medicine men insisted that the Red Men had not built the walls. The Indians claimed that long ago the Kanawha Valley was occupied by a 'fierce race of warriors, who killed off the prehistoric palefaces.'"[16]

At 50 pounds, McConahay's thirty-six-inch long stat-

> uette had been carved from a single block of chestnut, pock-mocked with numerous insect holes. The pedestal on which the figure stands measures eight inches high, and thirteen inches in diameter, with a three-to-four-inch hole bored through the center.... Its partially eroded facial features were still discernible by surviving elevations and depressions. The left ear was intact, but the right was decayed. In general, the right side was less well-preserved than nits left.... The carved image is intact and on display in the museum of the Science and Culture Center [Charleston]. It has been dubbed the *Kanawha Madonna*, because of its resemblance to the Virgin and Child.[17]

Despite the object's modern nickname, its sex is indeterminate, but the figure held in its forearms is plainly not a human child, divine or otherwise, but more resembles a sheep. If so, then the statuette may represent Jesus, known as "the Lamb of God." In any case, Robert Pyle's 2004 radio-carbon testing of McConahay's find by Canadian laboratories dated in to circa 500 CE, about the time Saint Brendan was said to have landed in the Land of Promise.[18]

A time-related discovery of another kind was made during excavations of prehistoric burial mounds near Spencer Lake, in Burnett Country, Wisconsin, during 1935. Among the typically 6th Century Plains Indian items was the skull of a mature horse, a startling revelation, because scientific opinion mandated that the animal did not exist in the Americas before its introduction by modern Europeans after 1492. Word of the anomalous object spread like wildfire, and popular speculation grew over time to cast serious doubt on Christopher Columbus as the lone discoverer of the New World. For the next 27 years, archaeologists did not question the pre-Columbian authenticity of their find, until Ralph Linton, an original member of the excavation team that found it, published the statement of a

"Mr. P," who confessed to having intrusively buried a horse's head in the Indian mound during 1928, when he was a teenager. This explanation satisfied anyone willing to accept Linton's apparent resolution at face value.

Others had difficulty understanding how an entire team of experienced scientists could have failed to distinguish between a skull buried 1,500 years ago or during the early 20th Century, especially after the radio carbon-dating process became available to them in the 1950s. It was also hard to believe that these same professionals were unable to determine that the skull was an intrusive burial, when they had repeatedly made such distinctions at numerous other mortuary mounds across the state. Wondrous, too, was the teenager's extraordinary ability to so skillfully insert a horse's head inside a previously undisturbed earthwork that the university-trained excavators were successfully duped for more than two decades. Why he decided to bury it in a prehistoric mound seven years before the structure had even been investigated was not explained. Instead, the outside world had to rely exclusively upon the hearsay of a single archaeologist, who could provide nothing more than the alleged confession of an anonymous "Mr. P."

Had any cultural diffusionist offered such paltry "evidence" to make his case for ancient Old World influences in pre-Columbian America, he would have been rightly pilloried by the official guardians of consensus reality. Indeed, Linton's questionable version of events suggests that the horse skull found within a 6th Century context was an authentic artifact of that period, and its presumed destruction after his uncertain disclosure represented another serious loss to American prehistory. At least its associated time frame was revealing, because it corresponded to other artifacts connected with contemporaneous Irish missionaries in West Virginia and Kentucky.

Nor was the Spencer Lake discovery the only such find made in the Badger State. During summer 1984, civil engineering students and staff from the University of Wisconsin, in Madison, "excavated a small horse skeleton from one of the mounds" near Aztalan, an Upper Mississippian ceremonial urban center that flourished from circa 1200 to 1325 CE.[19]

The reluctance of salaried academics to even discuss such embarrassing discoveries was recorded by a student who endeavored to learn more about the Aztalan burial from an "archaeology professor in Milwaukee," who casually responded in a telephone conversation, "Oh, not much was written about it. A farmer had merely buried a horse in an Indian mound."[20]

Student: "Did the farmer say so?"

Professor: "No, that occurred before the present farmer moved to the farm."

Student: "Where did you grow up?"

Professor: "In New York City."

Student: "But farmers in Wisconsin either send their dead horses to rendering plants or drag them to the woods. They do not bury them, especially in an Indian mound. How do you know the farmer buried the horse there?"

Professor: "It must have been a favorite pet pony. The farmer had to have buried it, for the Indians did not have horses at the time the mound was built."

Student: "What was the radio carbon date on the horse bones?"

Professor: "Look, the State does not have money to carbon date farmer's horse bones."

"And this was supposed to be the end of the story," the student sadly reported. The professor was kind enough to get back later with information about an earlier horse burial that had been reliably carbon-dated to the 19th Century, but the Aztalan burial was not addressed.

Another writer for the *Ancient Lost Treasures* Website pointed out

> [I]t is generally agreed that the Spanish Conquistadores brought horses with them. We know that to be the case, since [Francisco]

> Pizarro defeated the Inca with a cavalry of thirty horsemen. However, the question then has to be asked: how did the Spanish war horse, generally the Andalusian, "escape" to become mustangs and pintos, the horses that seemed to be common among the Plains Indians? The Appaloosa of Eastern Washington and Idaho were raised by the Nez Perce. The Appaloosa is not related to any other horse of North America, although they do have common ancestors. The Appaloosa is most related to the horses of Scandinavia, and not the horses of Spain, indicating that it must have been here before the arrival of Columbus.[21]

Historians of the American West Jim Aston and Art Davidson write that the first Spanish explorers of the San Rafael Swell encountered horses native to the large geologic feature, approximately 75 miles by 40 miles, located in south-central Utah.[22] It would appear that at least two different breeds of horse were introduced to our continent, the first by medieval Welsh colonists and another by the Norse.

But not all Christians who arrived in pre-Columbian North America came from Ireland or Wales. During late October 2008, Brad Sutherland was overseeing digs for a private home in the southern Wisconsin town of Twin Lakes. Just 2 or 3 miles north of the Illinois border (almost midway between the cities of Milwaukee and Chicago) the immediate vicinity was sparsely developed and under-populated. As the site's rough carpenter foreman, he was responsible for clearing the property and excavation prior to construction. Sutherland was also a rock hound and, after work, eagerly sifted through the heaps of freshly piled earth for interesting specimens.

Among the pieces of common quartz crystal, feldspar and occasional fossil, a small, moderately different stone attracted his attention, particularly for its unusual, dark brown coloration. Tossed into a gathering mound of possible additions to his mineralogical collection, it was forgotten until the following February, when he got around to polishing and cleaning his latest finds. As water and brush were applied to the "brown stone," Brad was surprised to notice that it was actually a badly eroded brass or bronze coin, and it appeared to be very old. He could make out what appeared to be faint markings of some kind, but was unable to discern the coin's age or nationality.

It was described by *Forum Ancient Coins* (an Internet numismatic dealer) as a "bronze *follis*" (a coin of fixed weight associated with late or post-Imperial Times from the Eastern Roman Empire), minted in Constantinople, the former name of Istanbul, Turkey's most famous city.[23] The Website's coin approximated Wisconsin's version in weight (0.3 ounces) and maximum diameter (1.1 inches). The *Forum Ancient Coins' follis* featured an identical "obverse bust of Christ facing, wearing *nimbus criciger* [a sunburst halo], *pallium* [a large, woolen cloak worn by Greek philosophers and teachers], and a *colobium* [a sleeveless shirt associated by the Romans with civilized attire], raising his right [hand] in benediction, Gospels in left."[24]

The front face of the coin represented "Constantine X's bust facing, bearded, wearing crown and *loros* [a long scarf worn by an emperor on festive occasions], holding cross and *akakia* [a cylindrical, purple, silk roll containing dust, held by Byzantine emperors during official ceremonies, and symbolizing the mortal nature of all men]."[25]

The historical figure portrayed on both the *Forum Ancient Coins'* specimen from the ancient Old World and Brad Sutherland's Wisconsin find is Constantine X, who was crowned the Emperor of Byzantium in 1059 CE. Born Constantine Doukas, as he was originally known, and the son of a nobleman, he became politically influential through his marriage to the niece of Byzantium's leading patriarch. As such, Constantine X was something of a Christian puppet, who undercut his country's armed forces' financial support in favor of the Church. Shortly thereafter, the Seljuk Turks threatened from the east, while Norman invaders menaced from the north.

Panicked, the Emperor suddenly raised taxes to make up for the damage so recently inflicted upon the army. He initiated renewed recruitment drives, increased payroll salaries, and re-supplied the army with new weapons and equipment. His measures came too late to prevent the Norman conquest of virtually the entire Italian peninsula, a loss compounded by defeats in the Balkans and throughout Asia Minor. Aged beyond his years by these unfortunate events, despised by his over-taxed citizens, and sick with some incurable illness, Constantine X died during his 61st year in 1067.

How was it possible for one of his coins to have found its way into southern Wisconsin? That it was dropped as loose change by some careless numismatist strolling through the outback of Twin Lakes seems unlikely, as it was dug up from about 9 or 10 feet beneath the surface of the earth, indicating its deeply pre-modern provenance. Mainstream archaeologists nonetheless dismiss Brad Sutherland's discovery out of hand as insignificant and meriting no serious consideration, because it was not made by an accredited, university-trained scholar under scientifically controlled conditions. The appearance of a self-evidently legitimate artifact found in the Badger State, but minted more than 400 years before Columbus arrived in the New World, nevertheless demands a credible explanation.

Constantine X's Byzantium was in no condition to undertake transatlantic voyages, however. The formerly splendid Classical Greek urban center had been transformed in 330 CE by his namesake, who made it the Christian capital of the Roman Empire, which even before then entered into its decline. After Constantine I's death seven years later, the city was known as Constantinople—the "City of Constantine"—until the advent of Turkish reforms imposed by Mustafa Kemal Ataturk, in 1930. By the time Constantine X took over as emperor, the long extinct Roman Empire had been far less successfully supplanted by Byzantine imperialism, as politically decadent, as it was culturally inferior and spiritually benighted. Roman Civilization's precipitous descent was graphically spelled out in its own coinage, from the high works of art exemplified by the denari of Caesar

Augustus to the exceedingly crude workmanship evident in Constantine X's *follis*. Beset on all sides by military crises, the poor quality of his ships additionally contributed to the improbability of far-flung expeditions to the other side of the world.

He did, however, have in his service a group of foreign mercenaries already well acquainted with the rigors of oceanic travel and in possession of vessels sturdy enough to successfully negotiate the seas that barred other peoples from long-distance voyages. These were the Varangians, Vikings from Sweden, who sailed southward down the Volga River, through Russia to Constantinople, as early as 842 CE. In old Norse, the name is *Vaeringjar*, derived from *vaeringi* (literally, a "sworn man"), "a foreigner who has taken service with a new lord by a treaty of fealty with him, or protégé." Big, fearless men, skilled in warfare, armed with immense battleaxes, renowned for the steadfast loyalty, and commanding the most seaworthy vessels afloat, they hired themselves out as the Varangian Guard. After years of constant service, many of them returned to Sweden rich men. A few stayed on in the Byzantine world, but others, more true to Viking restlessness, sailed throughout the Mediterranean Sea and beyond in their incomparable long-ships.

Some may have ventured as far as North America, a supposition suggested by the coin Brad Sutherland found in southern Wisconsin. Its minting in the mid-11th Century coincided not only with Varangians at war along the far western borders of the Byzantine Empire. A Constantinople *follis* from that period found deep beneath the surface of the ground in North America suggests the presence of visiting Varangians, because they were, after all, paid in Byzantine coin.

That they actually arrived in southern Wisconsin is less probable. More likely, the coin Brad Sutherland discovered had been brought to Twin Lakes by an indigene, perhaps an ancestor of the Ho-Chunk, or "People of the Big Voice," who then, as now, reside in the area. It was possibly a trade item exchanged with another tribal Indian from the east, where the coin was originally received from the hand of a Varangian veteran in the service of Constantine X.

Even older Christian coins from Rome itself were found near Round Rock, in central Texas. As cited by *Science Frontiers*, Dr. Valentine J. Belfiglio, professor of government at Texas Woman's University (Dallas), stated that the circumstances of their discovery at the bottom of a so-called "Indian mound" dated to circa 800 CE confirmed their pre-Columbian provenance.[26]

Image 14-2: Silverbell crosses. Photo courtesy of Ancient American.

If these small, single objects constitute hard evidence for Christians in pre-Columbian America, caches of related artifacts found in the American Southwest and Upper Middle West amount to overwhelming proof. During 1922, the first of more than 30 crucifies, plates, swords, lances, batons, spearheads, and similar items emerged from a lime kiln gravel pit off Silverbell Road, less than 7 miles east of Tucson. Weighing as much as 90 pounds apiece, nearly half were found within a 6-foot radius. All were lead, with antimony alloy traces of copper, tin, and gold that had been crushed and smelted, then cast and shaped by hammering and smoothing.

Many were covered mostly with Latin inscriptions (a few in Hebrew) Dr. Frank Fowler, professor of Classical literature at the University of Arizona translated with little difficulty. They recounted a joint migration of Jews with Roman and British Christians fleeing chaotic conditions in Dark Age Europe. Disembarking from Calalus—the Latin form of Porto Cale, a harbor-city on the Portuguese coast—they arrived in Florida, but were soon after engaged in running combat with native peoples, who continuously drove them westward across the continent, into the Southwestern desert. Written by different scribes over the next 100 years or so, the last entry was dated in 880 CE. Dr. Gordon M. Butler, dean of the College of Mines and Engineering at the University of Arizona, personally removed two halves of a spear shaft from the Silverbell lime kiln.

Image 14-3: A copper calendrical object found among the more numerous terra-cotta Michigan Tablets. Photo courtesy of Ancient American.

"Even if we accept the hypothesis that the soil was washed down by the rains," he stated, "it is ridiculous to contend that the objects were buried there within recent years. There is no evidence of burial or of recent disturbance. To have 'planted' the soil in place would have necessitated moving tons of it at a time."[27] Moreover, the lead items were almost thoroughly encrusted with caliche, a naturally forming bond caused by chemical reaction salts with water in a gradual process requiring about 1,000 years.

James P.Grimes told *Ancient American* readers:

> There has been no suggestion that the cement-hardened caliche encased around the artifacts has been previously disturbed, indicating a complete lack of any attempts to perpetrate a hoax.... Indeed, these objects would have been very hard to fake in the 1920s, or

> even today.... The wording and syntax of both the Latin and Hebrew inscriptions are consistent with that used by the Romans of the 8th and 9th Centuries [just when the Arizona inscriptions date themselves and contemporaneous with the Round Rock, Texas, coins mentioned previously]. The main scribe who wrote the incised texts was not highly educated in Latin, coming as he did from Britain, but nevertheless, got his message across, despite misspellings, etc. If anything, his discrepancies lend added weight to the inscriptions' authenticity.[28]

Dr. Gunnar Thompson concurs, adding that the Silverbell texts "include numerous quotes from well-known Mediterranean manuscripts, such as Vergil's *Georgics*. Some phrases used in the texts, such as *Dei gratia* ("By the Grace of God"), were common mottos in medieval Europe."[29]

A far larger pre-Columbian Christian body of evidence began to emerge when early pioneers settled in Michigan, after the turn of the 19th Century. While clearing the land for their first farms, they leveled literally thousands of so-called "Indian mounds," exposing caches of copper artifacts, but more often beautifully beveled, slate plates engraved with imagery usually depicting familiar scenes in the Old Testament and New Testament. From the early 1840s until 1911, an incredible 10,000 such objects were found, mostly by farmers cultivating their fields. As in virtually all collections of such magnitude and popular interest, this one was plagued by a relatively few instances of fraud.

Many of the "Michigan Tablets" were unearthed in controlled digs supervised by reputable officials—antiquarians (as archaeologists were known then), school teachers, clergymen, law enforcement officials, doctors, surveyors, notaries, newspaper reporters, or local politicians—who signed affidavits documenting the authenticity of their excavations. Although the objects are often covered with a unique "toothbrush script" that continues to prevent translation of the texts, their images occasionally suggest Gnostic themes, which may explain the arrival in the Upper Midwest of religious heretics fleeing the persecution of fellow Christians back in Europe.

Apparently, "The light of Christ that shines for all" inscribed on John Hudnall's Dark Age oil lamp with which this chapter opened was not universally perceived by all His followers. In any case, a similar find was made during the early 1930s by Brant Welge, while digging in his family's backyard on Grove Street, not far from the harbor in Clinton, Connecticut.

The 12-year-old boy was surprised to unearth a layer of mollusk shells, from which he pulled an oval object made of fired clay, 4 or 5 inches in diameter and covered with ornate markings. Brant imagined it was a smoking pipe of some kind, and traded it to a friend, whose father showed it to the local postmaster some years later, when it was sent to Thomas Charles Lethbridge, keeper of Anglo-Saxon antiquities at Britain's Museum of Archaeology and Anthropology, in Cambridge. The renowned explorer and archaeologist responded that Brant Welge's discovery was an oil lamp made in the Byzantine Empire during the 7th or 8th Century, 200 or more years before the Byzantine coin found in Wisconsin by Brad Sutherland had been minted.

Professor Lethbridge never returned the artifact, which has since disappeared, despite concerted efforts by Connecticut folklorist Bob Bischoff to track down its whereabouts. "So, next time you stand at the foot of Waterside [dock] and gaze out over the entrance to the harbor," he writes in *The Mystery of the Lamp*,

> imagine not just stories of British gun-ships during the War of 1812, or even Native American canoes gliding gracefully across the open water. Rather, picture slipping through the parting mist, the ghostly image of an ancient trireme of the Byzantine Empire powered by banks of rowers and wonder, who were they?

Where did they come from? How did they get here, blown so far off course beyond the Pillars of Herakles, and what eventually became of those lost mariners?

Finally, consider what other mysteries may lie buried beneath the ground on which we stand, just below the level of our everyday lives, waiting to rise, bringing with them their own tales of awe and wonder at the simple turn of a young boy's spade.[30]

Notes

Introduction

1. Childress, David Hatcher. *Ancient Technology in Peru and Bolivia* (Ill.: Adventures Unlimited Press, 2012).
2. Waters, Dr. Michael, quoted by Marshal Payne in "New Evidence of Early Man: Suppressed." Bill cote/Bce Video (*www.bcevideo.com*, 2013.

Chapter 1

1. Bertman, Stephen. *Handbook to Life in Ancient Mesopotamia* (N.Y.: Facts on File, 2003).
2. Verrill, Hyatt, and Ruth Verrill. *America's Ancient Civilizations* (N.Y.: G.P. Putnam's Sons, 1953).
3. Khan Academy, *smarthistory.khanacademy.org/ziggurat-of-ur.html.*
4. Meeks, Dimitri, Chapter 4 "Locating Punt," in *Mysterious Lands* by David B. O'Connor and Stephen Quirke (Calif.: Left Coast Press, 2003).

5. Atwood, Roger. "A Monumental Feud." *Archaeology, a publication of the Archaeological Institute of America,* Volume 58, Number 4 (2005).
6. Thompson, Gunnar, PhD. *American Discovery* (Wash.: Argonauts Misty Isles Press, 1994).
7. Ibid.
8. Wanger, Willibald. *Comparative Lexical Study of Sumerian and Ntu[* (Stuttgart, Germany: W. Kohlhammer, 1935).
9. Fox, Dr. Hugh. *Home of the Gods* (Minn.: Galde Press, Inc., 2005).
10. Sagehorn, Robert, *en.wikipedia.org/wiki/Hugh_Fox.*
11. Heyerdahl, Thor. *Early Man and the Ocean* (N.Y.: Doubleday, 1979); and Fox, *Home of the Gods.*
12. Fox, *Home of the Gods.*
13. Ibid.
14. Ibid.
15. Bailey, Jim. *Sailing to Paradise* (N.Y.: Simon & Schuster, 1995).
16. Ibid.
17. Ibid.
18. Childress, *Ancient Technology in Peru and Bolivia.*
19. Verrill and Verrill, *America's Ancient Civilizations.*
20. Bailey, *Sailing to Paradise.*
21. Bertman, *Handbook to Life.*
22. Bailey, *Sailing to Paradise.*
23. Bertman, *Handbook to Life.*
24. Fox, *Home of the Gods.*
25. Solis, Ruth Shady. *The Sacred City of Caral-Supe* (Lima: Instituto Nacional de Cultura Peru, 2007).
26. Moseley, Michael E. *The Incas and Their Ancestors* (London: Thames & Hudson, 2001).
27. Joseph, Frank. *Lost Civilizations* (Pompton Plains, N.J.: New Page Books, 2011).
28. Ibid.
29. "Sumerians in Tiahuanaco?" Kemo's Journal *http://kemo-d7.livejournal.com/1458247.html.*
30. Fox, *Home of the Gods.*
31. Verrill and Verrill, *America's Ancient Civilizations.*
32. Thompson, *American Discovery*
33. Ibid.

34. Gindling, Mary. "History Mystery: Chief Joseph's Cuneiform Tablet" (*www.stumbleupon.com/su/8Pv0tq/www.helium.com/items/1636848-hisdtory-mystery-chief-josephs-cuneiform-tablet*, 2009).
35. Biggs, Robert D. "History Mystery."
36. Gindling. "History Mystery: Chief Joseph's Cuneiform Tablet."
37. Thompson, *American Discovery*
38. Farley, Gloria. "History Mystery."
39. Tiel, William. "Two Enigmatic Stones from Ohio," *Ancient American*, vol. 9, no. 58 (August 2004).
40. Although they agree that the four cuneiform tablets are authentically Sumerian, mainstream archaeologists dismiss them as insignificant. As described in *Lost Civilizations*, "Professor Owen 'suggests that we are not to make too much of the (Quaker City) find,' since 'tablets of this type were sold throughout the U.S. in the early years of this (the 20th) Century, and have shown up in various places, including garbage dumps and garage sales.' That does not explain Chief Joseph's tablet, which became public knowledge in 1877, more than twenty years before the alleged importation of Sumerian relics, nor the Hearn Tablet, which was dug up on property consistently owned by the discoverer's family since 1850. The Quaker City tablet itself was excavated from a depth of some two feet amid a cluster of Indian arrowheads—hardly the setting for a misplaced trinket from the early 20th Century. Moreover, a thorough Internet search by this author failed to turn up any suggestion that brisk sales in authentic cuneiform tablets occurred in the United States during the early 1900s, as Professor Owen stated without proof."
41. Keeler, Clyde. *Secrets of the Cuna Earthmother* (N.Y.: Exposition Press, 1960).

Chapter 2

1. Siegmar-Walter, Breckle. *Walter's Vegetation of the Earth* (Chicago, Ill.: Springer, 2002).
2. Childress, David Hatcher. *Pirates and the Lost Templar Fleet* (Ill.: Adventures Unlimited Press, 2003).
3. Casson, Lionel. *The Ancient Mariners* (Princeton, N.J.: Princeton University Press, 1991).
4. Meeks, Dimitri in *Mysterious Lands* by David B. O'Connor and Stephen Quirke (Calif.: Left Coast Press, 2003).
5. Thompson, *American Discovery*.

6. Jairazbhoy, R.A. "The Egyptians Were Here," *Ancient American* vol.2, no. 8 (Nov./Dec. 1994).
7. Johannessen, Carl L. "World Trade Between Civilizations," *Ancient American,* vol. 16, no. 94 (July/Aug. 2012).
8. May, Wayne. "Ancient Egyptians Sailed to America for Corn" in *The Lost Worlds of Ancient America* (Pompton Plains, N.J.: New Page Books, 2012).
9. Ibid.
10. Burgos-Stein, Hector. "Shared Star-Lore of Ancient Egypt and Pre-Columbian America," *Ancient American,* vol. 3, no. 23 (May/June 1998).
11. Hamilton, Ross. "Newark Mounds," *Ancient American,* vol. 4, no. 34 (Nov./Dec. 2000).
12. Lehner, Mark. *The Complete Pyramids* (London: Thames & Hudson, 2008).
13. Caroli, Kenneth. Personal correspondence with the author, November 3, 2005.
14. Hopping, Jane. "A Temple in Tennessee," *Ancient American,* vol. 10, no. 75 (May/June 2010).
15. Ibid.
16. Ibid.
17. Stafford, Russell B. "Ancient Egyptian Impact on Native Americans," *Ancient American,* vol. 2, no. 8 (June/July 1994).
18. Hopping, "A Temple in Tennessee."
19. Joseph, Frank. "Riddle of Ancient Haiti," *Ancient American* vol. 3, no. 11 (Sept./Oct. 1995).
20. Hopping, "A Temple in Tennessee."
21. Corliss, Richard. "Egyptians in Acadia?" *Science Frontiers,* no. 88 (July-Aug. 1993; *www.science-frontiers.com/sf088/sf088a01.htm*).
22. Mathieson, David Warner, The Mathieson Corrolary Blog (*mathisencorollary.blogspot.com/2011/07/case-of-micmac-hieroglyphs-powerful.html*).
23. Thompson, *American Discovery.*
24. Mathieson, The Mathieson Corrolary Blog.

Chapter 3

1. Castleden, Rodney. *Minoans* (N.Y.: Routledge, 1993).
2. Ibid.

3. Homer. *The Odyssey* (New York: Farrar, Straus and Giroux, 1998).
4. Colton, Harold Sellers. "Is the House of Tchhu the Minoan Labyrinth?" *Science*, 45:667–668 (1917).
5. Ibid.
6. Joseph, Frank. "A Minoan Pendent in Ohio," *The Lost Worlds of Ancient America* (Pompton Plains, N.J.: New Page Books, 2012).
7. Ibid.
8. DeLaCastro, Gregory. "Americans in Minoa, Minoans in America, and the Fear of History," *Ancient American,* vol. 7, no. 47 (March/April 2003).
9. Stapler, W. Meade. "Anchors of the Atlantic," *Ancient American,* vol. 4, no. 13 (Sept./Oct. 1997).
10. Miles, Jim. "Georgia Before Columbus," *Ancient American,* vol. 6, no. 51 (Jan./Feb. 2002).
11. Ibid.
12. Rothovius, Andrew. "An Aegean Script Stone from Georgia?" *NEARA Newsletter* (Vt.), 5:27–28 (1970).

Chapter 4

1. Gore, Rick, "Who Were the Phoenicians?" *National Geographic* Website (*ngm.nationalgeographic.com/features/world/asia/lebanon/phoenicians-text/5*).
2. *The World Fact Book* (*www.cia.gov/library/publications/the-world-factbook/index.html*).
3. Perry, Tom. "In Lebanon DNA May Yet Heal Rifts," Reuters (*www.reuters.com/article/2007/09/10/us-phoenicians-dna-idUSL0559096520070910*).
4. Strabo. *Geography, I: Books 1–2* (Cambridge, Mass.: Loeb Classical Library, Harvard University Press, 1917).
5. McMenamin, Mark A. *Hypersea: Life on Land* (Columbia, Mo.: Columbia University Press, 1994).
6. Toma, Bill. "New Discovery of Ancient Map Puts Phoenicians in America," *Ancient American,* vol. 10, no. 17 (May/June 1998).
7. Hoyos, Dexter. *The Carthaginians* (NY: Routledge, 2010).
8. Holley Rock, Barbara. "Ancient Egyptians of New Mexico," *Ancient American,* vol. 1, no. 3 (March/April 1998).
9. Ibid.
10. Langer, Jhonni. *Fenicios No Brasil* (June 20, 2002).

11. Martin, Gabriela. "Pré-História do Nordeste do Brasil," *Editora Universitária UFPE* (2008).
12. Gordon, Cyrus. "The Canaanite Text from Brazil," *Orientalia,* no. 37 (1968).
13. Cross, Jr., Frank Moore. "Phoenicians in Brazil?" *Biblical Archaeology Review,* vol. 26, no. 11 (1979).
14. Joffily, Geraldo Irenêo. "L'Inscription Phénicienne de Parahyba," *Zeitschriften der Deutschen Morgenländischen Gesellschaft* (Berlin), 122, 22–36 (March 1972).
15. Burns, Gerard Michael. Bad Archaeology Website (August 2012; *www.badarchaeology.com/?page_id=4212*).
16. Ibid.
17. Strabo, *Geography, I: Books 1–2.*
18. Carter, George F. *Earlier Than You Think* (College Station, Tex.: Texas A&M Press, 1980).
19. Thompson, *American Discovery.*
20. Millar, John Fitzhugh. "Did the Phoenicians Plant Grapes in Virginia?" *Ancient American,* vol. 12, no. 68 (Aug./Sept. 2011).
21. Morison, Samuel Eliot. *The European Discovery of America* (New York: Oxford University Press, 1971).
22. Ibid.
23. Millar, "Did the Phoenicians Plant Grapes in Virginia?"
24. Wirth, Diane. "California's Mystery Monolith," *Ancient American,* vol. 21, no. 68 (Jan./Feb. 2005).
25. Wonders, Lance. "A Brief Blaine Stone Provenance," *Ancient American,* vol. 13, no. 82 (Nov./Dec. 2009).
26. "Phoenician/Canaanite," Omniglot Website (*www.omniglot.com/writing/phoenician.htm*).

Chapter 5

This chapter features some excerpts from material previously published by the author in Atlantis Rising (www.atlantisrising.com) *and* New Dawn (www.newdawnmagazine.com), *with permission.*

1. Craig, Kingsley. "From Pharaoh's Punt to Solomon's Ophir," *Ancient American,* vol. 1, no. 8 (May/June 1994).
2. Avienus, Lucius Festus. *Ora Maritima* (Ill.: Ares Publishers, Inc., 1977).
3. In 1970, Edward Lee Spence discovered the wreck of the first operational submarine, CSS Hunley, lost for more than 100

years, and described by Dr. William Dudley, director of Naval History at the Naval Historical Center, as "probably the most important (underwater archaeological) find of the 20th Century."

4. Will, Dr. Elizabeth Lyding, in "Underwater Exploring Is Banned in Brazil," by Marlise Simons, *New York Times* (June 25, 1985; *www.nytimes.com/1985/06/25/science/underwater-exploring-is-banned-in-brazil.html*).
5. Fretz, Gary. "The First Europeans to Reach the New World," *Free Republic* (*www.freerepublic.com/focus/f-news/1038045/replies?c=1*).
6. Ibid.
7. Ibid.
8. Marx, Robert F. *In Quest of the Great White Gods* (New York: Crown, 1992).
9. Author's email correspondence with Robert F. Marx, and Simons, "Underwater Exploring Is Banned in Brazil."
10. Thompson, *American Discovery.*
11. Fretz, "The First Europeans to Reach the New World."
12. Childress, David. *Lost Cities & Ancient Mysteries of South America* (Ill.: Adventures Unlimited Press, 1986).
13. May, Wayne. "Romans in the Midwest," *Ancient American,* vol. 1, no. 4 (Jan./Feb. 1994).
14. Thompson, *American Discovery.*
15. Ibid.
16. Ibid.
17. Indiana University Art Museum (*www.iub.edu/~iuam/online_modules/wielgus/south_america/south_america98.html*).
18. Thompson, *American Discovery.*
19. Collins, Andrew. "Tiny Roman Bust Shows Pre-Columbian Contact With Mexico," Andrew Collins's Website (*www.andrewcollins.com/page/articles/romanbust.htm*).
20. Johnson, Clark. "Anthropologist Says Romans Beat Columbus," *Boston Globe* (February 10, 2009).
21. "Oldest Latin in America: Bust May Prove Romans Got There First," *The Express* (London), (February 10, 2000), p. 28.
22. Thompson, *American Discovery.*
23. Joseph, Frank. "Imperial Roman Artifacts Found in Wisconsin," *Ancient American,* vol. 17, no. 98 (March 2013).

24. "The Number Nineteen," Encyclopaedia Britannica Website ([]*www.britannica.com/EBcehecked/topic/1086831/the-number-nineteen*).
25. Friedman, John. "Wisconsin Lamp Is a Roman Artifact," *Ancient American*, vol. 15, no. 62 (March/April 2009).
26. Pratt, David. *An Ancient History of the North American Indians* (N.Y.: Praetorian Press, 1985).
27. Fell, Dr. Barry. "The Etymology of Some American Inscriptions," *The Epigraphic Society Occasional Publications* 3, Part 2, No. 76 (1976).
28. Thompson, *American Discovery.*
29. DeWitt Media (*www.dewittmedia.com/2012/12/page/6/*).
30. Ibid.
31. Pennington, Lee. "Roman Coins Found In Kentucky." *The Lost Worlds of Ancient America* (Pompton Plains, N.J.: New Page Books, 2012).

Chapter 6

1. Caesar, Julius. *The Gallic War[* (Mt.: Kessinger, 2007).
2. Engel, Carl. *Musica Myths and Facts, Vol. 1* (S.C.: Forgotten Books, 2012).
3. Ferrer, Alvaro Paredes. *Alonso de Ojeda: El Descubridor de Colombia* (Bogata, Colombia: Editorial Planeta Colombiana, 2006).
4. Lehmann, Martin. *Die Cosmographiae Introductio Matthias Ringmanns Und Die Weltkarte Martin Waldseemuellers Aus Dem Jahre 1507* (Vienna: Peter Lang Gmbh, 2010).
5. Conner, William D. "The Legendary Azgens," *Ancient American*, vol. 12, no. 76 (Dec. 2007).
6. Hamilton, Ross. "Holocaust of Giants," *Ancient American*, vol. 6, no. 40 (July/Aug. 2001).
7. Dragoo, Don W. *Mounds for the Dead* (Penna.: Carnegie Museum of Natural History, 1989).
8. Smith, Colette Thomas. "Legends of White Indians in the Americas," *Ancient American*, vol. 12, no. 77 (Feb. 2008).
9. Corliss, William R. *Ancient Structures,* "The Scottish Brochs" (Md.: The Sourcebook Project, 2001).
10. Scherz, James P., PhD. "The Kingman Coins," *Ancient American,* vol. 1, no. 7 (Sept./Oct. 1995).

11. *Diodori Siculi* (S.C.: BiblioLife, 2009).
12. Thompson, *American Discovery.*
13. Hansen, Evan. "The Elliot Pendant," *Ancient American,* vol. 1, no. 2 (Sept./Oct. 1993).
14. Scofield, Bruce. "Mystery Hill: America's Stonehenge," in *Sacred Sites: A Guidebook to Sacred Centers and Mysterious Places in the United States* (Minn.: Llewellyn Publications, 1992).
15. Bailey, *Sailing to Paradise.*
16. Diringer, David. *The Alphabet* (Mt.: Kessinger, 2010).
17. Buchanan, Donal. *The Decipherment of Southwest Iberic* (Vt.: Mid-Atlantic Epigraphic Society, 1991).
18. Cunningham, Bernadette. *The Annals of the Four Masters* (Dublin: Four Courts Press, 2010).
19. Fell, Barry. *America B.C.* (New York: Simon & Schuster, 1994).
20. Ibid.

Chapter 7

1. Josephus, Flavius. *The New Complete Works of Josephus* (Mich.: Kregel, 1999).
2. McCulloch, J. Huston. "The Bat Creek Stone," *Tennessee Anthropologist* 18 (Spring 1993).
3. Wolter, Scott F. "Report of Archaeopetrography Investigation on the Bat Creek Stone," *Ancient American,* vol. 14, no. 88 (Sept. 2010).
4. Deal, David Allen. "Ten Commandments and New Mexico's Mountain Citadel," *Ancient American* vol. 2, no. 9 (Oct./Nov. 1995).
5. Ibid.
6. Ibid.
7. Rome, Lydia. "New Mexico's Mystery Rock," *Ancient American,* vol. 16, no. 65 (Aug./ Sept. 1995).
8. Deal, "Ten Commandments and New Mexico's Mountain Citadel."
9. Oshmier, Samuel. "Pilgrimage to New Mexico's Mystery Mountain," *Ancient American,* vol. 16, no. 66 (Oct./Nov. 1995).
10. Rome, "New Mexico's Mystery Rock."
11. Dalton, Rex. "University Buildings Named on Shaky Ground," *Nature* 426 (374): 200–201 (2003).
12. Thompson, *American Discovery.*

13. ben Yoseif, Maggid. "Israelite East M'nashe Traced to the Four Corners," *Ancient American*, vol. 15, no. 90 (March 2011).
14. Carter, George F. *Earlier Than You Think* (College Station, Tex.: Texas A&M Press, 1980).
15. Thompson, *American Discovery*.
16. Craig, Kingsley. "From Pharaoh's Punt to Solomon's Ophir," *Ancient American*, vol. 1, no. 8 (May/June 1994).
17. Ibid.
18. Thompson, Gunnar, PhD. "The Search for King Solomon's Mines," *Ancient American*, vol. 5, no. 19/20 (May/June 1996).
19. Burgos-Stein, "Shared Star-Lore of Ancient Egypt and Pre-Columbian America."
20. Thompson, "The Search for King Solomon's Mines."
21. Childress, David Hatcher. *Ancient American* (Ill.: Adventures Unlimited Press, 2012).
22. Caroli, Kenneth. Personal correspondence with the author, April 20, 2006.
23. Griffith, Martin. "Obituary, Gene Savoy." Associated Press (September 16, 2007).
24. Thompson, "The Search for King Solomon's Mines."
25. Burgos-Stein, "Shared Star-Lore of Ancient Egypt and Pre-Columbian America."
26. Seneca, quoted in *The Jewish Encyclopedia* (*www.jewishencyclopedia.com/articles/13421-seneca-lucius-annaeus*).

Chapter 8

1. al-Umari, Chihab. *Masalik al Absar fi Mamalik el-Amsar* (Paris: Paul Geuthner, 1927).
2. Taube, Karl. *Olmec Art at Dumbarton Oaks* (Washington, D.C.: Dumbarton Oaks Research Library and Collection, 2004).
3. Haslip-Viera, Gabriel, Bernard Ortiz de Montellano, and Warren Barbour. "Robbing Native American Cultures," *Current Anthropology* (June 1997), University of Chicago Press.
4. *DesMoines Register* (*newspaperarchive.com/des-moines-register/1975-02-24/page-11*).
5. Van Sertima, Ivan. *They Came Before Columbus* (New York: Random House, 2003).
6. Barton, Paul. "New Evidence for Ancient Afro-Americans," *Ancient American*, vol. 10, no. 22 (Jan./Feb. 2004).

7. Stuart, George E. "The End of the Beginning in Maya Scholarship," *Antiquity* 68 (261): 867 (1994).
8. Leutze, Willard. "The First Americans, Red or Black?" *Ancient American*, vol. 3, no. 13 (May/June 1995).
9. Ibid.
10. Fields, Richard A. "Pre-Columbian Blacks," *Ancient American*, vol. 6, no. 42 (Nov./Dec. 2001).
11. Ibid.
12. Ibid.
13. Ibid.
14. Diehl, Richard A. *The Olmecs* (London: Thames & Hudson, 2004).
15. Fields, "Pre-Columbian Blacks."
16. Ibid.
17. Stirling, Matthew, "Early History of the Olmec Problem" Dumbarton Oaks Conference on the Olmec (Washington, D.C.,1967).
18. Hanke, Lewis. *Bartolomé de Las Casas* (Philadelphia, Penna.: University of Pennsylvania Press, 1952).
19. Martir, Pedro. *De orbe novo* (New York: Putnam, 1912).
20. Van Sertima, *They Came Before Columbus.*
21. Diehl, *The Olmecs.*
22. Ibid.
23. Grundy, Martin. "Pre-Columbian Blacks," *Ancient American*, vol. 3, no. 18 (May/June 1997).
24. Hanke, *Bartolomé de Las Casas.*
25. Leutze, "The First Americans, Red or Black?"
26. Fields, "Pre-Columbian Blacks."
27. Thompson, *American Discovery.*
28. Barton, Paul. "Olmec: Mesoamerica's First Culture," *Ancient American*, vol. 8, no. 47 (March/April 1999).
29. Ywahoo, Dhyani. *Voices of Our Ancestors* (Mass.: Shambhala, 1987).

Chapter 9

1. "Mitochondrial DNA and the Peopling of the New World," *American Scientist* (*www.americanscientist.org/my_amsci/restricted.aspx?act=pdf&id=2885494546964*).
2. "C. Loring Brace" (en.wikipedia.org/wiki/C._Loring_Brace).

3. Brace, C. Loring. *Old World Sources of the First New World Human Inhabitants* (Museum of Anthropology, University of Michigan; July 2001; *www.ncbi.nlm.nih.gov/pubmed/1148145031*.
4. Ibid.
5. Ibid.
6. Ibid.
7. Kindaichi, Kyōsuke. *Ainu Life and Legends* (Tokyo: Japanese Tourist Board, 1941).
8. Ibid.
9. S. Percy Smith. *Hawaiki* (NZ: Wellington Press, 1921).
10. Cowan, James G. *The Elements of the Aborigine Tradition* (Mass.: Element Books, 1992).
11. Spence, Lewis. *The Problem of Lemuria* (London: Rider and Co., 1933).
12. Heyerdahl, Thor. *Aku-Aku : The Secret of Easter Island* (N.Y. : Rand McNally & Co., 1958), p. 77.
13. Spence, *The Problem of Lemuria*.
14. Cavalli-Sforza, Luigi Luca. *The History and Geography of Human Genes* (Princeton, N.J.: Princeton University Press, 1996).
15. Turk, Jon. "New World's First Dwellers Japanese?" *The Japan Times* (August 16, 2007; *heritageofjapan.wordpress.com/pacing-the-paleolithic-path/did-the-prehistoric-people-of-japan-colonize-the-new-world*).
16. Ibid.
17. Davis, Nancy Yaw. *The Zuni Enigma* (New York: W.W. Norton & Company, 2001).
18. Yoshida, Professor. Personal correspondence with the author, April 7, 2013.
19. Ibid.
20. Turk, "New World's First Dwellers Japanese?"

Chapter 10

This chapter features some excerpts from material previously published by the author in Sacred Sites of the West, *courtesy* www.hancockhouse.com.

1. Wilford, John. "Chinese Outdid Columbus, Briton Says," *New York Times* (March 17, 2002).

2. Finlay, Robert. "How Not to (Re)Write World History," *Journal of World History,* vol. 15, no. 2 (June 2004).
3. Whipps, Heather. "Map Fuels Debate: Did Chinese Sail to New World Firest?" Live Science Website (February 6, 2006; *www.livescience.com/7002-map-fuels-debate-chinese-sail-world.html*).
4. Thompson, *American Discovery.*
5. Birrell, Anne, trans. *The Classic of Mountains and Seas* (New York: Penguin, 1999).
6. Andrews, Jack. "Did Ancient Chinese Visit the Grand Canyon?" *Ancient American,* vol. 6, no. 41 (Sept./Oct. 2001).
7. Ibid.
8. Nelson, Greg. "Did Chinese Visitors Leave their Mark in Prehistoric Arizona?" *Ancient American,* vol. 8, no. 50 (March/April 2003).
9. Thompson, *American Discovery.*
10. Andrews, "Did Ancient Chinese Visit the Grand Canyon?"
11. Ibid.
12. Towner, Cliff R. "Ancient Asians in Pennsylvania" in *Out of Time and Place* (Minn.: Llewellyn Publications, 1999).
13. Ibid.
14. "The Twenty-Four Histories," *New World Encyclopedia* (*www.newworldencyclopedia.org/entry/Twenty-Four_Histories*).
15. Ibid.
16. Palmer, Arthur. "Pre-Columbian Chinese Treasure Found in California," *Ancient American,* vol. 8, no. 54 (Dec. 2003).
17. Ibid.
18. Ibid.
19. "Jianwen Emperor," Wikipedia (*en.wikipedia.org/wiki/Jianwen_Emperor*).
20. Menzies, Gavin. *1421: The Year China Discovered America* (Calif.: William Morrow, 2008).
21. Childress, David Hatcher. *Lost Cities of China, Central Asia and India* (Ill.: Adventures Unlimited Press, 1987).
22. Berton, Pierre. *The Mysterious North* (Toronto, Canada: McClelland & Stewart, 1956).
23. Chow, Lily. *Chasing Their Dreams* (B.C.: Caitlin Press, 2000).
24. Childress, *Lost Cities of China, Central Asia and India*
25. Mackenzie, Donald A. *Myths of China and Japan* (N.J.: Gramercy Books, 1994).

26. Ibid.
27. Cyr, Donald, in *Sacred Sites of the West* by Frank Joseph (Wash.: Hancock House, 1997).
28. Brace, C. Loring. "Old World Sources of the First New World Human Inhabitants: A Comparative Craniofacial View," Museum of Anthropology, University of Michigan(July 2001; *www.ncbi. nlm.nih.gov/pubmed/ 1148145031*).
29. Ibid.
30. Xu, Mike. "New Evidence for Pre-Columbian Trans-Pacific Contact Between China and Mesoamerica," *Ancient American,* vol. 8, no. 50 (March/April 2003).
31. Ibid.
32. Ibid. Skeptics argue no one in the international scientific community endorses Dr. Xu's comparisons between Shang and Olmec glyphs. But one of his most outspoken supporters was Joseph Needham, elected a fellow of the Royal Society in 1941, and a fellow of the British Academy, 30 years later. In 1992, the Queen conferred on him the Companionship of Honour, and the Royal Society noted he was the only living person to hold these three titles. Long before, in 1964, eminent archaeologist Gordon Ekholm, then curator of Mexican archaeology at New York City's American Museum of Natural History, had already stated that the Olmecs owed their art style to Bronze Age China.
33. Thompson, *American Discovery.*
34. Ibid.

Chapter 11

1. Steede, Neil, and David J. Eccott. "Comalcalco: A Case for Pre-Columbian Transoceanic Contact," *Migration and Diffusion,* vol. 1, no. 5:5 (November 2001; *www.migration-diffusion.info.*
2. Ibid.
3. Ibid.
4. Ibid.
5. Ibid.
6. Ibid.
7. Ibid.
8. Ibid.
9. Ibid.
10. Ibid.

11. Cassaro, Richard. "The Balinese-Maya Connection," *New Dawn,* vol. 7, no. 1 (2013).
12. Bach, Caleb. "Michael Coe: A Question for Every Answer." Americas (Washington, D.C.), Organization of American States (January/February 1996).
13. Cassaro, "The Balinese-Maya Connection."
14. Ibid.
15. Ibid.
16. Dalton, Bill. *Indonesia* (New York: W.W. Norton & Co., Inc., 2010).
17. Childress, David Hatcher. "In Search of a Maya Pyramid in Java," *Ancient American*, vol. 1, no. 4 (Jan./Feb. 1994).
18. Caroli, Kenneth, in *Discovering the Mysteries of Ancient America* (N.J.: New Page Books, 1995).
19. Ibid.
20. Lewis, T.H. "The Camel and Elephant Mounds at Prairie du Chien," *American Antiquarian* (1884), in *Ancient Man* by William R. Corliss (Md.: The Sourcebook Project, 1978).
21. Putnam, Charles E. *Elephant Pipes* Iowa: Academy of Natural Sciences, 1885).
22. Ibid.
23. Farquharson, R.J. "The Elephant Pipe," in *American Antiquarian* (Washington, D.C.), 2:26–69 (May 1879).
24. Smith, G. Eliot. *Nature* 96:340–341 (Oct. 1915).
25. Doniger, Wendy, trans. *Hindu Myths* (New York: Penguin, 2004).
26. Ibid.
27. Thompson, Gunnar, PhD. "Maize Diffusion Before Columbus," *Ancient American*, vol. 3, no. 19/20 (Jan. 1998).
28. Ibid.
29. Ibid.
30. Ibid.
31. Ibid.
32. Cavalli-Sforza, *The History and Geography of Human Genes*
33. Valmiki. *Ramayana* (Calif.: University of California Press, 2012).

Chapter 12

This chapter features some excerpts from material previously published by the author in Atlantis Rising *magazine* (www.atlantisrising.com), *with permission.*

1. "Vinland Map Is Authentic, Expert Confirms," Medieval News Website (July 2007; *medievalnews.blogspot.com/2009/07/vinland-map-is-authentic-expert.html#!/2009/07/vinland-map-is-authentic-expert.html*).
2. Adam of Bremen. *History of the Archbishops of Hamburg-Bremen* (New York: Columbia University Press, 2002).
3. Skelton, R.A. *The Vinland Map and the Tartar Relation*(New Haven, Conn.: Yale University Press, 1996).
4. "Vinland Map Is Authentic, Expert Confirms,"
5. Archaeological Fantasies Website (*archyfantasies.wordpress.com/tag/anatase/*).
6. Thompson, *American Discovery.*
7. Ibid.
8. Anderson, Colonel W.R. "Little Known Viking Sites in America," *Ancient American*, vol. 1, no. 6 (June/July 1994).
9. Thompson, *American Discovery.*
10. Anderson, "Little Known Viking Sites in America."
11. "The Goddard Norse Coin," Maine State Museum (*www.state.me.us/museum/anthropology/norsecoinpage.html*).
12. Ibid.
13. Anderson, "Little Known Viking Sites in America."
14. Ibid.
15. Schoolcraft, Henry Rowe. *History of the Indian Tribes of United States* (Penna.: Lippincott Publishing, 1860). Schoolcraft was the first scholar to suggest that the text of West Virginia's Grave Creek Tablet, discussed in Chapter 6, was Keltic.
16. Gage, Mary, and James Gage. "The Manana Island Petroglyph," *The Maine Archaeological Society Bulletin*, vol. 44 (1) (spring 2004).
17. Hastings, Sammy. "Why I Prefer Being a Maine Coon," *Cat Lover's Magazine*, vol. 12, no. 7 (Feb. 2002).
18. Farley, Gloria Stewart. *The Heavener Rune Stone* (Ohio: Midwestern Epigraphic Society, 1990).
19. Ibid.
20. Ibid.
21. Wallace, Brigitta, in *Norse America* (Penna.: Bullfrogfilms, 2000).
22. Farley, *The Heavener Rune Stone.*
23. Anderson, "Little Known Viking Sites in America."
24. Holand, Hjalmar. *A Holy Mission to Minnesota Six Hundred Years Ago* (Minn.: Rune Stone Museum Foundation, 1959).

25. Rath, Jay. *The M-Files, True Reports of Minnesota's Unexplained Phenomena* (Wisc.: Trails Books, 1998).
26. Morison, Samuel Eliot. *The European Discovery of America* (UK: Oxford University Press, 1993).
27. Anderson, "Little Known Viking Sites in America."
28. Rath, *The M-Files, True Reports of Minnesota's Unexplained Phenomena.*
29. Ibid.
30. Ibid.
31. Ibid.
32. Ibid.
33. Ibid.
34. Ibid.
35. Ibid.
36. Holand, Hjalmar. *Westward From Vinland* (N.Y.: Duell, Sloan & Pearce, 1940).
37. Papers, The Viking Sword Museum (Ulen, Minn.; *vikingswordmuseum.com*).
38. "Ulen Sword," Wikipedia (*en.wikipedia.org/wiki/Ulen_sword*).
39. Holand, *Westward From Vinland.*

Chapter 13

This chapter features some excerpts from material previously published by the author in The Barnes Review (www.thebarnes-review.com), *with permission.*

1. Wolter, Scott F. *The Hooked X* (St. Cloud, Minn.: North Star Press of St. Cloud, Inc., 2009).
2. Ibid.
3. Wolter, Scott F. E-mail correspondence with the author, January 30, 2010.
4. Wolter, *The Hooked X.*
5. Finke, Heinrich. *Papsttum und untergang des Templerordens* (Münster: Verlag der Aschendorffschen Buch, 1907).
6. Nicholson, Helen. *The Knights Templar* (UK: Sutton Publishing, 2001).
7. Kaulback, Michael. "Was a 14th Century Templar Knight Buried in New England?" *Ancient American,* vol. 4, no. 26 (1999).
8. Sora, Steven. *The Lost Treasure of the Knights Templar* (Vt.: Destiny Books, 1999).

9. Kaulback, "Was a 14th Century Templar Knight Buried in New England?"
10. Ibid.
11. Hopkins, Tim, and Marilyn Wallace-Murphy. *Rosslyn, Guardian of the Secrets of the Holy Grail* (New York: Barnes & Noble, 2000).
12. Wolter, *The Hooked X.*
13. Ibid.
14. Ibid.
15. Bailey, *Sailing to Paradise.*
16. Wolter, *The Hooked X.*
17. "Newport Tower," Clan Sinclair Website (*sinclair.quarterman.org/600/970925.html#Newport_Tower*).
18. Freedman, Janet. "Report on the Inscribed Rock at Pojac Point," State of Rhode Island (2012).
19. Ibid.
20. Church, Chris. "Missing Rune Stone off Pojac Point Was Focus of Study," *South County Independent* (August 30, 2012; *www.independentri.com/front/article_d22659e4-f2a7-11e1-b5f1-001a4bcef887a.html*).
21. Freedman, "Report on the Inscribed Rock at Pojac Point."
22. Wolter, *The Hooked X.*
23 Hodgman, Reverend Edwin R. *History of the Town of Westford, Mass 1659–1883.* (Westford, Mass.: Westford Town History Association, 1883).
24. Kaulback, "Was a 14th Century Templar Knight Buried in New England?"
25 Ibid.
26. White, Richard. *These Stones Bear Witness* (Md.: Anchor House, 2010).
27. *The Lost Treasure of the Knights Templar*
28. Wolter, *The Hooked X.*
29. Leduc, Gerard. "Did the Templars Seek Refuge in Canada?" *Ancient American*, vol. 7, no. 44 (March/April 2002).
30. Ibid.

Chapter 14

1. Llwyd, Humphrey. *Cronica Walliae* (UK: University of Wales Press, 2003).

2. May, Wayne. "Mediterranean Lamps," in *Discovering the Mysteries of Ancient America* (N.J.: New Page Books, 2005); *Portsmouth Daily Times* (Oct. 2004).
3. Traxel, William L. *Footprints of the Welsh Indians* (N.Y.: Algora Publishing, 2004).
4. Osmon, Rick. The Graves of the Golden Bear (Ind.: Grave Distractions Publications, 2011).
5. Ibid.
6. Michael, James. "The Brandenburg Stone," *Ancient American* vol. 3, no. 19/20 (Sept. 1997).
7. Ibid.
8. Osmon, Rick. E-mail correspondence with the author, February 23, 2013.
9. Gallagher, John. "Connecticut's 5th Century Church." *Ancient American*, vol. 8, no. 54 (Dec. 2003).
10. Edwards, M.C. "Did Irish Monks Visit Kentucky 1,000 Years Before Columbus?" *Ancient American,* vol. 4, no. 30 (Dec. 1999).
11. Pyle, Robert. "An 8th Century Irishman in West Virginia," *Ancient American*, vol. 9, no. 56 (April 2004).
12. Ibid.
13. Clark, Nancy. "West Virginia's 5th Century Statue," *Ancient American*, vol. 10, no. 62 (May 2005).
14. Ibid.
15. Ibid.
16. Ibid.
17. Ibid.
18. Pyle, "An 8th Century Irishman in West Virginia."
19. "Pre-Columbian Horses in America," Ancient Lost Treasures Website (*www.ancientlosttreasures.com/forum/ viewtopic. php?f=50&t=1201*).
20. Ibid. (This quotation and the following dialogue.)
21. Ibid.
22. "Constantine X, Ducas, 25 December 1059 – 21 May 1067 A.D." Forum Ancient Coins Website (*www.forumancientcoins.com/ catalog/ roman-and-greek-coins.asp?vpar=826*).
23. Ibid.
24. Ibid.
25. Ibid.
26. Corliss, William R. *Science Frontiers* #90 (Nov.–Dec. 1993).

27. Koenig, Earl. "Roman Relics found in Arizona," *Ancient American*, vol. 5, no. 36 (Dec. 2000).
28. Grimes, James P. "Calalus, A Roman Era City in Arizona," *Ancient American*, vol. 10, no. 66 (Feb. 2006).
29. Thompson, *American Discovery*.
30. Bischoff, Bob. "The Mystery of the Lamp," *Kelseytown (Conn.) Gazette* (*kelseytown.com/History.html*).

Glossary

Amerindian A term for American Indian used in anthropological contexts.

amphora A tall ancient Greek or Roman jar with two handles and a narrow neck.

anatase A tetragonal mineral consisting of titanium dioxide and used especially as a white pigment.

culture-bearer A migrant individual who carries or transposes cultural traits between societies.

cuneiform A system of writing used in parts of the ancient Middle East.

effigy A sculpture or model.

Gerzean ware Decorated pottery from Egypt during the late pre-dynastic period, 3600–3200 BC.

Logogram A written character or symbol that represents an entire word or phrase.

Mesoamerica The region of southern North America during pre-Columbian times inhabited by the Olmecs, Mayans, and Aztecs.

Midden A dunghill or refuse heap
New World A term often used to refer to the Americas, especially during the time of European colonization
Old World A term used to refer to Europe, Asia, and Africa in a historical context.
pachyderm A large mammal with hooves or thick skin.
paleolinguistics The study of human history by linguistic means.
petroglyph A carving or inscription on a rock.
philology The study of language, especially in written historical sources.
polyculture The simultaneous cultivation of several crops in a single area.
potentate A monarch or ruler, especially an autocratic one.
sepulcher A small room or monument in which a person is buried
tegula A flat roof tile often used in ancient Roman roofs.

For More Information

American Historical Association (AHA)
400 A Street SE
Washington, DC 20003
(202) 544-2422
Website: www.historians.org
AHA provides directories of useful historical resources and publications for students.

Canadian Museum of History
100 Rue Laurier
Gatineau, QC K1A 0M8
Canada
(800) 555-5621
Website: www.historymuseum.ca

The Canadian Museum of History has exhibitions, online collections, research, and educational activities for students on Canadian history.

Canadian Museum for Human Rights
85 Israel Asper Way
Winnipeg, MB R3C 0L5
Canada
1 (877) 877-6037
Website: www.humanrights.ca
Canadian Museum for Human Rights has exhibitions and galleries dedicated to showcasing the history and current development of human rights, including a gallery on Indigenous perspectives.

Institute for the Study of the Ancient World (ISAW)
15 East 84th St.
New York, NY 10028
(212) 992-7800
Website: isaw.nyu.edu
ISAW hosts exhibitions and provides information on publications, current research projects, educational events and lectures relating to the ancient world.

Museum of Archaeology and Anthropology, University of Pennsylvania
3260 South Street
Philadelphia, PA 19104
(215) 898-4000
Website: https://www.penn.museum/
The Museum of Archaeology and Anthropology offers several collections of recovered artifacts as well as events, research, and resources for students.

National Museum of the American Indian (NMAI)
Fourth Street & Independence Avenue, SW
Washington, DC 20560
(202) 633-1000
Alexander Hamilton U.S. Custom House
One Bowling Green
New York, NY 10004
(212) 514-3700
Website: www.nmai.si.edu
NMAI holds exhibitions and events, and also has games and resources for students.

Websites

Because of the changing nature of internet links, Rosen Publishing has developed an online list of websites related to the subject of this book. This site is updated regularly. Please use this link to access this list:

http://www.rosenlinks.com/DAA/colonies

For Further Reading

Davis, Dr. Graeme. *Vikings in America.* Edinburgh, Scotland: Birlinn Ltd 2011.

Dunbar-Ortiz, Roxanne. *An Indigenous Peoples' History of the United States.* Massachusetts: Beacon Press, 2014.

Huyghe, Patrick. *Columbus Was Last.* New York: Hyperion, 1992.

Ingstad, Helge and Anne Stine. *The Viking Discovery of America.* New York: Checkmark Books, 2001.

Lowenstein, Tom and Piers Vitebsky. *Native American Myths and Beliefs.* New York, NY: The Rosen Publishing Company, 2011.

Mann, C. Charles. *1493: Uncovering the New World Columbus Created.* New York: Random House, 2011.

Menzies, Gavin. *1421: The Year China Discovered America.* New York: HarperCollins, 2003.

Menzies, Gavin. *Who Discovered America?: The Untold History of the Peopling of the Americas.* New York, NY: William Morrow Paperbacks, 2014.

Miller, Mary Ellen. *The Art of Mesoamerica: From Olmec to Aztec* (5th Edition). New York, NY: Thames & Hudson, 2012.

Resendez, Andres. *The Other Slavery: The Uncovered Story of Indian Enslavement in America.* Boston, MA: Houghton Mifflin Harcourt, 2016.

Schobinger, Juan. *The Ancient Americans: A Reference Guide to the Art, Culture, and History of Pre-Columbian North and South America.* New York, NY: Taylor & Francis, 2016.

Sertima, Ivan Van. *They Came Before Columbus: The African Presence in Ancient America.* New York: Random House, 2003.

Toth, Henrietta. *Christopher Columbus: Explorer and Colonizer of the New World.* New York, NY: The Rosen Publishing Company, 2017.

Wallace-Murphy, Tim, and Marilyn Hopkins. *Templars in America.* Massachusetts: Red Wheel, 2004.

Williams, Robert A. Jr. *Savage Anxieties: The Invention of Western Civilization.* New York: St. Martin's Press, 2012.

Bibliography

Bey, Aziza Braithwaite. *Pre-Columbian Contacts* (S.C.: Book-Surge Publishing, 2010).

Childress, David. "Sumerians in Tiahuanaco?" *Atlantis Rising,* no. 88 (July 2011).

Covey, Cyclone, PhD. *Calalus* (N.Y.: Vantage Press, 1975).

DeCosta, Benjamin Franklin. *The Pre-Columbian Voyages of the Welsh to America* (South Africa: Ulan Press, 2012).

Enterline, James Robert. *Viking America* (N.Y.: J.R. Enterline, 1972).

Gordon, Cyrus R. "Stone Inscription Found in Tennessee." *Ancient American*, vol. 14, no. 88 (September 2010).

Gordon, Cyrus. "Authenticity of the Phoenician Text From Paraiba." *Orientalia,* no. 37 (1968).

Goudsward, David. *The Westford Knight and Henry Sinclair* (N.C.: McFarland, 2010).

Heyerdahl, Thor. *The RA Expeditions* (New York.: Doubleday & Company, Inc., 1971).

Hitoshi, Wanatabe. *Possibilities for Ancient Migrations* (Urbana, Ill.: University of Illinois Press, 1993).

Holst, Sanford. *Phoenicians—Lebanon's Epic Heritage* (Cambridge & Boston Press, 2005).

Howgaard, William. *The Voyages of the Norsemen to America* (N.Y.: Kraus Reprint Company, 1971).

Huyghe, Patrick. *Columbus Was Last* (New York: Hyperion, 1992).

Jairazbhoy, R.A. *Ancient Egyptians and Chinese in America* (N.Y.: Rowan and Littlefield, 1974).

Jones, Peter N. *American Indian mtDNA, Y Chromosome Genetic Data, and the Peopling of North America* (Boulder, Colo.: Bau Press, 2004).

Joseph, Frank. *Advanced Civilizations of Prehistoric America.* (Vt.: Bear & Company, 2009).

———. *Unearthing Ancient America* (N.J.: New Page Books, 2008).

Leland, Charles Godfrey. *Fusang: The Discovery of America by Chinese Buddhist Monks in the Fifth Century* (S.C.: Forgotten Books, 2007).

Mallery, Arlington, and Mary Roberts Harrison. *The Rediscovery of Lost America* (N.Y.: E.P. Dutton, 1979).

May, Wayne. "Minoan Artifacts in North America." *Ancient American* vol. 20, no. 76 (2008).

McMenamin, Mark A.S. "The Phoenician World Map." *Mercator's World* 2(3): 46–51 (1997).

Mertz, Henriette. *The Mystic Symbol* (Wisc.: Hayriver Press, 2004).

Nielsen, Richard, and Scott F. Wolter. *Kensington Rune Stone* (Minn.: Lake Superior Agate Publishing, 2005).

Nielson, Richard. *The Rune Stones of Oklahoma* (Calif.: Epigraphic Society Occasional Publications, vol.16, 1987).

Pearson, Richard J. *Ancient Japan* (N.Y.: George Brazilier Publishers, 1992).

Pohl, Frederick J. *The Lost Discovery* (New York: W.W. Norton & Co., 1952).

———. *The Viking Explorers* (N.Y.: Thomas Y. Crowell Co., 1966).

Smithsana, Don. "Japanese Place-Names in Ancient America." *Ancient American,* vol. 2, no. 10 (July/August 1995).

Thompson, Gunnar. *Nu Sun: Asian-American Voyages, 500 B.C.* (Chicago, Ill.: Pioneer Publishing Company, 1989).

Van Sertima, Ivan. *African Presence in Early America* (N.J.: Transaction Publishers,1987).

———. *Early America Revisited* (N.J.: Transaction Publishers, 1998).

Von Wuthenau, Alexander. *Unexpected Faces in Ancient America.* (New York: Crown Publishers, 1975).

Wallace-Murphy, Tim, and Marilyn Hopkins. *Templars in America* (Mass.: Red Wheel/Weiser, 2004).

Zimmerman, Fritz. *The Nephilim Chronicles* (Create Space, 2010).

Index

About the Author

Frank Joseph was the editor-in-chief of *Ancient American,* a national archaeology magazine, from its inception in 1993 until his retirement 17 years later. His work as an alternative science investigator has received award recognition from Ohio's Midwest Epigraphic Society, Japan's Savant Institute, The Burrows Cave Society (Columbus, Ohio), and Michigan's Ancient American Preservation Foundation. His titles include T*he Atlantis Encyclopedia* and *Opening the Ark of the Covenant.* Joseph edited and contributed to *Discovering the Mysteries of Ancient America, Unearthing Ancient America,* and T*he Lost Worlds of Ancient America.*